JESUS
LOVES
WOMEN

Life's one imperative is to become who we are.
—*Thomas Merton*

Each and every moment of finding balance between the extremes
of self-mortification and indulgence is a perfect replica of the
great Middle Way to liberation. Each moment of balance is an ar-
ticulation of the entire path in its completion. Liberation not
only is the goal of the path but is also found in its continually un-
folding process. On the Middle Way, we find freedom not just as
the end of the journey, but in the middle, and in the middle of
the middle, and in the middle of the middle of the middle. Each
step on the way to freedom is freedom.
—*Sharon Salzberg, from* A Heart as Wide as the World

JESUS LOVES WOMEN

A MEMOIR OF
BODY AND SPIRIT

TRICIA GATES BROWN

Foreword by
James Loney

DreamSeeker Books
TELFORD, PENNSYLVANIA

an imprint of
Cascadia Publishing House

Cascadia Publishing House orders, information, reprint permissions:
contact@CascadiaPublishingHouse.com
1-215-723-9125
126 Klingerman Road, Telford PA 18969
www.CascadiaPublishingHouse.com

Jesus Loves Women
Copyright © 2011 by Cascadia Publishing House.
Telford, PA 18969
All rights reserved
DreamSeeker Books is an imprint of Cascadia Publishing House LLC
Library of Congress Catalog Number: 2011027383
ISBN 13: 13: 978-1-931038-91-1; **ISBN 10:** 1-931038-91-0
Book design by Darryl Brown and Cascadia Publishing House
Cover design by Darryl Brown

The paper used in this publication is recycled and meets the
minimum requirements of American National Standard for Information Sciences—
Permanence of Paper for Printed Library Materials, ANSI Z39.48-1984.1984

Library of Congress Cataloguing-in-Publication Data
Brown, Tricia Gates.
Jesus loves women : a memoir of body and spirit / Tricia Gates Brown ; fore-
word by James Loney.
     p. cm.
  Summary: "Jesus Loves Women is the memoir of a girl raised in a fundamentalist Christian milieu she casts off at a young age and of her quest to find
wholeness and home, spiritually and sexually." "[summary]"--Provided by
publisher.
  Includes bibliographical references (p.   ).
  ISBN-13: 978-1-931038-91-1 (5.5 x 8.5 trade pbk. : alk. paper)
  ISBN-10: 1-931038-91-0 (5.5 x 8.5 trade pbk. : alk. paper)
  1. Brown, Tricia Gates. 2. Christian biography--United States. 3. Spiritual
biography--United States. I. Title.

BR1725.B689A3 2011
277.3'082092--dc23
[B]

                              2011027383

   17 16 15 14 13 12 11   10 9 8 7 6 5 4 3 2 1

*To Martin
who gave me three names:
"Tricia of the Restless Heart"
"Tricia of the Risen Life"
"Tricia of the Healing Voice";*

*and to Gilberto Arciga,
with love and gratitude.*

Contents

Foreword

Jesus Loves Women is a book for every man who loves a woman, every woman who has struggled to become whole, and every person who has ever felt a failure.

I remember being astounded, the first time I read it: Tricia, of all people, trapped in an emotionally abusive relationship!

Tricia and I had gotten to know each other through Christian Peacemaker Teams (CPT) and developed a real bond as writers. We had just finished collaborating on a book Tricia was editing about the hostage crisis when she told me she had written a memoir. As I was about to embark upon writing a memoir of my own about my experiences in Iraq while being kidnapped, I asked her if I could read it. What I learned shocked and surprised me.

Tricia was someone I looked to as an elder sister in the writing life. She was so confident and capable, a published author and an accomplished editor, a successful PhD candidate and former lecturer in theology, a woman who was offering important leadership within CPT. It made me realize, if Tricia had ended up in an abusive relationship, it could happen to any woman. Her story was a window into the story of all women.

Jesus Loves Women is a rare memoir. Some Christians may even find it surprising, for it is both a sexual and a spiritual autobiography. With unflinching candor and a poet's sensitivity, Tricia tells the story of her fundamentalist upbringing, her first marriage at the age of eighteen, her fall into the role of a submissive house wife and the emotional abuse she endured because this is what her faith and her church seemed to require of her. She tells of her decision to leave her husband and strike out on her own with a two-year old daughter, how she wandered for years in a fog of depression and anxiety, how she struggled to regain the sense of herself that had been destroyed in her marriage. She tells the story of her continuing search for love (sometimes in the wrong places!), her passionless second marriage, her anguished decision to divorce a second time in the face of disapproving family and friends.

Above all, *Jesus Loves Women* is a story of grace, of how through the healing beauty of the Pacific coast and the friendship of a Trappist monk, Tricia awakens to a mystical understanding of God's unconditional love. It is the story of how one woman finds freedom from the shame, social conventions, and religious pieties that constrict the lives of all women. It is a story she tells with generosity, compassion, and an unusual ability to glean extraordinary insight from the ordinary circumstances of our lives.

As a man, *Jesus Loves Women* helps me to better understand the experience of women who must come of age in a society that objectifies their bodies and diminishes their spirits. As a Christian, it nourishes my faith and calls me into deeper solidarity with the suffering of women. As a pilgrim searching to find his way through life's inevitable disappointments and complexities, it challenges me to honestly face who I am and to live from my deepest desires. As a writer, it inspires and pleases me. Thank you, Tricia Gates Brown, for giving us *Jesus Loves Women*. It is a book that emboldens my heart.

—*James Loney, Toronto, Ontario;*
  author of Captivity: 118 Days in Iraq and the Struggle for a
  World Without War

Author's Preface

This book is the story of a life, or a partial life as all memoirs are. It is "the story of a heart," as my monk friend said upon reading it. And since life emanates, in every sense, from the heart, his description is right on the dollar.

Writing about one's life is like taking a long walk through a rainforest in late spring. One is surrounded by innumerable animals, plants, and other natural phenomena—from an old-growth cedar to a flea, from a twisting stream to a paramecium, invisible to the naked eye. But as one walks through a forest, one is struck by just one thing among the multitude, then by another, then by another. One might notice the tiny pink bells of the salal, then a white butterfly looping W's across the sky, then a layer of moss twitching under a quilt of animate creek water. What catches one's eye will be different from what catches the eye of the next sojourner, and what catches one's eye will be a small fraction of all that is there to see.

It did not take much writing practice for me to ascertain the central themes of this memoir. What I'm drawn to, amid an array of memories, life stimuli, and experiences, is the complex interplay of body and spirit, of the sensual and the spiritual, the sexual and the spiritual. For another writer, the focal point of a memoir might be vocational struggles, or authority figures, or friendship. But I have been and always will be attuned to the beautiful, delicate, difficult balancing act we perform as embodied, sexual, spiritual creatures. We are not sexual creatures on one hand and spiritual creatures on another, as if the Gnostic dichotomy of spirit and body had proved true. We are one whole. Still, by and large, most modern people continue to live as Gnostics.

To tell the story of how one awakened to the goodness of being a sensual, sexual creature, and of all the mistakes and confusion leading to that awareness, is a challenge. I choose to tell the story not only because it is the truest accounting I can offer of my life, but because I believe it's important we hear such stories. In my experience, they are hard to come by.

Every memoir is a redemption story, and my story is about redeeming the body, although not in the old, pious way you might imagine. It is about dissolving the illusion of dualism in my understanding and life and coming to a deep awareness of the body's goodness, of the goodness of our senses and our sexuality, of the stunning beauty of how we are made. It comes out of *wonder* at how all the factors and laws set in motion at the beginning of time were set to bring us this life we know—the cornucopia of sensual and emotional experiences and the consciousness that allows us to apprehend them as wondrous.

Yet many individuals, both religious and non-religious, cling to dualistic understandings of body and spirit because of the unique power of our sexuality. Like all things imbued with power, the body has the ability to devastate as well as to bless. As human beings, we are faced everyday with the paradox that all good things can be twisted and used to bring harm. But rarely have we paid such a high price for this paradox, this fact of free will, as in the realm of the body. Because of this paradox we have allowed ourselves to shroud in shame what is arguably the most awe-inspiring achievement in creation: the human body and its experiences. Most of us assimilate this shame from a young age, and this shame is, I believe, what keeps us from talking about sexuality and the body freely and in a context of wonder. It keeps us trapped in unhealthy ways of thinking about our sexuality and how it is interwoven with all that we are; specifically, with our spirituality, with our experience of and relationship to God.

Shame does two things. It impedes honesty and it impedes humility—the two things most essential to awareness and the deepening of our humanity. Shame causes us to hide things from ourselves and others and to lie. It makes us *want* others to hide things, because we are afraid of what we will see. Shame causes us to be defensive and guarded in a way that keeps us prideful and causes us to judge others. Both dishonesty and pride then perpetuate an unhealthy attachment and relationship to our sexuality. Shame is not the same as recognizing missteps and lapses in judgment. It is not the same as doing something unhealthy and recognizing later that it was not such a good idea (the "I saw that happening differently in my head" experience). This kind of recognition and awareness is the antithesis of shame, which keeps us blind and manufacturing excuses. Every time a mistake is met with honesty and awareness, allowing us to see and recognize who we are a little more clearly, we are enriched. We have stepped closer to humility and love for ourselves and others. We are becoming more fully human. Therefore, mistakes are among our greatest teachers and our greatest gifts. Shame utterly robs us of these lessons, of the great gift of acknowledging, *in a grateful way*, and learning from, mistakes.

I would like to see this change. I have noticed it changing with regard to certain types of mistakes. In the United States, we are much more comfortable with acknowledging the powerful, healing lessons learned, say, by addiction or by awakening to our greed. As a society, we can celebrate with a person who has deepened in honesty and humility by learning from gluttony or by recognizing the consequences of addiction to money and work. This progress in embracing our mistakes as master teachers is something to celebrate. But when it comes to sexual missteps, we as a society are so blinded and bamboozled by our shame that we silence our most powerful teachers, the mistakes we make against and by way of the body, mistakes that are often made in a fog of unknowing, a whirlwind of love, longing, loneliness, and often fear.

In my experience, this is especially true within religious communities. I cannot tell you how many times I have seen this played out in various churches. A sexual misstep is reported; someone has to go. If both in the relationship are within the same congregation, it is not uncommon to name one party as the more egregious offender, and like a scapegoat, to send that person away. Out into the desert, often go honesty, humility, learning, and ultimately, our deepest humanity. Shame is given the last word. Shame, therefore, is self-perpetuating. Who wants to honestly and humbly acknowledge sexual missteps and lessons if the price one has to pay within society and within religious communities, is estrangement?

I have hope that this can change, that we can begin a new conversation about sexuality and the many lessons we learn through the experiences of the body and in our significant-other relationships. I am especially hopeful that a change in the conversation can happen among young people. As with our bumbling in other aspects of life, our bumbling with our bodies and within our significant-other relationships can be a powerful catalyst to spiritual and personal growth, but only when we bring them into the refreshing light of awareness and humility. This has certainly been my experience, and so I share the experience within these pages. My stumbling into grace and truth, into a profound, healing experience of God's love and of the goodness of sexuality, came as a result of such mistakes, God bless them.

As I reflect back on dabblings in unfaithfulness, promiscuity, and sexual experimentation outside of love-commitment, I view these actions as mistakes. I also view them with a profound sense of gratitude. I would not be where I am now, in a much clearer, freer place, more fully appreciative of sexuality and its integral interconnections with spirit and sacredness, and more fully myself, if I had not had those experiences.

Because much of this book is written in the present-tense voice, I write about thoughts and feelings on sexuality and commitment that, while spoken in the present-tense, I no longer have. I tell of experiences and actions from the past that I have grown beyond. Yet any growth that came throughout my life came as a result of, not despite, those experiences. Thus, I am thankful. Shame has no place in the telling of a life story, in telling of the living and learning that make us human.

Our bumbling can only serve as a catalyst to growth, however, when we can break down the barriers that keep us from celebrating the lessons learned in a context of grace.

I can already hear the voices saying (and rightly so) *BUT*. . . . But what about the people harmed by sexual misconduct—sometimes the very vulnerable, such as children or women (or men) who are victimized? That is a legitimate and crucial concern. I don't in any way minimize the wrongness of sexual violations within the context of role-generated or other power imbalances. I do also think that the types of violations we might call "sexual aggression" or abuse are bred in a context of shame and secrecy about our sexuality. A context in which sexuality is no longer shrouded by shame should *lessen* sexual aggression and misconduct, not enable or promote it.

A context for developing a healthy sexuality is one in which sexuality is surrounded by honesty and humility, and especially in the home, openly talked about in this spirit of learning and acknowledgement of sex's goodness. This can breed a healthier atmosphere in which to mature as sexual creatures than our present atmosphere of tandem shame and far-fetched, often violent, fascination—the flip side of shame.

Others will find my title, *Jesus Loves Women*, daft: "Of *course*, Jesus loves women! Why even say it?" In a way, that is the point. Sure it should be obvious that Jesus loves women. But for many girls, the statement is anything but obvious. Instead we hear from earliest age that women are somehow inadequate or unfit, even dirty. Jesus loves women? For many females, this revelation comes later in life as a knock-us-off-our-boots surprise. For women from patriarchal religious traditions other than Christianity, an analogous statement might be "Mohammad loves women," "Krishna loves women," or "Yahweh loves women"—but it would ring with the same audacity in the ears of many female listeners from those traditions or to women with no religious tradition at all.

Others will find "inappropriateness" where this is none, or will think, for example, that my friendship with the old monk named Martin, whom readers are soon to meet, is somehow strange. Yet Martin is one of the most pure-hearted people I've known. Would that all people could know and be loved by such a soul. I suspect that reactions of this nature come in part from shame and at times from the short-sightedness of Anglo culture. Non-white cultures, Latino cultures among them, are often less squeamish about affection, warmth, and expressions of love within platonic relationships. Thank God for that. I recently visited Mexico. I have never been kissed so many times by so many people in the course of two weeks. It was heavenly. How refreshing to be among a people who, despite whatever their own cultural blind-spots may be, have formed a deep appreciation for the physical.

Finally, this book is a story of coming home, coming home to my self and to God as a fully awakened sensual, sexual person, fully alive in her body, and fully integrated as a spiritual/physical whole. The road I took to get home was circuitous and rocky and often engulfed in fog. But the learning along the journey brought me to clearness, to a position on sexuality I would characterize as "nuevo-traditional" and that I elucidate at the end of the book.

The story is not unlike the great parable of the Prodigal Son, which for all its sadness is truly a celebration story. The parable ends with a feast, and the obvious shadow character is the shame-addicted brother who cannot bring himself to join the party. The parable illustrates what the life of the spirit is all about. It is about confusion, and making mistakes, and learning—all of which are ensconced in divine love. "First there is the Fall," as Julian of Norwich said, "then there is the recovery from the Fall. But both are the mercy of God."

Both are the mercy of God. This is the miracle of the spiritual life. *Jesus Loves Women* is about finding my way home and discovering at the end of the journey a grace, a love, bigger than the universe. It was there at the beginning, in every misplaced step along the road; and it will always be there. Always.

—*Tricia Gates Brown*
Nehalem, Oregon

Introduction

I arrive at Our Lady of Guadalupe Abbey just after compline, the last lauds of the day, when the monks chant Psalms by candlelight to the strains of a worn out guitar. It is fifteen minutes past sundown, and the sky falls over the chapel like a silk mantle, dusky cerulean fading to deep cobalt that fades at last to navy. The evening air, dense with the erotic fragrances of summer—pollen and grass and day-old growth, is starting to cool. Acres of lively woods behind the abbey seem to hold their breath till morning, when birds will burst into chorus and deer cut paths to the paltry streams sauntering through the hills. For now, all is deceptively still.

I reach the stairs that lead to the abbey's guesthouse, and a weak light flickers on. The figure of Martin, apparition-like in his black, hooded robe, hobbles to the door, cradling a bulging brown bag in the nook of his arm. Opening the door, I see his face, all full of light and smiling. We hug as he hands me the bag, containing six large burritos wrapped in foil.

I am headed to retrieve my thirteen-year-old daughter Madison from her dad's before driving the two hours home to Cannon Beach. It is a Wednesday, and on Wednesdays at the abbey, Martin cooks. The third day of the week is thus anticipated by the broth-ers, especially if Todd, a young monk with ascetic leanings, has cooked on Tuesday.

Nothing beats following a day of tempeh stew with a peak-cholesterol serving of Martin's burritos. Not only are they dripping with cheese and chorizo fat, but they're actually toasted in butter before serving. Martin, born to Mexican parents in La Mesa, Cali-fornia, and a monk for fifty-some years, has earned a reputation. He crafts the tastiest burritos state-side, *hands-down*. But he won't receive any medals from the American Heart Association. You could say Martin relishes the small pleasures: eating and cooking rich food, listening to torch singers like Natalie Cole on tapes in his cell, watching night fall in the abbey garden, and especially, ap-preciating the beauty of a tree. Whenever Martin makes burritos, he sets six aside for me. He has even been known to mail them. Last night, however, he phoned, knowing I'd be passing through town. *Would you swing by the abbey a minute? I have something for you.*

Martin and I walk a few steps to the reception counter, behind which glows the only light in the guesthouse. I put the burritos on the Formica countertop as Martin speaks through a coy smile: "I've been praying for your heart today." He laughs silently, with his eyes, and I guess what he is thinking. On the phone I'd told him I met an attractive Mexican. He was pursuing me, and I was considering seeing him—seeing *all* of him, though I don't divulge as much to Martin. Martin wipes his face with his hand, the way a mime wipes away one face to reveal another. But the second face is the same. Shaking his head and laughing, Martin leans his elbows on the tall counter. I adopt the same posture beside him. It's the "couple at a bar" posture.

"Tricia, you know, you're just always gonna love a lot. And don't ever change. The saddest people I know are people who close up their hearts and won't love." He looks into my face with urgent eyes.

"A lot of men are going to love you. You are a poet, you sing. . . . You're just gonna have to love a lot of people. I know people don't understand. It's something married folks don't talk about.

But when you write that book about how Jesus loved women, you will understand." This time we both laugh.

"It's not easy, though, which is why you have to pray a lot." Martin puts his hand on my shoulder. We stand up straight and face one another. "Just don't ever change, Tricia." He takes hold of my arm, both a gesture of affection and an attempt to steady arthritic knees. "You're ahead of the game, though," his eyes aglow, "you have a monk here praying for you." Again we laugh. "I'll be praying for your heart!"

I give Martin a hug. "I love you, dear," he says, cheek to my cheek.

"I love you too."

With the inescapable Mexican cheek-kiss, he sends me off.

♦

I met Martin for the first time in summer 2000, following an overnight retreat at the abbey. I was thirty; he was seventy-five. It was a simple case of lost and found. After my stay, a man found a book on a monastery trail, *The Spiritual Life* by Evelyn Underhill, and turned it in to Martin, who was attending the guesthouse at the time. Martin recognized my name on the book tag and sent me a letter. It was the first of many I'd eventually receive from him.

Though my memory of collecting the book is shadowy, Martin's memory is not. In a note dated June 27, 2005, he wrote: "Since Mass this morning at 6:45 a.m., I keep thinking of the day you came to the guesthouse counter inquiring about a small book on prayer . . . by an English woman writer. I saw your eyes and something happened. I wanted to be your friend. Only God and I knew that desire. . . . They seemed to be eyes that looked at God."

A year and a half pass after our lost-and-found exchange before Martin enters my memory in a detailed way.

It is early 2002. I again visit the abbey on retreat. This time I bring a large canvas, a set of oil paints, and my standing easel. I am eager to use an expensive tube of paint I recently bought, bright acid green, and to make the retreat an art get-away. With easel perched beside my guest-room window, beyond which lay a misty spread of waterfall and pond, I paint a large portrait of Madison, using a semi-abstract style with a bright green background. Over the course of two days, I paint for many hours, working on the picture late into the night, surrendering myself to an activity I don't often do. The strong, vivid colors, the texture and smell of the paints, are my soul-food.

On this retreat I visit Martin, and it is our first one-on-one. In the past we'd chatted at the abbey reception desk, me leaning on the reception counter, him quizzing me with questions between phone calls and inquiries from guests. But this time we sit. Scooting two chairs together on the sprawling porch of the guesthouse on a day alive with grasshoppers, dusted in pollen, Martin launches in to talking, beginning a conversation that will go on for years. And I do mean *talking*, as Martin's style is characterized by storytelling, not dialogue—a manner likely to evoke rage in more chatty interlocutors. But Martin's style has more to do with postwar hearing loss than an inability to listen. He relays tale after tale: people he's known, marriages ending, children wandering, addictions and epiphanies and grace. I rest into the nest of lives woven before my eyes, marveling at the lack of judgment in Martin, the tireless concern imbued in his stories, the epic range of his love.

At the end of the retreat I show Martin my painting. "You are full of spirit!" he exclaims to my surprise. Tears pool in his eyes as he looks at me and my picture. *And it is not so spectacular,* this painting. Yet I feel like Mary encountering Elizabeth during her pregnancy—like Martin has seen something inside of me others cannot see, something mysterious and hidden from plain sight, hidden even from me. Something manifest in the layers of linseed oil and acid-green paint that gives away my goodness—the way Jesus could see a woman's goodness pouring from an alabaster jar. Whatever it is, Martin is moved. "I can tell you spend time looking at God," he says. I chuckle. Half of me even believes him.

Early in our friendship, Martin began to say, "Someday I want you to write a book about how Jesus loved women!" He said it over and over again, every time I saw him. *When are you going to write that book about how Jesus loved women?* It became his Tricia *schtick.* In 2000, I had finished a PhD in Theology, New Testament Studies to be precise. I figured Martin envisioned a book exploring

Jesus' relationships with women, women who supported him like Susanna, or women like Mary Magdalene who befriended him, something about the cultural prescriptions for women in the Circum-Mediterranean and how Jesus transcended them. The book sounded important, but I knew others had already written similar books. And after several years of research in biblical studies, I was plum bored. The book conjured no enthusiasm.

So I humored Martin: *Sure, someday I'll write that book.* A harmless fib. Over the next few years, as my relationship with Martin deepened, he mentioned the Jesus book less and less. We had other things to talk about.

◆

Our friendship grows exponentially for the next three years. I visit the abbey and he writes letters—three in 2002, nine in 2003, then even more in subsequent years. By the glistening summer of 2005, we are, you could say, best friends. We confide deeply, leaving our dark sides bare. I find in Martin the most honest, unalloyed Christian I have ever met. He is like the grandfather I never had, so proud of my every triumph and so empathetic in my pain. With him I share my good news and bad days, and we hold one another in our hearts like a prayer.

By that summer, I have spent two tumultuous years bursting my life-encrusted cocoon of fear and conformity. I have been living apart from my husband for a year. Three weeks prior, I had phoned Martin telling him I was leaving my marriage, making real the separation from Darryl. I had not seen Martin since the news.

I ascend the hill toward the guesthouse to see Martin waiting on the porch. The sun paints broad triangles of light on the wood decking, and Martin's smile radiates. He sports his ratty jeans and a faded polo shirt, the ball cap of his beloved Notre Dame, looking like he belongs at a hacienda, not a monastery. "Are you the mystic of Cannon Beach?" he calls out, his usual greeting (sometimes he says "mermaid").

We exchange a hug. We then head to the pond behind the guesthouse where we most like to talk. "You look good," Martin says with a note of relief as we walk down the graveled path, "the best ever! You look full of joy and peace." I turn to check on him as he negotiates a small hill leading to the pond and his pace draws heavy and slow. Each step is a painful bend of swollen knees. "I've been worried about you," he adds, "But here you are, a real gift to my heart!" Looking up, I see my favorite hawthorn trees heavy with red berries and full of sunlight. The hillside flaunts thousands of tiny purple periwinkle.

We take seats in plastic Adirondack chairs under a cherry tree that stretches over the pond.

I start in.

"It feels good to be free of my marriage, Martin." My voice trembles with words I can no longer hold back, like air escaping a balloon.

Martin nods his head and smiles. "You remind me of my friend Father Thomas. He has a parish in Seattle. He comes to the abbey on a regular basis, but the monastic life perplexes him." Martin leans forward, briskly touching his hand to my knee, and laughs. "He just can't imagine the rules, the constraints." Martin has a slightly husky voice, like a boxer from the Bronx, somehow masculine and emphatic at the same time. In his younger days, Martin had been an athlete, playing baseball, jogging daily well into his seventies.

"That's how I feel about marriage," I say, grateful he offered the analogy.

"For me, the monastery is what makes me feel free. When I go out into the world, I feel like I'm in prison. The monastic life gives me the structure I need to open my heart, to love and rest." With eyebrows arched, Martin's face looks serious and full of compassion. Martin joined the abbey a few years after returning from World War II combat duty in the Philippines and Japan. He'd been with the men who first marched into Japan after "V-J Day." Martin's first years of homecoming were filled with drinking and brawling and occasional visits to jail until finally the spiritual life beckoned him. His search led to Our Lady of Guadalupe Abbey.

"I find constraints stifling," I say wistfully. "I'm more like an eagle. I need boundlessness. I need to *soar*." Watching a pair of ducks waddle to the water's edge, I add, "Sometimes I get snagged by a bear . . . but then I heal and fly again."

Martin laughs at the image, his eyes twinkling, head tossed back. Then I bristle. My husband is nothing like a bear.

"I don't have a super addictive personality," I continue, rattling off my self-misperceptions. Martin, a recovering alcoholic for about twelve years, participates regularly in AA meetings and understands addiction. "I don't need a lot of restraints to keep myself in check. . . . Some people use marriage as a straight-jacket," I blather on. "But I'm pretty self-disciplined." Even as I say this, blind spots dance before my eyes like skeletons escaping a closet. "If I am addicted to anything, it is total freedom. I dislike marriage. I can't hold a full-time job to save my life."

Martin nods, still smiling in utter acceptance. He never lets on he sees through me. But then, so deftly I fail to notice, he veers to the subject of men, my primary addiction.

"You need to give your heart some rest," he says, "to enjoy silent love."

"I feel like I've been loving silently for eight years!" I burst, referring to my lukewarm marriage. "I need some non-silent love for a change!" Martin's face offers understanding. "I appreciate expressiveness," I continue. "I want *expressiveness* in love, not silence." We get to talking about Mexican culture, and Martin describes how the twice-yearly bilingual services at the abbey bring the place to life. I realize how attracted I've become to the vivaciousness and warmth of Latin cultures.

"That's what I mean about how Jesus loved women," Martin says, back to his old refrain. "You know, when Jesus spent time with those women . . . when the woman wiped his feet with her hair, he *loved* her."

"Yes, and he didn't love women like a eunuch either, he loved them like a *man*," I say.

At this, Martin's face lights up—a baseball stadium on a summer night. He knows a missing piece has fallen into place. "Yes!" He leans forward. "Certain women he loved like a *lover*, like the best lover ever." I nod my agreement. I imagine Jesus having a crush on a girl, or feeling mature, deep love for a woman.

"Sometimes I've imagined how it would be if some woman went up and put perfume on the abbot's feet, wiped them with her hair," Martin muses.

I picture the scene in my head: the looking away and snickering, the whispers, the condescending men who would lead the woman away by her elbows, the shamed woman, her head bowed low. "It would be scandalous!" I say.

"Yes, people would make a huge to-do about it. But Jesus just *loved* her." Martin's eyes are enormous. "He was not afraid to show it."

I see that Jesus wasn't frightened by what a man could feel for a woman. He wasn't scandalized or scared by sexuality. He knew it was good. Whether or not Jesus was married or *had sex* doesn't interest me. Either way, he was a *good* lover. And God loves good lovers.

"Jesus would have been the best of lovers," Martin continues. "*He knew how to love.*"

My eyes fixate on a firefly hovering by a tip of tall grass. Expanses of algae float on the water. Silky white water lilies open themselves, like fragile young women, to the light. In late summer, the pond's vitality and virility literally buzz. *Of course Jesus loves women!*

I have on occasion run into monks at the abbey, either traversing the grounds or in the guesthouse, who seem scared of women. In female presence they are as awkward as fourth-grade boys on Valentine's Day. I actually pity them their discomfort. I find myself pulling my jacket around my chest as I pass. But Martin is so at ease with women (as are many of the monks) and so at ease with sexuality, even as a monk dedicated to celibacy. How could someone live in such a place, such a pulsing, life-begetting-life environment, and not be? Who, in such a place, would not be awake to, and honoring of the sensations of sexuality? *Jesus was awake to them*—I am sure of it.

Intense afternoon light washes out the colors of trees beyond the ponds, and the grass of late summer is parched and yellowed. But under the shade of the trees where we sit, Martin and I are surrounded by vivid color: the variegated greens of the grasses lining the water, the silver and blue of dragonflies, the intense neon-green of tiny insects traversing our arms and the blood-red flash of ladybugs, shiny, scarlet cherries overhead, golden buttercups growing wild on the incline to the pond, the fathomless canopy of sky. Even the koi I spot every few minutes in the water blaze with color. The world, so sensuous, so vibrant. *God is a lover!*

"You know," Martin says as he leans forward to rise, "my love and support are with you *para siempre* and no matter what, okay?" He takes my arm to steady himself as he stands. He hugs me like a grizzly bear, in an embrace that feels more loving than anything I've known.

When we return to the guesthouse that day, I start to write this book about how Jesus loves women, though not the book Martin had in mind when he suggested it. Instead, this book is about my struggle to believe the audacious statement "Jesus loves women," and all that it implies. This is the story of how, after all Martin's cajoling, I finally understood it. And it is about how crazy-hard it was to understand. In the course of my life I nearly drowned for love, I altered my identity for love, I betrayed a friend for love, I ended up in a small town police station for love—but I then finally got it. Jesus *loves* women.

Jesus loves women, and not because they are being nice, and cleaning up messes, and accommodating others. Jesus loves women when they are stumbling in the dark and breaking things. Jesus does not just love women who exemplify chastity (whether in the Victorian or the monastic sense) and who quell the earthy sensuality that distinguishes our menstruating, ovulating, child-bearing, lactating *women*-ness, that causes us to wax and wane with the moon. Jesus loves women in all our human fallibility and imperfection as well as in our God-like goodness and sensuality. With all that love encompasses, Jesus loves *women*.

Profligate

Just look how we circle, a flock
of gulls, vying for love like a tear of fish.
Arched backs, dreadful necks outstretched,
shrieking our greed cries. When
I look this way, ask me when love has
run out on me. Remind me how it clings
like manna to the soles of my feet, how
love, like a dandelion, blankets my fields.
Love, that keeps knocking me down and
pulling me up, that makes me naked
and poor, and always full. When fear
blazes in my eyes, take my hand, fly me
like a ghost above my life, to the places
love has crumbled battlements and raised
the dead. Be profligate with love, tell me,
and it will astound you. Spend it all.
Now. *Go.*

JESUS
LOVES
WOMEN

CHAPTER ONE

Restless Heart

I left the police station realizing how Jesus loved women. Well, perhaps it took a few weeks and considerable sobbing to encounter the full realization, but when Miguel wrote my dog's name on the hotel window in masking tape, I realized Jesus loved women the way I had come to love Miguel.

I had lost touch with Jesus' love somewhere along the way— not in the sense it was no longer around, but in the sense it was invisible, like a love letter that has fallen behind the radiator only to be recovered in another lifetime in that surprising, messy place. But how on earth had it come to this? My childhood did not suggest I would find myself walking across town to the local authorities, cradling an answering machine under my arm like unexploded ordnance. I had been the meekest of meek, an every Sunday churchgoer, a child shaking in her patent-leather shoes. I was a brave girl who did not know I was brave; a smart girl who did not know I was smart.

I was *girl*-smart. And this was not smart enough. Not if you didn't excel at math. Not if you didn't understand football or learn to ride a bike on schedule; not if you weren't tough. I was hopelessly female. I threw, as they say, like a girl. I cried easily. My truest essence was sensual, deeply attuned to the experiences of the body, and was, I assume, from Day One. I have tried as an adult to climb back into my childhood brain and rattle around the memories stored like pearls, or stuck in the corners like irritating grains of sand. I have tried to understand where my questions arose, where I came to doubt divine love encompassed me. . . .

. . . At the age of eight, I am meticulous. My paper dolls are grouped by style and color, tucked into envelopes; my books are flush with the shelf and arranged by size. Shoes stand in neat rows on my closet floor. Mother is busy making chores-charts using a yardstick and felt-tip pens on colorful poster board, or culling the house for superfluous items for our annual yard sale. But her housekeeping is haphazard. I survey the mild disorder of our house with an irrepressible urge to tidy. In my spare time, I straighten magazine stacks or sort the glassware in the cupboard from the Tupperware and the mugs that multiply like jack rabbits. I want our house to look like the houses of *other* mothers, ones who keep the towels in the hall closet separate from the slippery pile of sheets.

Otherwise, my small hands are just like Mom's. They stitch and draw and bake with little effort, as if moving to some ancient female rhythm instilled at conception. They sew their first garment at the age of nine, a dress of plaid-patterned broadcloth with a boat-neck collar and a drawstring waist pulled taut with ribbon the color of sky. They learn to make pies before middle school and know that coconut cream is Dad's favorite. With a little coaching, they master every domestic art.

And mine is a woman's mind, prone to detecting how people feel and intuiting others' thoughts. Tears come frequently, as often for the misery of others as for the constant needle pricks life administers to my own heart. Pain seems an invisible sea people wade through. As in the news footage I'd seen of flooded towns, people go about their daily lives wading through the rising floodwaters of pain. Some people take respite from it on their rooftops, or blaze over it with the force of a speedboat, but it is still there—everywhere. There is no escaping it.

Being a somewhat sheltered child, I first experience the flood of others' pain through the neighbor children who come to my door. There are the attractive sisters who live three blocks down, with beautiful red hair and cute noses to hold their freckles, whose handsome brother is brain-damaged. To look at him, you would think he is a heartthrob or a jock, but he wears a helmet he never takes off and has a childish voice you wish he would never use. There is the girl who first comes to our front door in underpants, homely and overweight since birth and the butt of every cruel child's joke. Her house hasn't seen paint in decades, and her parents are nonexistent. She lives with her grandmother and a brother my parents warn me to stay away from.

Yet for all the water at our ankles, most people seem happy and dry, and nothing perplexes me more. No one else seems to carry a heart like mine—as fragile as dime-store china, always threatening to fall into the raging current. I want to be tough and unbreakable so my dad won't say: *Don't cry!* or admonish me to keep a "stiff upper lip." I want out of my heart that cannot bear the atrocities of the world. I want to be strong and in control, *like a boy.*

But one summer day at the age of seven I sit at a Giants baseball game in San Francisco—my dad, older sister, and I on a special father-daughter outing. We have driven three hours from home. In the lulling white sunshine of that June afternoon, I struggle not to fall asleep. My eyelids begin to droop. I press my back to my seat in mock attention! But my eyelids droop again, feeling weighted by lead.

Boredom bears down. I imagine taking a nap, a straight-shot ride into heaven. No rounding the bases. No waiting for the next guy to get a hit. Just blankets of cloud and a fluffy pillow. But the innings drag on like miles stretching across the dead landscape of northern California, and the glare of the blazing clear sky hurts my head. Waiting for that game to end is worse than waiting for Christmas, worse than waiting all day for distant relatives to arrive, worse than the long drive to Disneyland. The announcer's voice drones hypnotically. *You are getting very, very sleepy. . . .*

To my befuddlement, Dad and Sister seem to be having a great time. How can they cheer, exhort the batter, bolt popcorn?

My dad is stern and short-tempered, and I want to please him. I know he planned the outing with earnest fatherly intentions to create a fun time. So how could I be such a spoil sport? Mustering all of my energy, I sit up straight in that hard plastic chair and feign alertness, forcing my eyelids open with every ounce of endurance. I strain a smile if Dad glances my way and clap when my sister claps. But even at seven, I realize I am utterly hopeless.

How could anyone enjoy this? I inwardly moan. Even the players in the field look bored, shifting from one foot to the other, sweating like hogs in their black polyester uniforms. *That's Reggie Jackson*, my dad points out. And all I can think of is daydreaming in the cool of a mimosa tree eating the *Reggie Jackson* candy bar. I know it is not the game. It is me. I am a hopeless baseball *loser*.

I may be seven, but I know my feelings will not change. Try as I might, I will not pitch my tent in a field of my father's liking. The field where I pitch my tent will be anything but a ball field. Yet by seven I already understand the importance of male opinion, and I am bent on cultivating male love: with teachers, friends of the family, my friends' fathers, men at church . . . it doesn't matter really. I need men to love me if I am going to be worthy.

I work hard at it. I stuff my sobs when hit by a ball. I repress my feelings like a hand at my crotch when I need to pee. At night, I leak all over my sheets, stained the yellow of a bed-wetter. Sure, I act interested in things like sports, I *act* undaunted by bullies, but my charade fails to convince. Thus, I have important work to do. If my traits don't curry favor with my dad, I will find other males.

Mission: get men to like me so I can be great.

♦

Trouble was, my choices in men were so limited. I spent the ages of three to seventeen in Red Bluff, California, a gassing-up point in the vast blandness of the northern California 1-5 corridor, a place people stopped for a night and then left, on their way to the glamour of central California, the fast-paced fun of southern, or the natural splendor of Oregon. During the summer months, Red Bluff was a veritable oven, occasionally reaching the low 120s. No wonder people were in a hurry to leave.

We did have a river: the Sacramento. Water-skiing with my parents, sister, and family friends, I filled my nose with the river's pitchy-ripe aroma. The lapping sound of a wake on boat-side and shore piqued my delicate, embryonic senses, as did the stippled light on the water—millions of skittering flashes, broadening rings emanating from leaf and water-skipper, glassy reflections of oak trees spreading into one another like ink. All and their mother tried to teach me how to water-ski, but I never learned. I was born a swimmer. Entering the water, thrilling to its cool touch, I absorbed the burble and roll. I let the river's wild green encompass me. That river was the first subject of my love-affair with nature.

Our family seldom camped apart from church retreat and never went for hikes. Thus, my experiences of nature love occurred on the fringes, when I wandered into them: into the dusty, oak-sheltered trails that laced mysteriously through Forward Park, into the creek where my friend and I panned for fool's gold, and into the field of swaying feather grass I used to lie in. The connection I felt in those places was exhilarating and bittersweet, like catching a glimpse of home while enveloped in homesickness. It would be years before I understood nature's importance to my soul. My family's activities were oriented around our trim-and-side-walked neighborhood, and the carpeted room where the television sat chattering from morning till night.

Like many smaller towns isolated from urban areas, Red Bluff bred a particular kind of boredom. There was little doin' by way of arts or entertainment in our town, and teenagers went drinking to kill time or have fun. Before that, kids had the movie theater, and before that, friend's houses. Not a vast set of options. From a young age, I stayed the night with friends. My parents approached the subject with uncharacteristic liberality, letting me stay in homes they knew little about. But spending the night was what kids did in Red Bluff, and besides, all of my friends were from church or Catholic school. They were presumably safe.

♦

I stay with a third-grade classmate whose father keeps stacks of *Playboy* magazines on a low shelf in the garage next to his sports car. This garage is not the locus of domestic neglect characteristic of many homes but a well-swept room full of secret treasures. The house, a large, airy box of contemporary design, sits in the country, surrounded by artful expanses of switch grass. Perched on storage boxes on the cool concrete floor, my friend and I dip into those magazines surreptitiously, hoping her older brothers won't find us. Her parents don't seem to be home. The magazine stacks are neat little cubes, all charged with curious, forbidden energy, full of a power I have never encountered.

Such intense sexual feelings for such a young age. Such bright, flaming intensity! I feel my insides bear down on me and a swooning dervish in my head. I feel an ache, for what I do not know, deep inside of me. Though the force of my guilt is nearly as strong as these sensations, it can never compete. I could bask in that energy, that intensity, until transformed to a small pile of cinders on the floor.

After the magazines, beside an isolated stream not far from her house, my friend and I emulate the scenes, taking off our clothes and lying back in sun-touched sand. The hands of this girl—world-wise for an eight-year-old and bold as a house on fire—find their way to my shy flesh. Exciting and warm, they touch me aimlessly, like a blind driver with no concept of the workings of a car, only the general direction she intends to go. Still, the feeling is good, even if, from that day forward, the secret burns a bright hole in my superego.

◆

Shortly after moving to Red Bluff, our family steps into the First Church of God on the corner of Luther & Jackson Streets—a run-of-the-mill evangelical church with some taste for the charismatic. The church, which meets in an L-shaped, single-level structure of '60s design, has a congregation of fifty to seventy people, and the same pastor who dedicates me at age five baptizes me at eight, in a ceremony beneath a bridge spanning Dog Island Creek.

At the baptism, church members line the bridge singing Andre Crouch's "To God be the glory, to God by the glory…," the song descending like a swarm of gnats and disorienting me. My heart pounds as I trudge into the dense brown water that rises higher and higher, licking my clothing inch-by-steady-inch. I fold my arms across my heaving, rainbow-emblazoned chest, full of unnameable expectations. Will I emerge from the water in glory? Will I be free?

I baptize you in the name of the Father, and the Son, and the Holy Spirit, the pastor says, his hands firm on my back and crossed arms. As I submerge, a burning flood of creek water fills my nose. I gasp, pulled back toward the light, water streaming from my hair. My soaking bell-bottoms, weighing fifty pounds, scrape the ground as I drag myself to shore, the chorus of voices filling the creek-side hollow around me. *To God be the Glory.* My thin T-shirt clings like a bandage to my chest. *I have been made new.* Tears cloud the eyes of my mother and her friends where they stand on the bridge beaming. Yet it is a sacred moment that, somehow, my heart does not show up for—the first of many such moments.

In my young mind this can only mean one thing: I am degenerate, a disappointment to God. I am, for some reason, a bad egg.

My experience at a charismatic church camp confirms this. As a child, I suffer severe leg cramps and these leg pains or "growing pains" torment me without fail at church camp because of the cold. On this occasion, I lie on a metal bed in a drafty, rustic cabin, covered by a sleeping bag and quilt. The throbbing in my leg brings tears. The room is lantern-lit and shadowy, and bodies hover about whispering. I despise my susceptibility to leg cramps! Am humiliated by my inevitable sobbing! None of my friends seem to have such pains. Aside from leg cramps, I am prone to headaches, sometimes migraines, and miss activities with geriatric regularity. I want to rail at the injustice!

Help arrives in the form of Mr. Flanagan, a neighbor friend whose family has accompanied us to camp. As he stoops over my cot, I notice the faint stubble on his chin and admire the bloom of red curlicues on his ample cheeks. A gentle hand rests on my head; he starts to pray. Mr. Flanagan is a stout, Irish-looking man of rounded belly and whitening hair; there at my bedside he whispers with authoritative clarity, "We rebuke you, Satan. We demand that you leave this child alone!" As he does, a conundrum of fear and security envelop me. *Why would Satan be in me, causing me this pain?* I ponder. *Am I bad? Maybe I am bad.* Whatever the reason, I am relieved to know Mr. Flanagan. He must have power over the Devil. His attention that night means I am important, even if his prayer doesn't immediately diminish the pain. A powerful man like Mr. Flanagan is praying for me! *He must think I am special.*

♦

Our family visits church two or three times a week. I sing in kids' choirs, help lead Sunday school, attend church camp, and go to Wednesday night service with my parents followed by Wednesday night youth choir. Church is the sun around which our family orbits. I know what lies behind every closet door of that church, where to find salad tongs in the church kitchen, what to do when the communion tray full of thick-walled thimbles of grape juice passes my way. *Wait for the tray heaped with tufts of torn bread. Take one tuft. Wait till the trays move out of your aisle. Chew the bread. Lift the cup. Hold the empty cup in your hands and look down.*

Though I seldom connect with God at church, I bask in the glow of human love. This expansive love is the sun that I orbit, the love of my parents' friends who watch me grow. Without my knowledge, they nourish my spirit, hovering over my steeple-clad terrarium, emboldening each small leaf of courage, every tender new stem of self-forgiveness, flooding my spirit with the energy to photosynthesize. This love is the gift that church gives me.

Both my mother and father converted to Christianity when I was a toddler—or "became saved," as they would say, since they'd had no real religion to convert from. Their enthusiasm for all things Christian is the primary energy buzzing through our house during my childhood. We listen to Christian music, attend Christian festivals, speakers, and concerts, talk about Christianity when people come for dinner, pray to Jesus before bedtime and meals, and know that we, unlike most of the world, are going to heaven. It is a peaceful world because our feet are firmly planted on the right side—on the solid rock, as the old hymn goes.

My mom and dad, whose marriage was stormy in my baby-years, find a unifying thread in Christianity. They share a fervor for Jesus and a mission to learn everything they can about their incipient faith. They visit and teach Bible studies and read Christian books, some of an apocalyptic bent whose covers glow with frightening red sunsets. Their shared beliefs not only lend them common principles but convince them to prepare for a global cataclysm, at the climax of which Christians will be raptured. The fervor works like glue, binding together my parents' formerly fractious union.

In addition to their concern about the rapture, Mom and Dad have life's daily cataclysms to hold them together. They bond around parenting, around expenditures of family finances, around what to plant in the yard and where to take family vacations. They schedule eye appointments and dental cleanings like clockwork and hold family meetings to announce developments. *We are going to Disneyland! . . . We have decided to build a house and move across town. . . . Our family is adopting a baby from Korea. You will have a little brother!*

My sister Kristen and I nestle between our parents on a brown plaid loveseat, their arms around us on either side as they explain that our new brother has already been born. When he comes to us, he will be a year and a half old, they explain. "Korea is near China," Mom says, picking a country my older sister Kristen and I both recognize. We think Asians all look like people at the Chinese restaurant. "Your mom will need lots of help with your new brother when he comes," Dad says, intent on including us. "You will come with us to Los Angeles when we pick him up at the airport." It is the most exciting news of my young life.

When the social worker visits the house to interview Mom, Kristen and I stifle giggles that escape in sputtering bursts at the photo of our brother, Hun Jung. He is polka-dotted, head shaved in patches around a smattering of invisible boils. My mother tries to look respectable, sitting in her middle-class living room with a stereo system, floor-to-ceiling drapes, and knick-knacks strategically placed, as Kristen and I take photos of Hun—one head shot, one full-body shot—and stick them together like a carnival gag, that big miscreant head on his small, tapering body. Our faces turn a deeper and deeper red as we sputter helplessly, a couple of mufflers bound for the junkyard. When my brother arrives, I love him with an intense concoction of adoration and intrigue. He is beautiful and cuddly and eats only rice. I want to be his best friend.

The family meeting four years later announcing the conception of my younger sister leaves an even stronger impression. *My parents are having a baby?* I ponder at nine years of age. *That means they have sex.* I can hardly brook the thought. My parents seem as asexual as any human beings I have known. I've seen photos of them as newly weds, at nineteen and twenty years of age, my mom in a high, '60s pony-tail with a gingham maternity shirt, standing on a log and holding up a blanket so the camera can't see my dad taking a leak behind it. My dad's smiling face peeks above the cloth. *Maybe those people had sex,* I surmise. Not the people sitting before me. I want the baby to come from a stork.

Despite the burden of raising more kids, Mom sewed us beautiful creations: dozens of floppy-limbed dolls with faces embroidered on muslin, with braided cotton-yarn hair and dresses of ruffled calico. She made us gorgeous clothing, from rick-rack trimmed skirts and lace-trimmed dresses to quilted jackets with matching corduroy gauchos or denim knickers, all the latest styles. Mom doled out love in straight, even stitches.

Dad doled out love in whatever way he could, which mostly meant heading off to work each day to provide for us and coming home to work in the garden—always the primmest in the neighborhood. But Dad also expressed physical affection with a dedication approaching duty, since his parents divorced when he was young and were unwaveringly unaffectionate. Our dad refused to deprive his children of the hugs and pecks he had so missed out on. Thus, he frequently told us he loved us. He touched us on the shoulders and kissed us on the head and said how special we were. He told us he was proud. He doted on us.

Yet for all that, Dad was never at ease with children (grownups either, for that matter). He was strung as tight as a buzz-saw and frequently snapped. *Kids, be quiet! What are you thinking?! Get that mess cleaned up right now! If I have to come into that room. . . .*

That said, my siblings and I were assiduously, if not luxuriously, provided for. Mom and Dad gave us as steady a home life as a child could want. From ages three to seventeen, I moved only once, from a 1970s H-grid development on one side of town to a rambling, rural, mish-mash on the other. The block where I lived through fourth grade was a newer neighborhood with single-level ranch houses in shades of brown and olive green. It was tidy and respectably middle-class. Each house had small front and back yards with neatly trimmed shrubs and lawns that stretched to the curbs. While older trees were few, our family had a huge oak in the back, with 2x4's nailed to the side to make a ladder. Nestled in the crotch of that oak was a tree-house with windows and neatly painted olive-green siding and trim, furnished with hand-made table and chairs. On the other side of the yard stood a new swing-set and an above-ground pool with a tiny adjoining deck. I had a floppy, adorable mutt named Mopsy whom I loved, and the Catholic school I attended from kindergarten through fourth grade sat, within view, a block up our road.

Our family could have starred in an insurance company ad, "security" written all over us. Caring parents, financial security, freedom from violence and abuse—we had it all. My siblings and I were talented, praised, and could, mostly do what we wanted with our spare time. We were surrounded by affection and love.

◆

So why was I always afraid?

Fear gathered around me like a haunting, ever-present aura. It pulled at my throat and beat on my breast. It whispered torments to me from the moment I woke up in the morning to the moment my eyelids gave out to sleep. It stole my voice and made me cry in public. It made me hide in my room, like Dorothy in the eye of the tornado. I was afraid of people, afraid of talking, afraid of what people thought of me, afraid of teasing, afraid of rejection, afraid of making a fool of myself, afraid of sports, afraid of reading aloud, afraid of being exposed for being bad, afraid of teachers, afraid people were looking at me, afraid of kids' parents, afraid of God, afraid of eternal punishment, afraid of my mom and dad.

I was always, *always* afraid.

Why this was is ultimately a mystery. But I know my mom's life was tumultuous when I was an infant—my dad overseas in the Navy, my sister only eighteen months older than me, and Mom living with her and a new baby at her parents' home in southern California, then inner-city Oakland in an apartment she was afraid to leave. By Mom's telling, my parents were unhappily married at the time, with Dad absent, volatile, and wandering, and Mom weak. Prone to anxiety, my mom was beset with worry during the formative years of my life, anxiety being a family poltergeist that drove her father to breakdown and her brother to substance abuse. Maybe I imbibed her fear like infant formula.

Whatever the case, I think I missed an essential baby lesson in safety. Babies are intended to connect with their parents, especially their mothers, in a deeply secure way that teaches them the universe is good. On our parents' laps, looking into their eyes and encountering absolute security and love, we are to pick this up. We are *supposed* to pick this up. But somehow this lesson in universal benevolence was lost to me. From my earliest memory, the universe seemed endlessly, relentlessly threatening.

My mom survived the chaos of my baby years to land in a decidedly settled housewife life. No one I know values settled-ness more, and Mom used the housewife role to create stability and routine for other people. Almost every night she tucked me into bed. Many nights she soothed my sadness and fear with soft fingers at my temples, her voice sweet as mulled wine, numbing the pain, lulling me to sleep. She was fine featured as a young woman, thin with short dark hair and gray-blue eyes. She had soft, small-boned hands with fingernails that arced like the back of a seal.

Mom grew up in San Bernardino, California, in a life that must have looked a bit like "The Truman Show." The patina of normalcy spread over her family's existence was thick and polished to a blinding sheen. Handsome, charming, and irresistibly likable, both of her parents spent their leisure time at parties or the golf club. Nana and Papa dwelt among the beautiful set and were more attractive than most for their inescapable love of one another.

Quite unlike my father's parents, my mom's parents experienced in their lifetimes a great love. Papa had such dark, Frenchman features and coloring he could have passed for Hispanic. My Nana was a strawberry brunette with eyes the blue of delphiniums. She had a house that smelled of roses where you'd find a dish of colorful soaps on every bathroom counter, alongside a tray of half-empty perfume bottles. My grandparents knew how to dance—and frequently did—and shared an infectious laughter. They loved Hollywood movies and cocktails and Sinatra. No unpleasant word was spoken in their house. No unpleasantness was acknowledged.

But the tension between this appearance and the realities of their life must have challenged their two children, my mother and her brother. Besides a condition that would be classified an "anxiety disorder," which landed Papa in the hospital for a nervous breakdown on more than one occasion, my grandfather had a heart condition that hung over him like a guillotine. He died of heart failure in his fifties, the same night he and Nana celebrated their wedding anniversary, and Nana lived the rest of her days waiting to join him. Mom's brother inherited both the anxiety disorder that plagued his father and an affection for liquor. He developed nervous conditions, reclusiveness, and alcoholism until he discovered a recovery program at a ranch where he stayed on to live and work as a handyman. Relatively speaking, Mom is a pillar of strength. She steers wide, open circles around risk, managing her anxiety by this careful avoidance and by adherence to conservative Christianity, which gives her rules and a rule-book.

My dad's parents are another story. According to my paternal grandmother, she had not received a whisper of explanation about sexuality from her strict Presbyterian parents when she married my paternal grandfather, who was something of a playboy. When he commenced on their wedding night to have sex with his young wife (or to attempt), my grandma accused him of unspeakable wantonness. *You want me to do what?!* She eventually submitted to his virile, newly wedded persistence, but with the enthusiasm of a woman being serially raped. The couple's wrangling over sex persisted for several weeks until my grandpa solicited the help of a pastor who lived next door. He knew that if an actual clergyman explained sex to his young wife, she would believe him. After the man discreetly handed my grandma a book on sexuality in marriage, she finally did.

But the resolution of the sex question was a single gain followed by a torrent of losses. The couple lost three girl babies at birth, before the survival of my father, the fourth born. They shared a marriage devoid of joy. Home was in flux. My grandpa chased logging and utilities jobs between California, Oregon, and Oklahoma until the time my dad was ten and his parents called it quits. My grandma left the marriage with little financial or paternal support and found herself working for a monolithic propane company in San Bernardino, California—a career of banal office work in a soul-sucking environment of metal, duct, and vinyl tile. Before the age of forty, she saw the beginning and ending of a second and third marriage and along the way, the birth of a boy twelve years younger than my father.

After a persistent people-phobia became so intense she couldn't bear to visit the office, Grandma sought early retirement. In her late fifties, she moved to a trailer park in Red Bluff, beginning her life as a veritable hermit, reading a clutch of bulky paperbacks every week and playing countless games of solitaire. When I visited her she fed me homemade fruit leather stuck to wax paper, or fresh muffins stored in an ancient cake tin.

Grandma pinched pennies like one of those small-town carnival machines. Once at the Mexican restaurant we visited together when I was twelve, Grandma poured the entire basket of complimentary tortilla chips straight into her purse. She did not fold them neatly into a napkin before depositing them or ask the server for a to-go container. She held that basket over her large, knitted purse and simply *poured*, a small horror to my tidy sensibilities. I imagined the granules of salt lodged behind her library card, the little spots of grease staining the purse's calico lining.

But Grandma didn't seem to care. She rarely seemed to care. She had suffered polio as a child and lived with stunted growth and a limp the rest of her life. As a result, she could not ride a regular bicycle and bought herself a girl's banana-seat bike, equipped with tassels on the handlebars and a white woven-plastic basket with orange and blue flowers. The ridiculous sight of her coming on that bike evoked in my child-heart a feeling akin to panic.

Yet she was my favorite.

And I, hers.

Where in the human genome does tact reside? My grandma inadvertently passed on her lack of tact, her hopelessly unbridled tongue, to her son, my dad. Dad was further handicapped by his utter lack of understanding of the female gender, likely the result of being a mostly only child raised by a mom who was remote and absent. But with off-handed comments he never intended as hurtful, Dad hurt my delicate feelings frequently, chiding me for my awkwardness at sports or my clumsiness. *Come on, you can throw better than that!* . . . He grew subtly aggravated when I couldn't do certain things, like say the word *purple* (which I couldn't say until second or third grade) or ride a bike (which I didn't master till fourth). He whittled away my fragile confidence like a dog gnawing on its own flesh.

Nonetheless, my Dad loved his kids as much as anyone I know loves his kids. He was simply unskilled at showing it.

The result in my life was pronounced performance anxiety. Afraid of doing anything wrong, I became a hopeless perfectionist, however persistently perfection eluded me. And it avoided me like dengue fever. . . .

◆

Color-coded booklets with matching question cards arrive on our desks. The teacher pulls a stop-watch from her top drawer. As she does, distraction and horror swirl through my head like loose trash in a strong gust of wind. I need absolute solitude and quiet to read, and my ability to comprehend or remember what I read decreases in direct proportion to my panic. I stare bleary-eyed at the SRA card, seeing one word, then another, standing apart from each other like strangers in an elevator. None of the words register in a sensible progression. I scan the card for words that appear in the questions, and read a phrase here, a phrase there. I guess at the answers. Glancing around, I see no one else struggling. Students are looking at the words, reading intently, drawing neat lead circles onto answer cards. My heart pounds in my ears as I stand firm against an onslaught of tears. The test places students in certain reading groups and my closest friends always excel, adding potential social ostracism to the confluence of SRA pressures. Somehow I avoid the lower groups.

SRAs are my worst grade-school nightmare.

Actually, no. My worst nightmare is P.E. class. And my worst, *worst* nightmares are 1) choosing teams for P.E., and 2) the annual humiliation of Presidential Fitness Testing. The practice of choosing teams for P.E. must have been invented by Pilate and his guards: *Whip and scourge her, then do team selection, then weave her a crown of thorns.* Presidential fitness testing presents its own humiliations, as kids are forced to hang with their chins suspended above a high bar—arms shaking like a chicken waddle—for as long as possible with their classmates looking on.

Big surprise this is named for the guy who sends "our boys" to war.

As fate would have it, my closest friend is innately athletic. Marie, who I've known since the age of three, is *cute*-pretty, all platinum-headed and round-nosed, and tall and slender. Though we bicker incessantly, hell-bent on outdoing one another, we call each other "best friend," an appellation that is as much a challenge as a term of endearment. Next to Marie I am clumsiness incarnate. I worship her agility and athletic skill. I certainly fear her, and my insecurity and fear compound my hopeless bumbling in her presence.

But when we put competition aside, Marie and I have good times. Marie has relatives from the South (who speak with accents, no less) and one of these relatives, Marie's southern grandmother, sends her tiny, lacey bra and panties sets made of red and black satin—girl-sized, flat cups and all. I think this must be the most extraordinary grandmother in the whole United States, and these undies sets the best gift I have ever seen. Red satin with black lace trim. Black with red lace trim. Little dress-up lingerie. At the age of six, Marie and I lip-sync Beach Boy songs for her parents and brother with tennis-racket guitars, clad in these lacey numbers in the middle of her family's front room. For us, it is the height of excitement and meets with an amusement by the audience that we interpret as sheer glory. How my performance anxiety allowed me to lip-sync surf tunes to my friend's parents while wearing underwear, I will never understand.

◆

I cannot say when, exactly, I began to question that Jesus loved me. I don't know that I ever believed it. It was the message of the first song I likely ever learned: "Jesus loves me this I know, for the Bible tells me so," as it was for countless church-going children. But "the Bible tells me so" didn't work for me, not even at a young age. In my gut, I knew it wasn't reason enough. I couldn't believe that love was the bottom line when I felt judged and watched, no matter what the Bible said. Of course, this wasn't formulated in my child-mind, it was what I *felt*.

One only needed to look around church to see what Jesus really loved. What Jesus really loved were men. Men stood in front of the service every Sunday morning and evening, and every Wednesday night. Men received respect and attention. Men served the communion, collected the offering, led the meetings, and taught the important Sunday-school classes, the ones only adults attended. Men sat at desks in offices with locking doors and dictated memos and sermons to the church secretary—a woman—who sat at a public desk anyone and her brother could get into. Men wore important-looking suits and led wedding ceremonies and baptized people who got saved.

Certainly one would wonder what was wrong with women. *Something* was wrong with them, or God would have wanted them to serve in these important roles. That they were not seen as fit for leading roles in the church could only mean one thing: women were not good enough. God did not value women as highly. Jesus did not love women as much as men. The story of Adam and Eve made this obvious enough. Wasn't Eve's sinfulness and deception the cause of all suffering and evil? Eve = Evil. It didn't take a genius.

Perhaps that was why girls had such a heavy moral burden. It was clear that girls were expected to be above-board even when boys were not. Girls were expected to stay quiet and help around the house when boys got away with fighting, tracking in dirt, and calling girls names. Maybe they could get away with these things because they were less indebted to God. Males had less to make up for. Females, on the other hand, were always and forever in the red.

Even if I couldn't parse out the theological messages making me doubt "Jesus loves me, this I know," I did get the drift at a pretty young age. I think many girls in conservative contexts do. It was certainly obvious to me that women needed men, girls needed boys. Males apparently exemplified all that was right with God. So if women and girls were to be saved, they had to be washed in the blood of the man.

◆

No wonder I start looking for male approval and attention so young. I remember having a crush on a boy in preschool. But true boy-love didn't strike till kindergarten, when Marie and I shared a crush on the same boy.

Obviously, this posed a dilemma for our friendship. Thus, we devised a plan to solve it. At lunchtime, on the far side of the school building, Marie and I arranged to meet the boy, Brian Perry, and demand that he choose between us. Brian, the son of a well-to-do farmer, was tall for our age and freckled. He had straight brown hair, velvety sweet eyes, and dense lashes that swept across his eyes like feathers. Our Catholic K-12 school was a featureless white cube that seemed monolithic. The windowless white plaster of the building stretched on mercilessly and was met by a wide swath of asphalt rimming the building's base. Brown September grass edged the asphalt and stretched across an expansive soccer field.

We told Brian to choose which girl he wanted for his girlfriend. It was a brilliant solution to the strain the threesome posed for our friendship.

It was, that is, until Brian chose Marie.

This pattern: girl loves boy, other girl loves boy, boy chooses other girl, would repeat itself dozens of times over the course of my young life, resulting in greater and lesser degrees of anguish for jilted girl. With this early start on boy-love, I got to suffer a whole lifetime's worth of romantic disappointment before learning how to drive.

My entire class at Sacred Heart School was, for whatever reason, prematurely amorous. I was given my first lesson in French kissing in third grade by a half-Mexican boy named Craig Padilla who won the school talent show by singing and playing "They Call the Wind Mariah" on a banged-up guitar as big as he was. He was a short boy with a tan, Charlie-Brown head and beautiful blue eyes. He gave me love notes folded into notebook-paper pouches that held pennies and nickels. But the kissing lesson was just that, a lesson. *This is what French kissing is, and this is how it is done.* Very straightforward. Several times in fourth grade, a group of us played spin-the-bottle behind the backstop in the far corner of the ball field where recess monitors couldn't see us. As I recall, those kisses were not French, but they were much more fun.

At the end of my fourth-grade year, my family moved to a new house across town and I transferred to public school. Here, in fifth grade, I had my first "boyfriend" (who lasted four weeks and held my hand during *The Fuller Brush Lady*, starring Lucille Ball, which we watched in the school cafeteria) and learned to cuss ("You bastard!" I'd say to Mark, the class tease, before kicking him in the shins and scrambling up the monkey bars). I had a crush on my Brazilian-American teacher who wore an Afro and went by the name "Fuzz." The sole highlights of the year were the cinnamon Certs Mr. Fuzz passed out for good behavior, and peanut-butter cookies from the school cafeteria.

Home Box Office (HBO) and Showtime, popular in the early Eighties, were a fixture in several houses I visited in these days, though our household abstained. On occasion, I spent the night with friends who could watch TV late into the night, unsupervised by parents. Late-night movies played on HBO and Showtime were pornographic at the time, and between fifth and seventh grades, I saw three such films.

On friends' living room floors, tucked into sleeping bags on soft shag carpeting, I saw my first graphic depictions of human sexuality, which were also scenes of female degradation. On one occasion, I watched, with heart racing, a large-busted woman being strapped to some sex contraption, and on another I marveled at the tangle of three women and one man. It was clear, from these images, that women were toys, fascinating objects to be used, like sports cars, for male amusement.

♦

I am in sixth grade when I form my first deep friendship. Her name is Sarah. Sarah has pixie-black hair and a round ashen face, a smile that could melt glaciers, and sable, almond-shaped eyes. She talks with a high-pitched, lyrical voice, and walks with small steps like a geisha. Sarah and I spend hours each day circling the school building together, divulging our secret longings and talking about the boys we love with not a small measure of insanity. "I think Jerrod was looking at me today during lunch. Do you think I'm imagining it? . . . I don't know what I'll do if he doesn't like me. I don't think I could ever, *ever* like anyone else. We're so perfect for each other. . . . " "Do you think I should ask Todd to dance with me at Friday's dance? . . . But I don't know if I could ever do it!"

When we aren't together, we write notes that often end with the adage: "with faith all things are possible." We take this to mean: *Dream big! Don't give up on your loves who barely notice you!* But I love Sarah as much as I love anyone. The way she and I understand each other and make each other brave, the way we share our deepest selves without threat of betrayal or belittling, the way we appreciate things about the other that no one else understands—it is the kind of friendship I've always hoped for.

But a year after our meeting, Sarah's mom moves her from Red Bluff to a far-less-rural location in central California, in an attempt to escape a cloying ex-husband and to craft a freer life for her daughter. I ache at the loss, before, during, and after Sarah's move. I see it ahead of me like a fast-approaching barrier I will soon crash into. I brace myself for it, I barrel into it, and I am shattered.

Sarah and I make every promise to stay close, to not grow apart. But we take up very different lives in very different places. Despite our solemn promises, I apprehend the gravity of her leaving. A seed of loneliness takes root in the crevice of my broken heart, begins to grow, and over the course of years, produces a grim canopy. The pain of losing Sarah sends out rays, like a cartoon stun-gun, wavy, psychedelic rays that distort the appearance of everything. As a result, I lose my footing in a brutal junior high school.

After the loss of Sarah's friendship, I floundered. Hanging out with the "popular" girls, I attempted to get nearer the popular *boys* I was most interested in. Ratcheting up the ladder of popularity, I went to parties, became head of the cheerleading squad, wore the latest fashions. But I was a reeking failure at popularity, far too sensitive and serious to succeed as a party girl. By the middle of eighth grade, when the popular crowd I hung out with started drinking, I leapt like a skydiver from the plane of popularity. Since submission to overt peer pressure went against my independent nature, and since abstaining from alcohol while hanging out with the drinking crowd is just plain lonely, I had no choice but to jump. I made a conscious effort to befriend the nice kids, the so-called "nerds" who congregated in the science room and played chess during breaks. Turns out they were vastly more interesting.

The popular girls I abandoned at that time decided—with a vengeance only junior-high-aged girls can muster—to make my life a veritable hell. My exit from their hoard was the ultimate snub, and I would have to pay, since in junior high, nothing costs more than nonconformity.

As a result, the girls I once called friends aped my mannerisms behind my turned back and called me a "bitch" and a "nerd." I remember sitting in a classroom on Friday afternoon when students were finished with class work and milling about. Someone asked tauntingly, "What are your Friday night plans, Tricia?" "I don't really know," I replied tragically, aware of the trap and longing for a comeback that never came to mind. "That's because she's a *homebody!*" chimed a girl from the corner of the room, inviting snickers from her cluster of petty, mean friends.

These same girls scrawled BITCH across my locker in eye-pencil. They whispered and laughed when I spoke in class. They toilet-papered my house with what must have been the entire supermarket's supply of TP (Dad went out early to remove the catastrophe before I woke up, but I caught him). They snickered at my clothes and spread rumors that I'd made snobbish remarks I hadn't made. These girls positively *loathed* me. In contrast to this, the brainy kids embraced me like a goddess, despite the negative attention I drew their way. They were incontestably smarter than I but never once implied it. They are probably now rocket scientists, every one.

In many respects, that year shaped the next chapter of my life. I had failed at being popular, and found I had little taste for the popular set. I was analytical and intuitive. I dwelt comfortably in the shadows, where darker emotions could exist unhidden, where the fascinating underside of things was explored, and where compassion was nurtured. I belonged with the poets, not the mall rats. But I had learned to be ashamed of my nature. What counted was having friends, being the life of the party, being liked by boys. What counted most was being *fun*. Yet in eighth grade at public school, my best efforts proved hopeless and humiliating.

I was also deeply depressed. I descended into a melancholy that was, in part, a homecoming. It turned me all lyrical and introspective. Yet it was likewise a descent into clinical adolescent depression. I say "clinical" because of what I know now, not because I received a diagnosis or treatment for the condition. This was before therapy was mainstream in small towns, and my parents, like most evangelical Christians of the time, were a tad leery of psychology.

◆

Around this time, I start dating.

Out of the blue and just a week before classes, my parents give my sister and me the option of attending *Catholic* high school. If my parents had announced that a gorgeous exchange-student-slash-professional-surfer was coming to live with us, it would not have been more welcome news. I felt as though I'd been whisked from a burning building, since I'd spent the summer dreading my clutch of enemies awaiting me at the public high school. Kristen, who attended the public school her freshman and sophomore years, also transfers to the Catholic institution, which is appropriately, amazingly, almost *allegorically*, called "Mercy."

Perhaps out of competition with my sister, I take an immediate liking to a boy in her grade, two years above mine. He is Indonesian-Swiss with finely chiseled jaw and cheekbones, a perfect mouth, and a thin but well-proportioned body. His alluring brown eyes follow me across the gym—volley of voices, squeak of sneakers, and I am *noticed*. He has a head of silky, thick black hair and an intriguing name: Hector. His aspect seems serious and intelligent, almost mysterious.

Hector is my first lesson in how dramatically looks can deceive. After deciding through the agency of mutual friends that we both like each other and want to go out (though we've said less than ten sentences to each other), we end up on a double date, a car date in my friend's parents' white station wagon with blue velveteen interior. I am thus afforded an opportunity to get to know the ineffable Hector.

I soon realize Hector rarely crafts an intelligent sentence. His jokes fall flat as communion wafers. He is the inevitable butt of his friends' sarcasm and laughs a bit like a *clown*. "Dork" is the word echoing in the back of my mind, but I do not listen to it, nor do I heed my gut, which shouts: *Nip this thing in the bud while you still have some dignity.*

But the dignity slips away too quickly to arrest it. In the back seat of the car on the way home from a movie, I fall victim to what I later learn are Hector's infamously fast hands. Somehow, in a sitting position, he manages to get his hands all the way into my underpants and onto my breasts. His hand is as skilled as Houdini's, navigating clasps and zippers like a man escaping with his life.

I am a fourteen-year-old who's had virtually no practice at finding my voice with boys, who cannot lift a hand to stop him or shape my tongue and harness the breath to form the word "No." I feel *helpless*. Nonetheless, I do have limits. When Hector places my hand on the stiff little roll in his pants, I take it away. All the while Hector is kissing with pointy tongue and not-so-fresh breath, as I try to remember what could possibly be desirable about kissing.

Throughout the entire scene our comrades in the front seat, who are apparently well aware of Hector's fast hands, snicker and pant tauntingly. The radio mumbles Jim Morrison's "Light my

Fire" and windshield wipers slap back and forth, back and forth
against pouring rain. *Goodbye, sweet dignity, goodbye.* It is a good
thing, almost, that it slips away so completely, for there is none left
to lose when Group Car Date 2 rolls around and Hector wets his
pants. Yes, wets his pants.

Car Date 3 never happens.

◆

For the remainder of my freshmen year, I used up eight-tenths
of my cognitive energy on a boy named Peter, overanalyzing each
and every look that passed between us, each glance striking me like
a small electric shock, each magical smile or nod. Peter was a tall,
skinny boy with shiny, flaxen hair cut in the one-tier style of the
'80s. He had sparkling eyes of deep umber and a melting smile
with a mole on the side of his lip. His parents, divorced and rich,
encouraged their children to watch documentaries on public television and to take college-prep courses. After graduating salutato-
rian, Peter went off to college at Occidental, a school I was too
middle-class to have heard of. Peter was funny in a self-effacing,
quirky way I found irresistible. He had a way of *shucking* himself,
raising his shoulders and tilting his head when he said something,
as if to appear humble. Perhaps this veneer of humility is what en-
gendered the impression I had a chance.

Despite the fact that I was a freshmen and he a junior, I asked
Peter to a Sadie Hawkins dance, an informal dance to which the
girls ask the guys. The evening of the dance, I wore my fashion signature: a sweatshirt and full skirt hemmed a few inches below the
knee. At fifteen, I'd yet to discover the power of my body and thus
kept it well hidden (the first clue I understood nothing about
boys). On our date, Peter drove and insisted on paying for dinner,
a meal at a Chinese restaurant I remember little about. I was too
busy trying to remember what the hell I'd been thinking.

In life there are times we mistake stupidity for courage, and for
me, the Sadie Hawkins dance was such a time. I had felt brave asking Peter to the dance, which in fact I was. I was a ninth-grade no-
body while he was a popular upperclassman. At the dance, Peter
spoke hardly a word to me. He spent the entire night laughing and

dancing with girls from his class as I distracted myself with my good friend Aamir, trying to blend into the wall, pretending to be the Invisible Girl.

Some would have dropped the crush like a hot biscuit after that night, but my crush on Peter persisted through part of my sophomore year.

One interaction with Peter remains in my memory as if it happened yesterday. . . . I am at an all-day weekend rehearsal for The Pajama Game, sitting with a group of friends on bleachers in the gym and listening to music on headphones.

Peter asks what I'm listening to.

"Grieg," I tell him, glad that he asked. I doubtless chose classical music to impress him.

"Who's playing it?" he asks.

"Grieg," I reply, thinking he hadn't heard me.

"No, who's *playing* it," he says again.

Again, I reply, "Grieg." A look of mounting frustration befalls him as our friends on the bleachers begin to tune in.

Perplexed and sinking, I look in his eyes. When I finally catch on to his meaning, my entire insides wilt. I hand him the tape jacket and stare at my lap.

"It's okay," he says suddenly, recognizing my embarrassment. "No problem." He is trying to be nice. Yet if there is one thing worse than being thought dumb by the boy you like, anything *approaching* the mortification—it is being the subject of his pity.

◆

As an adolescent, I was still dedicated to the pursuit of male approval and attention—yet nine times out of ten, was a wretched failure with males. The moment I set my eyes on the conquest of such attention, everything possible would go wrong. I'd end up making a ding in the drivers' ed. car the moment my teacher started to like me, or I'd splatter red punch on my crush's tan chinos. Just when the horizon would start to look bright, a storm cloud would gather above my head and let loose.

Not only did I fail in my attempts to get the right boys to like me, but I rarely got on well with male teachers, whom I started to have in middle school. My inability to maintain good relations with male teachers was in part because they teased. And I was both sensitive and sarcastic, a toxic, regrettable combination. My reaction to teasing was to muster a bit of attitude and return the razzing, causing the teasing to devolve into an all-out tournament. The teacher seemed to enjoy this, but it was disastrous for someone with feelings as fragile as mine. By the end, I'd be teetering on the edge of tears.

On the other hand, as a teenager I had several enjoyable friendships with "the guys." Things went well with boys I didn't much care to impress, as was the case with my guy friends. But the moment I developed a crush, or the friend got a crush on me: friendship doomed.

At this stage of my life, I still believed male opinion mattered more than female opinion. I certainly still felt, in a visceral, irrational way, that God preferred men. Yet at this time of life, I also began to catch glimpses of what I'll call "resonances of the transcendent." The Father God associated with church sermons, Sunday school, and many stories of the Bible still felt distant and exacting. This Father God loved you only so far as you towed the line and pleased him, insofar as your life was pure and holy, especially in the sexual sense. And this Father God was most certainly a Him. In my mind I inadvertently pictured this God looking like Moses in the Charlton Heston depictions. This God was male, authoritarian, and angry with women. Think of a white Ayatollah Khomeini.

Nonetheless, it was during my early teen years that I started to earnestly pray to Jesus when I needed help. I associated Jesus with compassion (though his association with the Father God cast aspersions on his attitude toward women). I also began, at this age, to experience reverence.

Compassion and reverence were my first and nearest experiences of divine love. From a young age I experienced deep compassion, both in my own response to people's suffering and in the responses of certain individuals to my suffering, especially those of my mother, a few adults at our church, and the youth pastor who counseled me for six months when I was fifteen. In eighth and ninth grades I became involved with youth-group service projects, including delivering food baskets to families in need at the holidays, working with inner-city youth at a drop-in center, and visiting the elderly in nursing homes. In sharing compassionate love with people in need, I touched something that seemed like transcendence, like a beyond-this-world force of love—like God but not the Charlton Heston one.

I had inklings that this compassion had something to do with God's essence. I had formulated no ideas or explanation for this, I just felt it as a hunch. And the times I felt closest to God were in the surrounding aura of that compassionate love. That, and in the enveloping wonder of nature.

In encounters with nature, I sometimes experienced resonances of the transcendent. I vividly recall a time our church youth group took a retreat outside of Grass Valley, California. Our group went often to the camp for retreats. On one occasion when I was sixteen, I and five friends decided to stay out late viewing stars in an open amphitheater on a night as clear as spring water. So numerous were the visible stars, it seemed the universe had split open for us. We could see stars far beyond the usual ones—stars zillions of light years away. And the number of shooting stars one sees when this number is visible, is mind-blowing. Shooting stars went off like fireworks. We all lay on the ground on our backs, heads clustered together, bodies fanned out like spokes of a wheel. We were overcome. Someone started singing a church song, and we all sang along, followed by another hymn-like song, then another.

It was a spontaneous worship service under the stars, but we were drawn into singing and reverence not by the telling of a Bible story, or an ideological speech from the pulpit. We were drawn to awe and reverence by the reminder over our heads of how immense and beautiful the universe really was, and how much love we felt experiencing it as close friends. We were overcome with reverence, reverence for that bigness, that beauty, for whatever force dwelt beyond it, and reverence for the source of love itself.

♦

Around car-driving age, I fell in love.

I was actually thirteen the first time I saw Tom. He was walking with his mom and younger brother (with whom my sister was acquainted) on a street in downtown Red Bluff. It was a sun-drenched April morning and lilting birds hung invisible streamers all over the sky. Tom wore a blue and white lettermen jacket and weathered jeans and had dense, short brown hair. His brother's name was Dan. At the sight of Tom, the words "Dan's brother is handsome" actually passed my eighth-grade lips. Maybe I was overcome with the titillations of spring, maybe I was channeling Audrey Hepburn—but "handsome" is a word of rare usage among middle-schoolers. Nevertheless, this guy, five years my senior, was eighteen, a man; and men were called handsome. From that day until the approximate age of thirty, I had a major *thing* for Tom, though it would be two years before I actually got to know him.

Tom's mom, a single mother, insisted her sons attend church, and (sing hallelujah!) it was my church they attended. After my first glimpse of Tom, I spent most services worshipping his inspiring visage and daydreaming our shared future. In observing him as he sat through church or chatted afterward with his friends, I learned Tom was not only handsome but funny and confident and intense.

The infatuation was, at this point, a one-way street. Tom had yet to discover my inspiring visage. Then one day while I was yet in eighth grade, I sang a tender, earnest song before the congregation, a song and performance Tom found memorable though I did not. The song's subject was the desire to see things through God's eyes and how that mattered more than what other people thought. Tom took notice. He was nineteen.

◆

Tom and I have been stealing penetrating glances of each other for many months when our paths finally cross in, of all places, San Francisco. It is the summer before my tenth-grade year, and I am fifteen years old. My limited dating experiences have included the pants-wetting Hector and the humiliation of Peter.

In my reckoning, I am ready for a man.

Tom had trained with the army reserves right out of high school and works a few weeks each summer in a medical capacity at a VA hospital in San Francisco. I am involved in my church's youth group, which each summer spends several days in San Francisco assisting a youth drop-in center in the worst part of town, painting, cleaning, entertaining kids. Though Tom no longer attends church, and though he lives forty-five minutes from Red Bluff in the university town of Chico, he is a friend of our youth leader. In the evenings after working at the VA hospital, he joins our group for a little urban nightlife.

Four quivering, salty San Francisco nights. Tom and I launch huge Chinese fireworks. With the group, we eat pot stickers, see a movie, and visit the wharf. Every taste and smell is new-born. What could be in this air, filling me with such an ethereal hope, making my head light? I have never seen so much beauty concentrated in one place—the lights on water, the pungent sea air, the city's texture and vitality. The voices I hear are angelic, and the noise even of cars is a symphony. Every step I take is a leap.

On the fourth evening of our stay, our group takes a midnight stroll through Golden Gate Park. With air damp and ripe, the night smells quintessentially urban, delightfully different from home. The lights of the city and the occasional streetlamp diminish the darkness of the park, but it is a big-city park in a relatively high-crime area, and I thrill to walk it at night. The stars in the dense, indigo sky are few, but each one, on that night, shines for us.

Up to that point, the signals between Tom and me were eye to eye: the way he stared at me across a table as I talked, his look as he passed his coat to stop my shivering, our frequent interlocking gazes. At the Chinese restaurant, my fortune speaks of finding love, and I scoff as I read it aloud. "Yeah, right," I say, in my most sarcastic tone.

Tom looks straight into my eyes, "You just haven't found the right guy."

But now, sitting in a menacing park on a mystical night, with friends on either side of me, Tom and my signals advance to *touch-*

ing. Tom stands behind me where I sit on the park bench, looking down on a grassy hillside overshadowed by ghostly maples and towering oaks. Leaning his hips into my back with deliberate flirtatiousness, Tom settles his weight against my shoulders, and my head rests gently on his belly. No one but us can know what is happening, but a fire passes between us, a charge that seems to rise up from the center of the earth. It sparks the most intense sensations I have ever experienced, and sets my heart spinning in a tornado of feeling. I want to reach my hand up and grasp his; I want to turn and face him as he lowers his head to kiss me. But instead I sit frozen and silent as a glacier, not moving a hair, just letting the impact of the touch pass between us—our secret. Now Tom and I will graduate to a new stage of romance. I am sure of it. He will love me and I will love him. I will *love* him.

When we drop Tom off near the hospital before returning to our ramshackle hotel in Oakland, he looks straight into my eyes. "See you tomorrow," he says. My heart turns a pirouette.

The next evening we arrive at 6:00 to pick him up. We wait thirty minutes in a near-empty parking lot outside Tom's quarters, on a hill overlooking the city.

And he never shows.

There is only the amber thread of the Golden Gate, the deep-sinking bay.

◆

I pocket my disappointment discreetly. No one would have believed me had I told them Tom and I shared hints of an unspoken romance. I am fifteen and famously insecure; Tom is twenty, well known around town for his talent, and is soon to ascend the ranks of the theater program at Chico State, where he attends college. He is magnetic and humorous and entirely out of my league, though he occupies my mind nearly every waking moment of every day. By mid-September, the pressure is unbearable.

Around this time I receive a coveted privilege for a middle kid of four living in a four-bedroom house. "Tricia," my mom says to me one day, "I believe it's time you have your own room." I can hardly trust my ears! My own private space! My own room!

Turns out I am granted my own room while my older and younger sisters, separated by a twelve-year chasm, share one. Since neither of them complain, I proceed to inhabit *my own room* with astonishment and without a trace of guilt. Whenever possible, I sit alone in that solitary paradise. I fling my colors everywhere: old four-poster bed passed on to me by my parents, a simple quilt handmade by my mother with holly green edges and squares of roses, lily wallpaper, my Grandma's cedar chest, and a satin ribbon stretched across the ceiling from which I hang vintage hats with clothespins. One wall is reserved for James Dean. My desk is full of art supplies: tubes of acrylic paint, drawing pencils and fixative, and smudged white erasers with rounded corners. The desk's surface displays my latest work-in-progress.

On a particularly lucid fall evening, sprawled across the bed of my neo-independence, my secret sneaks out, like a pin-prick leak in a balloon, in a conversation with my mom. Mom and I still talk regularly. She often visits my room at bedtime, peeking in to say, *How are you, Dear?* At times that year, I have been desperately depressed. Mom sits at the edge of my bed, stroking the hair from my forehead as I release a deluge of tears.

"What's bothering you, honey," she asks one night, voice like a velvet glove, fingers traversing my warm, throbbing head.

"I'm just sad," I sob. "I don't know what to do."

She measures out her words in the stillness as she would measure a bolt of cloth, holding the fabric between her shoulder and outstretched arm. Thoughtful, reticent. Looking past the window, she gently rests a hand on my shoulder. "Don't know what to do about what, Dear?"

"I," I stammer, "I miss someone. . . . I miss Tom." Mom knows of the Tom-crush I have had since eighth grade. She knows he accompanied our group in San Francisco.

Mom sits quietly for several moments as my shock at saying the words stops up my tears. The room becomes hauntingly still. The light of a partial moon softens the hard edges of the bed-posts, the walls, making everything gauzy and gray.

"Well, maybe you should write him a letter," she finally says. "Let him know you're thinking of him." Her words spill onto my bed. It is a moment of liberality I expect she lived to regret. But the words are nonetheless there. They sit on the bed like a gift waiting to be opened, waiting to be picked up and used. I pick them up. Later that week, I write to Tom.

♦

That fall I sink deeper and deeper into a hormonally induced depression that lasts for months. For some, including me, the transition called puberty is a monstrosity.

I have told none of my friends about Tom. Who would believe me?

Then, on a school trip to the Oregon Shakespeare Festival in Ashland, Oregon, I bump into my old friend—my walk-around-the-school, dream-sharing, "with faith all things are possible" confidante, Sarah. Strolling across a wide courtyard, I see her, sitting with a group from her school, her smile emanating surprise. It turns out my and Sarah's school groups are in the same hostel. After the day's scheduled events, when our groups have returned to the hostel for the night, I sneak into Sarah's room, a small second-story bedroom with beveled ceilings shared by two adult chaperones snoozing placidly in their corners. The room is dark.

Sitting with legs crossed on the end of Sarah's bed, I start at the beginning. . . . "So he was walking to church with his mom when I first saw him. . . . " I narrate the story to the end, speaking in emphatic whispers. . . . "Somehow I just know he'll write back to me . . . or something will happen." "Sarah, I *know* he cares about me," I whisper. "It is crazy, in a way, but I know it in my gut."

"Then you must be right," she replies.

Sarah and I sit on her bed talking and stifling laughter for hours, releasing our cache of stale secrets late into the night. She is the first friend to know about Tom. I know she will tell me to dream, and she does.

Even so, there seems no sense in expecting the improbable. Thus I divert my attention toward Peter, my crush at school, reckoning I'll at least have someone to flirt with.

Then, around mid-October 1985, a month after I'd written

to Tom, I receive a letter. It has Tom's name in neat letters across the top.

I carry the letter to my room, staring open-mouthed at the envelope as if it holds Willy Wonka's golden ticket. I simultaneously dread and anticipate its contents. Perhaps it is a letter sent to apologize for raising my hopes, a letter gently instructing me to back off. Perhaps it is an ardent proclamation of love. My heart races in my chest, and I feel elated and nauseous and dizzy with shock. I shut the door and slowly tear back the flap.

Tom has written to ask me on a date.

He asks me to accompany him to a play in Chico in early November, *Come Back to the Five & Dime, Jimmy Dean, Jimmy Dean.*

I scream and toss the letter in the air! I run to tell my sister, whom I'd pushed out of the room to read my letter in privacy. That invitation, written on the inside of a greeting card, is my golden ticket—my golden ticket out of silence. I will tell my friends! I will tell the world! *Tom asked Tricia on a date?* friends will muse. Finally, it is real. I am fifteen years old, and *Tom Hendricks has asked me on a date.*

Tom is of medium-height, 5'8," with spritely eyes that spring cartwheels when he smiles. He has a self-assured, almost bounding gait and spreads happiness around like a puff of dandelion. He excels at school. He wins people's affection with humor. All who know him well know he is a gifted actor.

Yet I sense in Tom, who frequently steals sincere, penetrating glances at me across a room, a brooding seriousness he keeps hidden. Over the years, I learn my sense is correct. The brooding part of Tom is enormous, and it is the part that draws me.

Tom's parents divorced when Tom, his younger brother, and younger sister were kids. His mother—a friend of my parents'— worked full-time, struggling to keep her family afloat, and as the eldest son, Tom assumed the role of responsible, affable child. His brother is rebellious, his sister the baby, several years younger than her brothers. Tom is easy-going and undemanding, the delight of his mother, the delight of his teachers, everyone's absolute delight.

Growing up middle class, I have the luxury of not noticing money. I notice when rich friends at school have more than I do, designer clothes instead of off-brand, spanking-new cars instead of used. But I take for granted my nice house, the fact my needs are met without my noticing how. For five years our six-member family has lived in a spacious new ranch house of my parents' design, with stucco-and-brick siding and a tile roof. It sits on a half-acre lot with expanses of lush green grass (watered via sprinkler system), a large, productive garden, a dozen fruit and nut trees, and assiduously groomed flower beds. A hedge of low-growing juniper borders the road and three maple trees stand like sentries out front.

I honestly do not notice Tom is poor. I notice he has one pair of dressy clothes he wears for every dressy occasion but figure he cares little about clothing. I notice he borrows his mother's old car to take me out but reckon this is standard for college students. Maybe they don't need cars while away at school. I have never driven through Tom's neighborhood.

Tom notices he is poor. And he notices I am not.

♦

Our date to *Jimmy Dean* finally comes. At the time I am partial to vintage, somewhat-flamboyant fashions, but on this occasion I choose velveteen, charcoal-gray pants, a black sweater with a red scarf, and black flats. I have short-bobbed hair lightened slightly to true blond, and no bangs. Good hair. Tom picks me up and drives the forty-five minutes between Red Bluff and Chico, answering my questions about college and life without bouncing questions my way.

"So, what do you want to do with a biology major when you graduate?" I ask.

"Well, I suppose I'll teach," Tom says, "or maybe do something in the medical field." We drift again into an awkward quiet. I try to dream up more questions. I'd been hoping for a longer answer to the biology thread. "But who knows," Tom finally chimes in, "I might change majors and throw everything into acting."

"I've heard you're very talented. . . . I didn't actually get to see your plays in Red Bluff when you were here. . . . "

What a dumb thing to say! I suddenly realize, berating myself. *I* heard *you're very talented! . . . I should have told him how much I liked his plays! I should have lied!*

"Well, I love to do it, anyway," Tom replies, face hinting at a knowing smile.

We drop by Tom's apartment before the play to fetch a book, and I am struck by the tidiness of the place, a spotless college bachelor pad—basic white-wall, white counter sort of place, with parking spaces out front.

Tom and I are excruciatingly polite.

We sit on Tom's bed making stilted small talk about old films and the energy in the room stagnates, as if the passion has been sucked clean out of us with a Shop-Vac, though I'd imagined myself there a hundred times.

We head to the play and arrive early, sitting in the quiet theater bereft of words, watching couples mill about and take their seats, greeting friends they know and chatting about the people in the program. During the play we sit two inches apart, laughing at all the right moments, apportioning seriousness as needed. I cross my legs and sit up straight like a woman. I am fifteen. When a lady trips and falls during intermission, Tom and I exhibit an appropriate level of concern, then look away, averting our attention and gaze from awkwardness to emptiness. We are so bloody well behaved, we are boring.

I hear nothing from Tom for weeks. I write him at least one letter, in which I keep matters light, despite the fact I've fallen headlong into a sea of depression: *I've drawn a picture for you for Christmas. Maybe you can stop by my house and pick it up.*

Then, well into my Christmas vacation, while in the throes of yet another virus (physical illness being the favored bed-fellow of psychological illness), I receive a surprise visit from Tom. It is late morning, brisk in a California kind of way, and shining with golden winter light.

I sport green sweatpants and a faded, oversized baseball-T of my dad's. I haven't brushed my teeth. Tom and I visit on my parent's overstuffed, blue velour couch in the front room and exchange gifts: my drawing for him, a paperback "how-to" on successful theater auditions for me, before perusing photo albums stored under my parents' glass-topped coffee table. The whole incident bears the greenish hue of fiasco.

"This one's nice." Tom points to a picture of me dressed as "Aunt Gertrude," a part I played for my baby sister when I was in middle school, when I entirely convinced my sister of Aunt Gertrude's existence. Gertrude has large, stuffed bosoms and a generous stuffed behind. She speaks with a high, proper accent and wears a wig, glasses, and ample red lipstick.

I roll my eyes. "Yes, thanks. Sort of embarrassing, isn't it?"

"No, it's cute." Tom and I sit slouched into the sofa, shoulder to shoulder, but I feel unforgivably ugly. I obsess over the thought I have morning breath.

"Let's look at your family photos next time," I offer sarcastically.

"You really don't want to see those."

I ask Tom what classes he'll take next semester, whether he's auditioning for plays—the most grown-up questions I can think up.

"Yeah, I have a lot going on," he says, "I'll be busy." *A blow-off,* I surmise. *I obviously won't be hearing from him.* "You know, they call it working on a 'play,'" he continues, "but there's not much playing involved." He fiddles with the photo album. "It's very hard work sometimes." I nod in agreement, as if I know. "But it beats driving a tractor." His eyes twinkle as he smiles.

"Thanks for the drawing," he says. It's a dark pencil sketch of James Dean all slouched in a corner with sunlight cutting across his cap. "It's good."

"You're welcome," I say, feeling suddenly embarrassed, wondering if I've gone overboard with such a personal gift. "Thank you for the book," I add. "I'll definitely read it."

At the door, Tom raises his hand goodbye. He smiles and offers me a hug, but it's a "You're a great friend" sort of hug. I smile back, then walk inside and wilt. *What happened to the heat we experienced when we were near strangers?* I contemplate in exhaustion. *What is this stifling politeness?*

♦

It is early spring when I see Tom again, February 1986, a festival in downtown Red Bluff. Nighttime parade. Crisp daffodil evening, starry lights in the trees along Main Street. My sister and I meet friends at a cafe. On the way back to our car, through crowds of people on the street, I notice Tom attempting to cross a jam-packed side street. He rushes past people in an obvious hurry, apparently trying to catch someone far up the road, and my heart snags on a sliver of hope. I continue walking bolt-forward like a soldier. Half a minute passes. Then a quarter of a minute. Then, I hear my name.

Tom asks if he can drive me home.

Before leaving downtown, we go for sodas, and this time the air around us veritably *buzzes*. Unlike our prior two meetings, I feel confident and natural. Tom sits looking at me, quiet and serious, with the unavoidable shade of a smile on his face—the way you look at someone you're happy to be with. By this time I am almost sixteen, more aware of my body, my sexuality. I feel beautiful with Tom and desirable. Tom is twenty-one.

On the drive home he tells me of a film coming out, *Out of Africa*. Will I go see it with him, in two weeks? He will call about arrangements. When I get out of the car I look into his eyes. We feel it, both.

Suddenly, I want to live.

CHAPTER TWO

Book of Love

The days stretch on like a Utah highway, but the time of our date finally arrives. On the drive to the movie theater thirty minutes north of Red Bluff, Tom and I converse easily amid long, charged silences. As we watch the film, a love story, the temperature slowly rises in the room. We say almost nothing on the return drive to Red Bluff. We don't have to. Pulling into town, near the turn-off to Ide Adobe Park, Tom asks if I'd like to take a walk. I nod yes.

The night is luminous and misty, not quite cold, a springtime night in northern California, with crickets and frogs trilling and air ripe with the scent of cut grass. Ide Adobe Park is the historic site of an early pioneer homestead standing in replica, from log cabin to stables, where the original homestead once stood along the Sacramento River. On this night, the river is laden with fog.

Standing by the water, Tom and I gravitate toward one another until we are woven together. Our kisses melt one into another. Hands on faces and backs and arms. Strong embraces and laced fingers. Tom's eyes wet with tears. Why have we not been here before, this close to each other? How did we resist this strong pull, more powerful than age or time? I want to stay there in that place where the fog hides us from restriction and reality, where we are just sweethearts by a river, and the night feels like home. I want to claim the mossy grass, the musky smell of river, the vaporous air and the liberating dark, to make them ours forever. Alongside the river that night, Tom and I release one scant ounce of our pent-up sexual energy, crossing a threshold between distant admiration and physical expression. My spirits soar. In the car, on the way to my house, Tom leans toward me and strokes my hand so tenderly, I can never doubt it is love.

◆

I wrote to Tom a few times after that night and received no response. I saw and heard nothing of him for eight months.

. . . Eight . . . months.

Eight months. To a lovelorn teenager, this is eternity. Never have I wanted something as intensely as I wanted closeness with Tom at that time—not before or since. But to think of him then, to remember the look of his hand on mine, the longing I'd seen in his eyes, was to *contract* with pain. For some reason, Tom had rejected me, or rejected *us*. He had chosen distance over connection. He had ignored my attempts at communication, shutting me out like a needling noise. For all I knew, we would never experience again what we experienced that night.

My heart leaked blood by the drop those first months. No matter where I thought of Tom, in the grocery store, at church, in history class, I fought back tears. Tom had drawn close to me only to disappear. An apparition. An insanely bad joke.

◆

That spring, desperate for distraction, I apply to a church-based service organization for teenagers and am placed with a team headed to Playa del Carmen, Mexico. We will complete a building project. I raise the necessary funds, pack my army-style duffel bag and wide-brim sun hat, and leave home for two months. I can hardly wait to be away.

The natural phenomena I behold in the next two months dwarf every ounce of exhaustion and homesickness I must endure to encounter them , every ounce of despair I have left behind in my attempt to escape. Playa del Carmen sits on the Caribbean Sea. And believe me, it is hard to be miserable on the Caribbean Sea. White sand like talcum powder. Low, cupcake clouds hanging like fringe on the edges of pristine sky. Warm, lucid water the color of desire. I have beheld nothing like that blue. The gentle bend of co-conut palms, the atomic orange of indigenous orchids, the rain-bow-hued fish that lace through my feet as I wade—I encounter it all as pure gift.

On one excursion to visit a remote island, I see a thin band of pink draw closer as our ferry nears the island. From miles offshore, I first spot it. *Is it a mirage?* As I wonder, a cluster of dolphins sidles up to the boat, skimming and dipping through the water. Then we draw closer to the island, close enough to see the solid, cotton-candy shoreline. One long edge of the island is covered in pink flamingos. Layer upon layer of the flaming birds, clustered to-gether, too beautiful to apprehend.

The water of the Caribbean is velvety smooth. Its hue fades from a delicate turquoise, to the color of aquamarine taffeta, to a deep lapis. Far out in the water one can still see the white-sand bot-tom of the ocean floor, which tapers very gradually. Water, raptur-ous water! On this trip I fall in love with the Yucatan, the Caribbean, with Mexico. A needle of longing wedges in my blue-as-sapphire heart that will remain until the day I return.

I arrive home acutely sensitized to small pleasures. I thrill to the sensation of a hot shower. I devour good food. Despite the memorable sights of the trip, the physical experience was ex-tremely demanding and the team leaders megalomaniacal, and I return home amply homesick and fatigued. I will be switching from Catholic high school back to public in one month, in part to save my parents' money, in part because the Catholic school's new principal instituted strict new policies, such as a dress code, that I couldn't abide. Another transition awaits.

◆

It is late September 1986, and I am sixteen years old. I am tak-ing an acting class at my high school when one afternoon, out of nowhere, Tom shows up at my class. My drama teacher is a close friend of Tom's, his former director from high school, and he pays a visit to watch her teach, perhaps hoping I am one of her students.

As I walk toward class, I see him in the late afternoon shadow of a tall building, wearing his usual weathered Levis jacket. His face lights up as we say hello—and when his face lights up, it really lights. *Shadows, be gone.*

Tom and I keep silent throughout the class, shifting our eyes if they meet. We say less than ten words to each other. I am golden brown and sun-bleached from my trip to Mexico, my hair streaked-with-corn-silk blond. I wear little makeup. Immediately after class, Tom and I offer a shy goodbye.

I run into Tom three more times that winter. On these occasions, we trade news like old friends. Still, we maintain a careful distance, a shrouded mysteriousness. After I see him, my mind is a cyclone of hope and remorse, passing memories over and over again in a storm of confusion and regret.

The following spring, on the day I'm scheduled to take the SAT test in Chico, Tom is in a play. Rather, that *night* he is in a play: Sam Shephard's "True West." He is both directing and acting. I call Tom telling him I'll be in town that day, asking him to set aside a ticket. He replies with an enthusiastic yes and invites me to the theater to visit after my test.

When I arrive for the visit, it is early afternoon, with Tom on a break from rehearsing. We talk eagerly for almost an hour, sitting atop a table, Tom's legs bent and crossed at the ankles, locked in his arms, mine perched on the table's edge with feet dangling. I have an undeniable sense that he thrilled to see me. Not just pleased, but thrilled. Before returning to rehearsal, Tom asks me to supper at his house—just the two of us—promising to cook me pasta before the show, then I watch him rehearse. His pounding energy resounds in me. I let my old feelings fan out inside, opening all the windows I had carefully latched. My emotions stretch to the far corners of the room where they mingle with Tom's. We are in love. I know it. The grand build-up begins again.

I am flammable.

By the time we get to Tom's house, he is way behind schedule. He asks me to help run lines with him, but there is no time for dinner. He recedes into quietness, his shoulders bowed and face sullen. *I've let you down*, he apologizes. *I'm sorry we cannot do dinner. Another time, okay?* I sit at the thrift-store table in his kitchen setting up lines while he washes dishes piled in the sink and dries them with a frayed-edge towel and rehearses. But when we finish, I feel insecure and diminished. Tom rushes around the apartment grabbing items he needs for the play and I feel like an obstacle there in the middle of his room, something he must plot a route around. He seems as nervous and withdrawn as a snail sucking back into its shell.

When we arrive back at the theater a gorgeous woman—blond and smiley and appropriately college-aged—stands at a table arrayed with gigantic cookies for sale. She has long, wispy limbs and radiant straight hair. When Tom greets her with a hug and introduces me, I know immediately who she is.

She is Tom's girlfriend. Her name is Amy.

In a dark, quiet corner of the theater, in front of a table of cookies, Amy and I stand awkwardly, making broken conversation as Tom runs through scenes pre-performance. Tom had introduced me to Amy as "an old friend from Red Bluff. She came to see the play," he tells her.

On stage that night, Tom is a volcano. A suicide bomb. A chemical explosion of deep-seated angst. I have never seen the likes of it. Off-stage he is largely subdued and bottled-up, politely *appropriate*. But that night on stage, he rages. I recognize that Tom's passion is more than an enlightened performance. I see him releasing his feckless, conflicted swell of emotion. I am sixteen, but I understand. Tom adores me. He has a girlfriend who is beautiful and sweet and, most importantly, his age. That night I feel closer to Tom, and farther away, than I ever have before.

◆

Late spring, I grow restless. I want to name my own experiences, to step out of my timid shoes into a life of my choosing. One day, wishing my mind away from school, I write the following poem in a notebook, scrawled between a ledger of history notes. The words are to be an anthem, words to live by—cymbals crashing in the background. I inscribe, in these lines, my next script, a manifesto. *This* is who I will be, I tell myself. I title the poem "Tomorrow":

> Believe not in tomorrow.
> Tomorrow is unsure today.
> Your wildest dream holds
> As great a probability
> As the next day . . .
> Today.
> So do not expect to soar tomorrow
> And decide to creep for now
> But spread your wings
> And live each moment
> For the next might bring
> A death to the moment past
> And you will wish you had
> Lived a little more
> Or loved a little stronger.

Within a month I have my first real sexual encounter.

Unlike my car-experience with Hector, which felt uninvited, I choose this encounter and participate in its planning with the other party. It is time to lose my virginity, I decide, and I will be in control. I choose as my partner a school friend with copious sexual experience, someone fit to guide me into the alien, unchartered territory of sex. He is not my type—not in the least—but I am sexually attracted to him. I have chosen a gregarious, quintessential jock, whereas my type is creative, deep, passionate, and quiet. The choice is strictly practical considering the goal.

Another unusual name: Donatello, half-Greek, half-Irish—a guy I had met and befriended in geometry class. I can talk to him about anything; he is open-minded and entirely non-intimidating. Not only is he a linebacker in reality and build, but he speaks with a dumb-jock accent that I learn, as I get to know him, is a put-on. He is smart. Not deep, not wise—but smart.

His parents are headed out of town for a night, so we devise a plan to rendezvous at his house around six. I shower and put on my favorite faded jeans, topped with a long-sleeved cotton shirt and a thrift-store cardigan. I drive to his house and park my parents' station wagon far down the shady block. He answers the door wearing jeans and an un-tucked oxford shirt, sleeves rolled up to the elbows.

Events advance quickly and we are on the floor within minutes of my arrival. His parents' house is a large, modern structure with high ceilings and new, soft shag carpeting. There is a leather sofa, a wet-bar, and a glass-topped coffee table. Clothes strewn across the floor.

After some kissing and foreplay, I tell Donatello to use a condom. When he goes to retrieve it, he says with a smile, "Hold that thought."

What a line! I think to myself as he walks away. *How many times he has said that before?!*

Lying on the floor, knees bent and bobbing together, I apprehend the loaded moment. A momentous line is about to be crossed, and I will be one giant step closer to adulthood. There on the floor of his parents' front room, I feel exposed, but in a way that is almost exhilarating, like stumbling onto a bold new perspective.

Donatello returns and we have sex.

It hurts like *hell*.

Ripping flesh, *excruciating* pain. I scream and gasp. With Donatello, I don't have to pretend—a key reason for my choice. But I don't experience an ounce of pleasure from the event and doubt he does either.

After our encounter, we ascend the staircase on our way to the shower. Under the stream of water, Donatello and I talk for almost an hour, the only pleasurable part of the experience. But despite the pain of first sex, the intimacy of the evening is new and addicting. Donatello and I repeat it one more time the following week, then go back to being just friends.

◆

In almost no time, the entire experience with Donatello became a surreal recollection. *Did that really happen? Did I really do that, with* him *of all people?* I tried not to think about it, tried to whisk the awkward memory under the rug of denial. Soon it was almost as if the whole thing never took place. This practice of shame, illusion, and denial became a pattern over the next five years of my life. *Do not acknowledge it and it did not happen.* Gradually my life became a patchwork of surreal, vaguely recollected memories I did not reflect upon. Still, the experiences of the time left marks that were impossible to erase. Of all the things that affected my spiritual development, denial was the most detrimental. Because of shame and fear, I found it nearly impossible to tell myself the truth.

Denial is different from a lack of awareness. At any given time in our lives, there are things that have not yet come into our awareness, things in our selves and our lives that are still shrouded in illusion. About the things we are aware of, we can be forthright and honest. But how can we tell the truth about something we don't yet know? At all times in our lives, there are things we just don't yet know. Denial, on the other hand, is hiding. Deep down, we are aware of something that we don't want to acknowledge, either because we are ashamed or because we fear what actions will be required if we openly acknowledge it. Thus we shove the thing out of sight, out of our conscious mind, and we proceed with our lives in denial of it.

At times, this may be a survival mechanism. We shove the thing until the time we are free and prepared to take necessary actions about it. Most of the time, however, the denial should not be necessary.

Denial is there because grace is not.

Denial is there because a liberating acknowledgement of our fallibility, of the inevitability of our making mistakes, is absent. An atmosphere of grace, where people recognize they will make mistakes and that mistakes are an opportunity for learning, makes denial unnecessary. It is the opposite of an atmosphere of shame. An atmosphere of grace says: mistakes don't make us bad. We *all* make mistakes. Grace says: this is an opportunity to learn and grow, so let's turn it into a gift. Grace doesn't make excuses for missteps, for things we do that hurt ourselves and others. In fact, grace makes excuses unnecessary. Grace lets us tell the whole truth, without shame or hiding, because grace lets us lift our chins and start over, acknowledging we can do better next time, that we will *be* better for what we learned. And the next time we make a mistake, we can be better again, and again. This is how we grow up.

Whatever the reasons, grace was not where I dwelt as a young person. I felt that any mistake I made, any choice that was somehow less than "pure," was an indication of my wrongness before God. It meant that I was not a good person. For people who don't come from religious settings, shame might issue from another place. It might tell them: you are not a good person because you were not strong enough, or smart enough, or mature enough, to keep from making that mistake. . . . You are a disappointment to [insert important individual]. But for me, and I expect many young people raised in strict religious environments, shame is deeply related to God. Shame says: you disappointed God. God does not love you as much as someone more righteous. You are not good enough to deserve God's love.

In light of this, my new forays into sex cast me in a rather poor light God-wise. At least with regard to the Charlton Heston God I still subconciously believed in, the flannel-graph God I had grown up with. If I had doubted before that God loved me and was pleased with me, my dawning sexuality made this doubly doubtful. Looking face-to-face with this God was out of the question, so I mostly stopped praying. I was too shamed to pray. I knew I couldn't hide from God, but I could choose not to think about God. I could live in denial that anything was wrong. So I did.

Denial affects our spiritual selves the way an ailment affects our physical selves. Denial weakens us spiritually, it makes us exhausted, vulnerable, confused, and less than whole. Our spiritual lives are our essence—whatever beliefs or symbols we use to define them and whatever are or are not our spiritual practices. Therefore, denial has a very detrimental effect on our essence, our overall wholeness and well-being.

Truth-telling, on the other hand, no matter what bumbling things we are up to, is healing and bolsters the spiritual life. It brings awareness into our lives. It brings even our most regrettable mistakes into the light where we can acknowledge them and learn something redeeming from them. It helps us to realize where we have hurt others and need to apologize. It makes us more loving. Truth-telling is like good natural medicine for the spirit. Truth-telling breaks down any walls we have built between ourselves and God, because we face God knowing we have no need to hide. On a spiritual level, our hiding was never successful. On a spiritual level, we cannot hide. And as long as we construct for ourselves reasons to hide, we will never be safe, because we will always be found out. Truth-telling eliminates the threat. In grace and truth, there is no threat. On the material level of our lives, we may lose things as a result of telling the truth, but in truth-telling we will be freer. On the spiritual level, there is total safety in telling the truth.

It would take many long years for me to learn this. In the meantime, I lived, to one degree or another, in denial, with lesser or greater impact on my spirit. In the meantime, I continued to feel largely estranged from divine love.

◆

A month after my sexual encounters with Donatello, I find myself at a friend's graduation. It is the first week of June, and again I see Tom. It is the graduation ceremony of Mercy High School which Tom had attended, and which I had attended my freshman and sophomore years. Tom has come with his best friend in hopes, I presume, of seeing me.

The graduation takes place in a park alongside the river, and Tom hangs out far to the back, looking around distractedly. I hang on the fringes as well. The air is warm, the fading grass streaked with shadow and edgy evening light. Kids shout on swings just a quarter-block's distance from the ceremony, and beyond the playground a man plays fetch with his dog. When I see Tom, I boldly walk toward him, as his eyes trace my approach. We walk away from the ceremony to talk, and soon find ourselves in a long, intense embrace.

I am seventeen. He is twenty-two.

Till four in the morning, Tom and I wander through town. We spend hours talking about our hopes for life, about films we had seen and plays Tom had read, about our friends and our disappointments. The sky is as open as a book that night, and the stars read like a detailed fortune, portending happiness, rich lasting companionship, portending true and matchless love. I am overcome with all my heart holds for Tom and has been holding for years, the seams stretched to bursting.

As we stroll past the old Safeway now converted to a library, I ask Tom the Question. "So, have you had a girlfriend this whole time—since our last date?" Several months earlier I'd heard a rumor Tom was living with a woman in Chico. I heard it three weeks after our *Out of Africa* date. Though on the surface I'd dismissed the news as rumor, I had carried it with me for over a year, like a summons to appear before a judge.

Tom huffs a denial and says no, as if the thought is ludicrous. "I mean," he starts, "I dated one woman for awhile, but it wasn't serious. Now I'm seeing Amy, who you met at the play. We've only been dating a few months, though. It isn't very serious." He stares intently at the ground in front of him, trying to maintain his buoyant gait. It is the most he has ever divulged.

"I'd heard you had a boyfriend at school," he continues. I think of Donatello. I assume Tom had heard of our brief dating and blown it out of proportion. *He thinks I am interested in someone else?!* "I didn't know whether you were serious about me," he continues. The explanation is hardly satisfying, but I decide to let it go. After that night everything will be different: honest, one-on-one, lasting. Hope swells my heart like a dry sponge at first contact with water.

At one point we stop by Tom's mother's house to borrow a car. Tom requests that I wait outside while he goes in, the dark sky a curtain I hide behind. He doesn't explain, but I know that his mom, a church-friend of my parents, will disapprove of his having me out late. It's the first time I've been to the neighborhood, and the houses, plain-faced and unkempt, display broken aluminum window frames, busted chain link fences, brown lawns, and old rusty toys out front. Hiding in the side yard while Tom retrieves a car feels sort of adventurous. But it also feels lousy, which I immediately deny. Tom's mom knows he has a girlfriend. She will know he is cheating. I am the girl who hides in the back yard . . . willingly.

Nevertheless, I am proud to be with Tom, in the breezy energy of a summer night, to have friends see us together. We talk on the steps of the old library, across the street from my best friend's house, waiting for her to arrive home. I want her to see me with Tom, and when she drives up, I glow with pride. After years of veiling our feelings, Tom's and my connection that night makes all things seem possible.

Red Bluff sits like a quiet, empty shell, and Tom and I fill it with passion and whispers, with potent caresses. There is not enough room inside of me for my love. It hurts, and I have never felt so happy. We spend the minutes sliding down dark passageways, through residential side-streets lined with large Victorians, stopping to sit and make out, to look in each others' eyes, to let our hands explore the youthful, smooth contours of hip and waist and arm, to explore where shoulder and neck meet and the tender lobes of the ear.

We drive to Ide Adobe Park, where moon-swept hills and mythic, shadowy oak trees create a perfect stage. We lie on the grass, covering one another with kisses, with our warm bodies. But it is there that I feel myself hold back, unwilling to drop the last layer of armor sheltering my heart. Tom doesn't touch a button of my clothing or lay a finger to a zipper. Yet I know what he must want. And I won't give it.

Around 4 a.m., Tom finally drops me off at my friend's house where I've arranged to sleep over with several others. I clamber through her bedroom window with a revelatory grin on my face. I will tell my friends all about the night.

I will keep Tom's girlfriend a secret.

◆

Several months prior, I had decided to leave high school early. I passed my GED, applied to the small Christian college my sister attended in Oregon—George Fox College (GFC), got accepted, and made plans to leave home a year early. I couldn't leave high school soon enough.

But after one night of honest passion from Tom, I am ready to scrap these plans *en todo*. My best friend Tracy will be moving to Chico late in the summer to begin school at the university Tom attends. Furthermore, it will be Tom's last year in Chico before moving away to start a Master in Fine Arts in acting. If life presents windfall moments that must be seized, this surely is one of them. Thus, I devise a new plan. I will start college at Chico State. I will live with Tracy. I will make an earnest go of it with Tom. I will, that is, if he will have me.

I call Tom on the phone from Tracy's apartment. "I could go to Chico State next year," I announce, and the silence following my announcement is short—but far too long. "That way we could have a chance," I offer, though I know he doesn't need an explanation.

"Well, that would be great," he finally replies. "I would like that." Yet the hesitation in his voice tells me more is coming. "But, I can't promise you anything. We'd just have to see what happens."

"Oh . . . I know," I quickly add. "I wouldn't be going just for you. . . . And I know we would have to just give it a try. . . ."

"As we talked about," Tom elucidates, "Amy will be away for a year." She will be studying at a university on the East Coast. "That would make it a good time to see what happens between us."

It is not the response I had hoped for, but I take what I can get.

"I don't want to break up with her, since I don't know if things will work out with you. But you and I could give it a chance. . . . It sounds like a good opportunity," he says, ever the practical guy.

I believe a chance is all I need.

I see Tom on several occasions that summer, though his girlfriend is still around. Tom is a lead actor in a summer-repertory program at Chico State, and gives me free tickets to all of his plays. After his shows, we take walks, the nights ripening, warm and vibrant. On one occasion his girlfriend is present on the night I attend a play and I wait out her and Tom's goodbyes before getting him to myself. During the play, she sits across from me in the small theater-in-the-round, and under the theater's dark shroud, I watch her. I watch her watching Tom, smiling as she observes him, so proud, so trusting. On another occasion I wait for Tom in the

Green Room after a play while many of his actor friends sit discussing the night's performance. *Do they know who I am?* I wonder. They all know Amy. *Who am I?* I ask myself. *Am I Tom's seventeen-year-old trifle? Is there a word for this thing I've become?*

With summer stock and two girlfriends, Tom has little time to spare. But one Saturday I drive to Chico to spend rare, contiguous hours with him. We stroll around town and visit a used bookstore, grab something to eat. Then later in his bedroom—all dark, wood-paneled and sparsely furnished, he pulls me into a passionate kiss. It is a sweltering northern California day and the room without air conditioning. Tom's open window spills grainy, midday light across his bed, revealing shafts of dust. On his desk sits a plate of cookies from his stunning blond girlfriend. *What's with the girl and cookies?* A card is attached. Signed, Amy.

My first experience on a bed with Tom, and all I can think of are those blasted cookies. I had run our love-making through my head a zillion times. I want in my deepest core to be Tom's lover, but on that day, I don't participate, like something inside of me is backing away, as if from an accident I have just observed, slowly stepping back and back. At that moment, I am all but asexual, his touch as stimulating to me as still air. At the time, I don't understand. I feel frustrated with myself. Yet it is the girlfriend. And the cookies. And the unacknowledged sense of being duped.

♦

I had put off informing my parents of my change of plans long enough. It is the middle of the summer and I am scheduled to head to college in late August. My older sister, Kristen, with whom I am to room at GFC, will be the first to know. She and I are house-sitting that summer at a woman's house not far from my parents.

Late in the evening I break the news to her. She throws a twelve-alarm tizzy. After our conversation, I head off to bed.

I am awakened at 11 p.m. by a phone call—my parents, insisting I come home immediately. Kristen has told them my plans. From the sound of Dad's voice, they are livid.

My dad's face turns chili-pepper red as he speaks. "Absolutely not!" he fumes. "You cannot expect us to just pay your way while you go off to follow a boyfriend!" My mother cries, "I'm so hurt by your keeping this from us." Both are entirely unsympathetic to my lovelorn plight. They seem contemptuous of Tom, who they've heard is "no longer even a Christian."

"You do not have the freedom to decide your destination next year," my dad informs, "if you are getting out of high school, you will go where we feel comfortable sending you." The clincher comes next: "You do not have the money to fund your own education."

"But Chico State would be so much cheaper!" I protest. By this time, I am sobbing. "Why can't I go where *I* want to go?!"

"You will go," my dad insists, "where your sister goes. . . . Or you won't go at all."

My choices are clear: go to GFC as planned, or stay home and complete twelfth grade. No exceptions.

I cry and yell as the four of us debate on my parents' bed, my mom and dad in their bathrobes with sullen, shocked faces. I insist I am worthy of trust, able to make my own choices. I will do *well* at Chico State. *Just trust me. Give me a chance. It is my only chance with Tom.*

No exceptions.

Since remaining in high school is not an option I can stomach, I am headed north to college—eight hours from home, nine hours from my one true love. I immediately share the news with Tom.

A week and a half later, outside of a theater in Chico, he gently breaks up with me.

For the remainder of that summer, depression, anger, and hopelessness hover around me, a wretched aura. My family moves that month from the family home to an older rental while Mom and Dad await construction of a new, smaller house. Since the rental has only three bedrooms, I sleep on a mattress on the floor of a converted laundry room. Black widow spiders appear in the yard, which is bordered by low arbor vitae draped in cobwebs. The house is sticky and dark. For summer employment, I babysit a rotten-spoiled, six-year-old girl I cannot help but loath, who whines like a slipped fan belt and whose baby-talking voice nudges me toward insanity. The hot summer air rolls over me, pinning me to my dull, claustrophobic space. The Red Bluff landscape, scorched and scarred, looks just like my derelict heart.

♦

Never in my life had I been as lonely as I was that following autumn. Loneliness wore me like a loose-knit shawl. It carried me places I never would have gone without it. I felt out of place among students I met at my college and I craved companionship. I was furious with my parents who had, I felt, screwed up my life irreparably. I had lost my sense of home. Oregon was a chilly, grim world compared with sunny California, and that year I dreaded dreary days and nights alone. I wanted distraction from the endless Oregon gray. Over time Oregon's swelling, wet ambience crept into my heart and became home, but that first year, I shook and chattered. I felt hopelessly Californian.

It was in this state, after my first few weeks at George Fox, that I met my first husband. We'll call him Alex. It was late September 1987.

Alex was a blockbuster—a bonanza of sound, action, and good looks, as mind-numbing and distracting as a Roman circus. There was much to love in him, but more simply to like, and most everyone liked him. He could be absurdly funny, flattering, powerful—the polar-opposite of how I felt. I expect this is what attracted me. At the time I met Alex, I felt silenced and helpless. Yet as someone working to fill the artsy niche at the rather homogeneous Christian college I attended, I stood out. And Alex was drawn to the unusual. He immediately took an interest in me, asking friends about me, showing up in spots I frequented, opening doors for me with a showman's flair. Alex was the same age as Tom.

What I didn't know was that he was seriously dating another girl. Had been for two years. I found this out the night of Alex's and my first date when she stole his car and we ended up walking home. I found it out after we had shared our first kiss.

But never had someone expressed such enthusiastic regard for me. Alex's attention drew me like a bee to red clover. He was handsome in a striking, unusual way, with deep-set dark eyes, a sharp brow and angular jaw line, a head of thick, wavy black hair. As an acquaintance, he was fun, and so different from me, I was intrigued. He wore a baseball jacket and, at times, a button-up shirt with a bollo-tie. He drove a souped-up '54 Chevy pickup. What drew me to him most, however, was how he made me feel: adored, beautiful, sexy, interesting. I was needy and narcissistic, and Alex made me feel like someone was paying attention, at last, to me. A month into school, I started dating Alex. Within weeks, I was virtually living with him. I was swept away like a dust bunny.

If someone had predicted who among my circle of high school friends would marry young and meld into the mold of the obsequious housewife, it would not have been me. I heralded social justice. I was a feminist. I was, at least in theory, into "movements." Though I often wore skirts and dresses, cultivating a feminine appearance, I didn't reckon myself a man's woman. At the time I met Alex I had been looking at art-college catalogs. I figured I'd endure one year of the Christian college scene to earn the freedom to choose my next fate. As I pictured it, Mom and Dad were sending me to art school.

Alex, five years my senior, lived off campus in an apartment with his brother and one other roommate. Prone to stunts like mis-shelving sections of books at the library, bringing his breakfast bowl, milk, and Kelloggs to a morning class and eating through the lecture, releasing a possum in the school cafeteria, Alex enjoyed playing the prankster. But he was quite conservative politically. He chided my liberal views and berated me for "defacing" an army jacket with a peace sign. But he did live dangerously. He was a little wild and he was wild about me. I figured I could keep my politics to myself.

I dated Alex for twelve months and fell deeply into what, I reckoned, was love. I now see it more as neediness. But at the time, I thought I'd found the One. Perhaps I'd been spared a relationship with Tom—who'd fallen from my consciousness like a car careening off the side of a cliff—because I was destined for Alex.

I started dating Alex at the beginning of October, and already, by November, I had shrunk a few inches in stature, slowly fading from the picture of my own life. Alex frequently got angry. He could get angry over anything: what I did, what I said, what I wore, what I didn't do, didn't say, didn't wear. I didn't know what to expect from one day to the next, so I slowly became *moderated*. I held every movement, every word, every step I made to an internal scrutiny, hoping to avoid the missteps that evoked his brooding anger.

One morning in mid-November, amid one of Alex's angry bouts, I sat on a stone bench in the center of campus, under a safe blanket of fog, waiting for class to begin. I wrote one of the few poems I would pen that year, or for years to come, recognizing with my pen what my heart hadn't the courage to acknowledge.

> On foggy days
> when the silhouettes of
> ghostly trees bleed
> into mist
> and the sodden ground gives beneath me,
> I stand and watch,
> wondering if the world has got up
> and left.
> It doesn't move.
> Only I am alive as leaves
> fall and crack beneath my feet,
> mind wandering,
> bed's cozy heat. . . .
> Somehow I hope to hide from
> this freeze-frame world today.
> I think I am afraid.
> I think I am afraid
> of not being strong enough to
> face the fog with a smile
> and a "hi."

Over the course of twelve months, I became transformed. My hair and skirts shortened dramatically, as did my sentences. My shadow said more than I did. Poetry-writing tapered off to almost nothing, and I stopped drawing. Though I did well in school, I was apathetic toward everything save Alex. Directly following classes I would head to his house and wait for him in his room. He was perpetually late. If he was to pick me up at my dorm, I sat at the curb waiting, waiting... waiting like a dog for its master. I wasted hours just waiting.

When I won a lead role in the spring drama, *I Never Sang for my Father*, I drifted like a phantom through play-rehearsals, disengaged, never quite present. When Alex learned I was to kiss the cheek of a male character in the play, my character's son, he gave me the silent treatment for days. Finally, I talked the director into changing the scene. When I explained to the director the reason for my request, he cautioned me about possessive relationships. I didn't listen. I had few reliable friendships apart from Alex's, and our relationship was a tightrope. One foot in front of the other, and the other, with tremendous concentration. It took everything. It was all I had energy for. In a photo taken the month of my play, I appear gaunt and pale as a corpse, perfect for the ailing eighty-year-old woman I portrayed.

Eventually I became sick, and over spring break underwent a tonsillectomy. Deep down I knew what was happening was ugly, that I was unhappy and losing touch with myself. But I felt abandoned in the world—by home, by God, by Tom, even by myself. Staying in the situation was not as scary as the loneliness of breaking up. The loneliness, I could not bear. So I chose denial.

◆

A year after our meeting, in October 1988, Alex and I married. I was eighteen.

I had piercing second thoughts the two weeks before the wedding. But the ceremony was planned, dresses and decorations had been bought, bridal showers had taken place. Relatives from out of town had bought plane tickets, and family friends had planned vacations around the event. "You can cancel, if you need to, Tricia," my friend Tracy exhorted as I sobbed on the phone. She was the one person who knew my true feelings, the one close friend I had in the world. "It really would be okay. It *sounds* impossible," she repeated, "but you could do it." From my perspective, it *was* impossible. I would let down a hoard of people. Canceling one's own wedding at the last minute would be a humiliating failure I could not face. I simply did not have the strength.

Alex's and my wedding took place in early October, in the Red Bluff church I had grown up in. I wore a flattering white-satin dress made by my mother, with hand-beaded bodice and train, and my signature red lipstick. I wore the most convincing smile a bride could wear. The ceremony was filled with drippy, sentimental songs and prayers and was graced with old and new friends who had gone out of their way to attend.

From the moment I showed up at the church to the moment Alex and I drove away in the black limo he had rented for the occasion, I was the model happy bride—a role I adopted knowingly. I stepped into it as if stepping aboard a train, a train that would take me so far from who I was that I would no longer remember what I'd been.

◆

My transformation continued over the next few years, very little of which I remember. Looking back on the time, I see a stranger. She walks around in my skin but wears different clothes than I would have worn. She styles her hair differently than I would have styled it. She *uses* my body. She is impeccably polished and fashioned, prudent to the point of banality. She holds no opinion on matters unrelated to family and home. This woman in my skin had bought it: the old-fashioned cultural prescription for women. I'd taken one large dose of mind-numbing elixir guaranteed to allay conflict with husband and family, to give the appearance of control, and to win the admiration and envy of female peers. Looking at photos of this woman, I *cringe*.

After the wedding, Alex and I moved into a small rental house that stuck out like a sore thumb in Newberg, the home of GFC and the town Alex had spent his entire life in. The house was oddly Mexican-style, with arched entries and red tiles running along the edges of flat roof. The siding, a blown-on, orange foam painted white, created a faux-stucco effect. Since the house was situated in a neighborhood in downtown Newberg sprinkled with historic bungalows, it was all the more out of place.

A huge holly tree and towering evergreen huddled over the small front yard, and in the side-yard, along the sidewalk, stood three enormous maples. At first I could not believe I had my *very own* house, my very own trees. I painted the walls a buttery ivory with robin-egg trim. I sewed eyelet curtains.

After the first year I pulled ancient, dank carpeting up to reveal shabby wood floors, which were a real improvement. I decorated with steamer chests and thrift-store finds, and cut lavender and roses from the yard to display in turquoise mason jars on my table. The house's west-facing front flooded with light each afternoon, sun spilling through the tall front window, brightening the plastered walls within. Just down the street from the rental was the newspaper where Alex landed his first post-college job, sports writer for his high school and college alma maters.

The house was charming in a run-down sort of way. It had a built-in corner cabinet with beveled-glass doorknobs. It had French doors opening off the dining room onto a tiny front patio, and old-fashioned bedroom windows with antique brass latches.

Nevertheless, the room I remember most vividly is the basement. I can still conjure the smell if I try, a scent like soil or stale theater costumes, the scent of organic matter dying.

For years, the basement had leaked. When someone finally installed a sump-pump to expel the water during winter, the room's layer of mildew was already ineradicable. It scented the room's entire contents, which consisted mostly of belongings from the woman who had died in the house before we moved in. Her son, our landlord, had never removed her belongings. Since Alex was a friend of his family, the son rented the house to us "as is" upon her death. The rent was cheap, and the woman's things were left to be used, ignored, or packed away. But not discarded.

♦

Unused, 1960s-era wrapping paper on long rolls, boxes of ancient Christmas decorations—plastic holly garlands that smell like Goodwill, green and gold glass balls wrapped in newspaper ads from the 1970s, wide red ribbon. It is all there in that basement. There are gardening tools we never use, parts of an old lamp with brown and olive-green glazes running down the pottery base, yellowed photos in chipping gold frames, dozens of near-empty spray-paint cans. None of this is thrown away. Instead, we shove these items into spaces between the half-walls and the ceiling, shelves running along the sides of the basement that reach far back into the earth. I despise the dark mysteriousness of those shelves. I despise that basement.

I never clean it. All those years of mildew and cobwebs, the rotting, crumbling brick—left as is. Nothing is cleaned unless I clean it, and the dirt overwhelms me. The dirt bears down on me.

Unless absolutely necessary, I stay out of the basement. Alex, on the other hand, keeps tools there. On winter nights when it is too cold to work in his drafty garage, he works in the basement, and if the need arises, I descend the stairs to ask him a question. The bald light bulb in the room's corner is our only light. The cold, musty air tightens my chest. Alex stares at his project as we speak, his answers to my questions short and calculated. He makes nothing easy. Answers have to be exhumed.

In one corner of the basement I keep a stash of mementoes: school yearbooks, dresses I'd bought in Mexico as a high-schooler, journals from my trip, old photos.

One night during our first year of marriage I climb into bed, Alex beside me. I have just settled under the covers when he says, "a Tom Hendricks called for you today." I don't say anything. I just start to shake. When I'm nervous, I shake—an earthquake running though my muscles until my teeth chatter. I still love Tom. I had never told Alex about Tom and had not said his name for many months. His name entering our bedroom is a collision of past and present, the before- and after-shots of my life. There, lying within the plaster walls of a bedroom I loath, in a dead woman's bed, in a house only I will clean: "Tom Hendricks called for you today." Crash.

I lay shaking in silence for three whole minutes before Alex finally adds: "He didn't really call."

Alex had read Tom's name in my journal in the basement that day, the journal from the Mexico trip when I was sixteen. *He didn't really call.*

◆

There are times Alex doesn't speak to me for days. I sleep beside him under eyelet-trimmed sheets and the rose-strewn quilt my mother made, cook his meals, clean his house. Silence. Hatred pulling his eyebrows into a tight "M." Maybe I had paid too much for groceries. Maybe I had spent too much time at my mom's (my parents had moved to Newberg), not been home to fix his supper on time. Maybe I had looked at him the wrong way.

Silence.

His brows relax as he speaks to a friend on the phone or laughs at a show on TV. But as soon as I speak, they furrow. After two tortured days of this, I beg forgiveness. I am a landslide of tears and groveling. Sometimes I beg for several days. *I am so sorry.* Only after Alex is desperate for sex does be give in. He rolls over in bed and ends the matter. As soon as I feel his touch, I know it is over. I respond with willingness no matter what I feel—hurt, frustration, disgust. I am desperate for an end to a silence lonelier than almost anything else.

◆

Whatever affection there was at our wedding breathed its last breath within two years of married life. I had been steadily attending school until, in my sophomore year, Alex decided to change jobs. I had a tumor in my ovary that had been diagnosed shortly before our wedding, and because Alex's health insurance was shifting, I needed to schedule surgery to remove it. The condition would have been "pre-existing" under a new policy. Therefore, I withdrew from all of my classes and had the operation, by which time the tumor was the size of an orange.

After my recovery, Alex refused to pay the bills. They were *my* bills, he explained, and I needed to pay them. Alex was the checkbook keeper and bill-payer of the household, but every month he stacked my medical bills neatly on the corner of the kitchen table, unopened.

I started working and didn't return to school for five years.

Granted, my earning potential was minimal and I'd made Alex shoulder the entire financial burden of the household. My ten-hour/week work-study jobs at the college library merely mopped up my small college bill—didn't buy groceries, didn't heat the house, didn't put gas in the car. Because Alex was the bill-payer, I was free from the worry of making ends meet, or failing to, and was admittedly naive about money. Unlike me, Alex desired expensive things: a sports car, shop equipment, a nice house, and I was the lead weight anchoring him to poverty.

My job experience allowed me few attractive prospects, and immediately after my surgery, I went to work at Subway. After Subway, I graduated to a ten-month stint—the longest I could endure—as receptionist at a large, upscale real estate office. A family friend landed me the job. Every day I sat at a desk for most of eight hours, repeating the name of the company, a literal tongue-twister, hundreds of times on the phone. By the end of the ten months, I could not untangle my tongue. My colleagues were fifty snazzy-dressing realtors who drove late-model German cars, wore cologne that cost more than my monthly outlay for food, and strove to outdo one another's vacations. The office manager with whom I worked closely was an embittered, fastidious, and territorial older woman who disliked me intensely.

The upside of the job was the positive attention I garnered from males around the office. In an office full of well-manicured, middle-age men mostly bored with their lives, I was a pretty, sweet girl sucking up male attention like a famished anteater at an anthill. So desperate was I, in fact, that I fell blindly—rather, *cannon-balled*—into a flirtatious relationship with a powerful man in the office that, had I been in my right mind, would have blared "*sexual harassment.*" But sexual harassment requires that words and actions be unwanted, and I was in such a needy emotional state I actually welcomed the man's smarmy comments about my body and its suitability for *Playboy*. Occasionally he'd throw in a comment about my mind, even calling me a "genius." I sucked it right up. Though I made a decent wage at the job, I spent too much money on clothing, hoping to fit into the high-fashion atmosphere I positively despised.

♦

Several months after my surgery, and after I'd quit my job at the real estate office, I became pregnant. It was the best news I had heard in years, and Alex shared my excitement. Some unhappily married women want babies to save their marriages; I wanted a baby to save my life. My own little baby—the perfect cure for my loneliness. During the pregnancy, I worked at a temporary library position three days a week, a job I found enjoyable and energizing. But outside of work, I was useless. My energy vanished as soon as I walked through Alex's and my front door.

I took long naps every day, enduring pregnancy with little grace. By the end of the nine months, I had taken on so much water I could have burst like a balloon with a pin's prick to the arm. I broke out in heavy acne on my chest and back. My migraine headaches, which I'd experienced since puberty, were intense and incapacitating. Every vexing problem one can have in pregnancy, I had. Heartburn? Mine could have powered a small electric plant. Hemorrhoids? Mine kept the stock of Wyeth, makers of Preparation-H, at an all time high. Back pain? Like that of a bench-pressing octogenarian.

◆

During one migraine headache, I ask Alex to drive me to the hospital. I have suffered intense pain for over thirty hours and it is a weekend—my doctor's office closed. Our Kaiser Permanente insurance requires we drive forty-five minutes to a hospital three towns away. In response to my request, Alex stomps through the house gathering his keys, a scowl on his face and the bend of anger heavy on his shoulders. He has better things to do than take me to the hospital.

The entire drive loud rock music rages on the car stereo. Alex expresses his displeasure with the gas pedal. At the hospital, a careless doctor administers Demerol without asking if I've eaten. Narcotics on an empty stomach. The doctor gives me the shot and sends me away. On the way home, I dry-heave repeatedly for two minutes straight, my abdomen convulsing and rock music blaring. When I ask Alex to please turn the music down, he clicks it off and fumes.

He is my child's father, and I hate him.

A male friend of Alex's tells him Lamaze classes are no use, so Alex refuses Lamaze. According to this friend, he and his wife didn't find Lamaze helpful during her labor (though of course, no one bothers consulting the woman on the matter). As a result, I enter labor entirely unprepared for what will happen, while Alex sits out most of my labor in the waiting room watching MTV.

On the delivery table, I actually go into a kind of shock. My temperature drops so low I quake for hours. Over and over I ask for heated blankets to bury my trembling body. Each contraction through my tensed muscles is a switchblade stab, even after the epidural, which is administered too late. I am white as the sheets I bleed on, cry on.

The nurse on duty during my delivery is a woman in her sixties who resents each minute separating her from retirement. She resents the demands of tormented women. She resents their doting, voyeuristic relatives. She resents the doctors who stroll in at the last hour and steal the glory and most of the pay. She resents me.

In response to my request that they turn up the heat, she bellows, *No way—we're roasting in here!* When I fail to push hard enough, she interjects, *If you're going to push like that you might as well not push at all!* The woman apparently learned nursing etiquette at boot camp, or hopes to get herself fired. As a saving grace, my post-delivery nurses are all Florence Nightengale incarnate.

My older sister, Kristen, who had recently had her own baby, stands by my bedside whispering breathing instructions throughout delivery. She sounds like our mother leaning over my childhood bed. I try hard not to hyperventilate or hold my breath. Kristen is my savior.

Madison comes twenty-one hours after the vice of real labor had tightened around my midriff. I hear her cry, and the pain stops. Like that. My body begins to stabilize, and I become a shade of pink again. My baby, for her part, is red as a raspberry, and achingly beautiful. As soon as I cradle her in my arms, her screaming gives way to silence, and we stare at each other. No hospital room, no bloody sheets, no IVs or humming monitors. Just she and I, enraptured. Madison has large, charcoal-gray eyes that will turn a deep cedar brown. Dark hair dusts her perfect, rounded head, and peeks from the pin-striped cap that adorns it. My blood makes burgundy, web-like designs on her pristine arms and legs. I love her so much it almost crushes me.

After the nurses and doctors stitch me up, they leave me alone to shower. Stepping into that stream of water feels like breaking through the clouds in an airplane, rising to a world of glaring sky, seas of dense, lily-white clouds. I wash away two days of sweat and filth, and the blood caked between my legs. I wash away a lifetime. A sudden ecstasy sweeps over me that lasts for two days, making it impossible to sleep. *How can I sleep with this baby to hold and adore?* Her fingers. Her eyes. It is like falling in love. It *is* falling in love.

I hold Madison all night the first night, and I hardly sleep. The press of her warm, soft body next to me is euphoric. When she wakes up hungry, she leans into my breast, makes a perfect "O" with her pink ribbon mouth, and roots around for sustenance, pecking her fragile neck like a chicken until I help her latch on. She breathes inaudibly as she sleeps, but I watch the rise and fall of her chest and back, which are the size of my hand and covered in tiny dark hairs. I stroke her skin—all velvety brown, of olive-complexion—and wonder how I could have made something so unspeakably handsome.

After that night I had to start sleeping. But I slept with Madison on my chest, her legs curled under her body so her bottom stuck up in the air, higher than her head. Or I laid with her beside me. I once read a story about young Holocaust orphans who spent months or years in a state of starvation. Even after their rescue and many ample meals, they could not sleep. They were afraid they might awaken to starvation, to a state of frightening deprivation that would never end. Their caretakers were at a loss. They had provided everything the children needed. So why couldn't they sleep? Then the caretakers devised a brilliant strategy: They gave the children a piece of bread before bedtime each night, and allowed them to sleep with the bread warm and soft in their clutches. The children slept like angels.

Sleeping with Madison was like that. It was sleeping with my bread.

Birches

Always look straight up at them.
Feet apart. Near enough to see
their sacred scars. Let them be
your halo, white, or your crown
of thorns. Birches, like women,
are more lovely without cover,
will dizzy you with their drive
to bud and drink and live.
When they shed their skin
you will want to write your love
on their passing girlhood, to press
it in a book. You will want to give
up all for a look at the sky
through their timorous arms, which wave
a summons to come.
Time to feel. Time to live.

CHAPTER THREE

Risen Life

It was New Year's Day when I left Alex, Madison's second birthday a month away.

A New Years Eve fight propelled me to my mother's kitchen the following day sobbing-tired. I had been there, in the same posture, too many times. The day was drizzly and cold. My life felt like a tall gray tower with no winding escape. My marriage to Alex was five years old, and though I had, in the previous year, largely severed my emotional self from Alex, I was still his wife.

I had maintained a precarious monogamy throughout the marriage but had become more and more distracted by the attentions of other men. In fantasy, I'd been leaving Alex for years. Still, I had never solidified the fantasy by admitting it to anyone. Divorce was taboo in the context I grew up in, and the taboo held me between a rock and a vow. *If I divorce, what will people think of me?* I faithfully attended church, the one place I was allowed to form relationships, and friends and acquaintances shared the taboo. If I divorced, my peers would pity or judge me. Despite themselves, they would look at me down raised, properly married noses.

Feeling judged and pitied is a sensation I'd experienced far too often growing up in a conservative religious milieu I did not fit in to, where boundaries and laws and exclusion seemed to have the last word. My life with Alex may have been miserable, but I was, at this time, safely within the boundaries—a good little wife, a conscientious, loving mother, an every-Sunday-church-goer. I was *acceptable*. Up to that day, January 1, 1994, I had not had the courage to leave Alex because I didn't have the courage to face the loneliness, the judgment and pity, to become once again, unacceptable.

But that afternoon my mom made a small suggestion, spinning out the words like a silk-worm spins silk, almost blithely. She suggested I needed space, time away from Alex. *Why don't you come stay here for a while?* she said, and a locked box inside of me opened up. Nine simple words. Nine words, and my mom took the fantasy of my heart and lent it animation. In saying those words, she proffered the small measure of acceptance I needed to contemplate leaving. Suddenly, it seemed less lonely. With a wet tissue wadded in my hands, my hands holding up my sagging head, I told her I wanted to leave my husband. As the words left my mouth, the impossible at once felt possible, and my decision was made. A New Year's resolution.

Alex was away from the house as I quickly packed Madison's and my suitcases. On the note I left behind, I called what I was doing a "separation," though I knew in my deepest heart I would never go back. I drove away from that house feeling like the women in *Thelma and Louise*.

My parents and younger siblings had relocated by this time from Red Bluff, California, to Newberg, Oregon, to be near my older sister and me. Madison and I moved into the grandmother-apartment attached to their house. They'd built the house just a year earlier, carefully reworking the plans to include an apartment for Nana, my maternal grandmother, who was battling colon cancer. Less than a year after its completion, she died. Two months after her death, Madison and I moved into her space.

Nana's scent lingered in the apartment, the smell of lavender lotion and rose-scented soap. The walls embraced us. In Nana's last days I had sat and held her hand in that room, where she lay in a hospice-issue hospital bed. I had trimmed her nails and brushed her hair and felt closer to Nana in that apartment than I had ever felt to her before. It featured all of her favorites: rose-colored carpeting, rose-colored Formica in the kitchenette, and a view of my father's flower garden. When Nana lived there, the walls had been covered in her ornately framed oil paintings, overpowering the tiny apartment's four hundred square feet.

Now those four hundred square feet felt expansive. For the first time in years, I had room to be myself. Madison's bed stood at an angle to mine, the two beds joined at the headboards. As Madison slept, I listened to her breathe. I stretched out, savoring every square inch of my double bed. *Were sheets always so soft and clean smelling? Was morning always so still?* Each week Madison and I visited the library and hauled home a giant stack of picture books. Before going to sleep, we would sit on my bed, Madison nestled into my arm, and read the entire stack. I felt at those times that I had been liberated, that the stifling path I'd been walking most of my life had folded out into a smooth and temperate plain of possibility arcing toward a horizon as enchanted as it was unknown.

Eventually, we made our mark on the place. I bought an unfinished bookshelf, sanded it, stained it, and filled it with books. We jammed two desks into place—mine the desk my parents bought me in fifth grade, which they had stored for years, Madison's, an old school desk with a hinged lid I had found at a yard sale. We situated a small dining table in the corner, blocking the closet doors. Opposite the table, three feet from the corner of my bed, we squeezed in a loveseat and coffee table, and a television that—for once—was silent.

Madison, at age two, had wispy, sable hair that curled on the ends, and large, impish brown eyes framed in dense, long lashes. She had peachy-round, rose cheeks and an olive complexion. Madison was a *beauty*. People stopped on the street to talk to her, telling me what a lovely girl I had, and by the age of four, she had been on the news four times. Madison seemed to be present (usually with her paternal grandmother) whenever a news reporter filmed at the zoo or the opening of the latest kids' movie, or when they filmed children playing at the beach. Without fail, Madison would be interviewed and put on the broadcast. From a young age she was animated and articulate, sometimes talking with a high-brow accent she adopted from videos or books-on-tape, prancing about the room with arms swinging, acting wistful.

But Madison had a fiery side. She was a Dr. Jekyl/Mr. Hyde kind of girl, and when Dr. Jekyl needed to come out, it was time to get home. During her first year of preschool, Madison's teacher effusively announced that four-year-old Madison was "a perfect child." At her parent-teacher conference, the woman gushed: "I can't think of one negative thing to say about Madison!"

If you only knew! I wanted to burst out. On a regular basis, Madison exploded. In polite company she was self-controlled, but in the comfort of home, she could throw a well-pitched fit. She'd been doing so since her colicky infancy. And boy, could she pitch. She was usually set off by not getting something she wanted, like candy or the privilege of watching a movie. At times she screamed for over an hour, looking like the girl in *The Exorcist* and saying things like "I hate you" or "you are a bad mom." After exerting all her energy yelling and kicking, she would collapse like a house of cards and sleep. Madison wasn't spoiled and, generally speaking, not "bratty." She had a deep core of rage, an inherent intransigence. At times that core needed venting. Usually I stayed calm and let her vent. Sometimes I tripped over the edge, yelling and spewing threats like Joan Crawford in *Mommy Dearest*.

From a young age, Madison dictated poetry to me. In a poem she wrote at the age of four, she said, "I love you my little storm / my little storm is just the thing / for God and twinkle and diamonds / of the world." Madison wrote the poem about her best friend, Cloe, but I stole the storm metaphor to describe the poet. Madison was "my little storm."

Within months of moving into Nana's apartment, I began to write poetry again. I began to read voraciously. I decided to return that fall to college, to major in biblical studies, and to pursue the degrees necessary to teach at the university level.

Over the prior two years, I had grown intensely curious about theology and theological resources, particularly the Bible. I harbored misgivings about the theology I'd accrued as a young person steeped in a fundamentalist tradition. I was not sure what Christianity meant, but I knew that a life lived in God had to be something inconceivably better than what I had glimpsed in my life as a churchgoer. I knew God had to be something more than a cross between Charleton Heston and Ayatollah Khomeini. Somehow I got the notion to read the entire Bible. By the time I reached the last verse of the last book, I was *captivated.*

I did not find an explanation of the variegated thing called Christianity. I was not sure what I'd found. The Bible didn't read like a moralistic, boring book. It didn't read like a typical, univocal *book* at all, not even a multi-vocal book with a unified theme. The Bible was more anthology-like, as multi-layered as an archaeological tell, full of eras to dig through and stimulating, unanswerable questions. Within its layers were exquisite truths and shocking absurdities, glory and horror. Parts of the Bible, such as the Gospels or Ecclesiastes, were comforting; other parts, such as the conquest narratives, were deeply disturbing. The image of God presented in the disturbing parts contradicted everything the Gospels seemed to say about Jesus.

I wanted to know why this was. When I located a Bible with academic notes, I found there were many different answers for the questions I posed, and many mysteries. For example, I learned that the authors of the Matthew and Luke gospels seem to have used an otherwise unknown book, which scholars called "Q," as a source. I stepped back. *Why, in the name of Sunday school, hadn't someone told me this?*

The deeper I dove into the mysteries of the Bible and the historical undercurrents of Christianity, the more questions arose. I spent hours deconstructing ideas about the Bible I'd been exposed to growing up. I gained a profound appreciation for the poetry, mystery, and intricacy of the Judeo-Christian Scriptures. In the end, I had what seemed an insatiable curiosity for the subject. The thought of being able to study it for countless hours thrilled me. It was the reason I chose to major in biblical studies.

I was also drawn to a life of academia, a life devoted to study. As a single mother, I needed to choose and prepare for a career. In all seriousness, the only job that appealed to me was that of an academic—hence, a professor. My choice to pursue academic work was practical: *I need a career, a career in academia is the only career that sounds interesting to me,* ergo *I should become a professor.*

The decision was in no way indicative of confidence either in my intelligence or my ability to succeed as a student or professor. By this point in my life, my confidence level hovered around 1 on a scale of 1 to 10. I believed I was intellectually inferior, I could barely speak in front of acquaintances, let alone strangers, and I felt watched and scrutinized in all human company save Madison's. I had, in the prior three years, developed a mild speech impediment, so that I would frequently run out of air and trip up in my speaking. I avoided speech whenever possible.

Ironically, George Fox (now University) was the school I was drawn to, the same school I'd felt forced to attend as a college freshman seven years earlier. But the college was five minutes from my house (where my mother generously babysat Madison), and I wanted as little time away from Madison as possible. I had also heard the Religion Department was progressive, and this proved to be true. Most of the faculty considered themselves Quaker.

So in August 1994, I returned to university, this time to study theology. I had no idea the discoveries I would make.

◆

During my marriage to Alex, I saw Tom Hendricks one time, during a trip to California for a friend's wedding. Before that I hadn't seen him since summer 1987, five years earlier, when we we sat outside a theater in Chico while he broke my heart.

Someone had told me Tom lived in Ashland, in southern Oregon. He was performing with Ashland's renowned Oregon Shakespeare Festival. I called directory assistance for his number and stumbled my way through a phone conversation I can barely remember. "Tricia!" he exclaimed on the phone, "how wonderful to hear from you!" It was all I could do to stop choking. We made a plan to see each other as I passed through Ashland on the way to the wedding. He asked for a phone number where he could call in case of a schedule change. "Don't call," I said abruptly. "I will call you to confirm." If Alex knew I had phoned Tom, all hell would positively unfurl.

♦

Tom and I meet in the festival courtyard. He smiles as I approach, and we hug deeply. His eyes dance in a way that is so unbelievably familiar, I cannot believe I'd forgotten it. "You look great!" he says when he sees me. Tom is in desperate need of a haircut. He wears a brown leather jacket and worn jeans and looks ten years older than the last time I'd seen him. He looks absolutely beautiful. I have on a white tank top and a sarong skirt that blows erratically in the wind. Tom invites me to his apartment for soup.

We arrive at his house after a brief walk. The place is tidy, though pictures lean against bare walls and boxes sit unpacked four months after he's moved in. I notice the white down comforter on his bed. "I made some lentil soup," Tom says, "Would you like some?"

"No thanks," I reply distractedly, "I don't care for lentils." Really, I have no appetite.

"Who doesn't like lentils?" Tom asks with surprise.

We take a seat on his small couch and spend one and a half hours perched on opposite ends. At first our conversation trips along clumsily. Eventually it steadies its feet. It winds its way back to the summer I had left California. Back to the bench outside that theater on the smoldering July night we said goodbye. "I was like Hamlet," Tom says, trying to explain his conflicted state at that time. "I couldn't make up my mind." Sitting in his apartment in Ashland, Tom looks drawn and weary, and at the same time edgy, like he is a tight ball of rubber bands. He cannot relax; his head seems too heavy for his body. Tom glances toward me and our eyes meet. Five time-bomb seconds pass. "Now here you are," he continues, "right here. . . . And you are so far away."

I drive out of Ashland that day like someone who just woke up from a coma. *How long have I been asleep?* I ask myself. *What do I do now that I'm awake?* Sitting with Tom I can see myself from his perspective, see how I have changed from the person I once was. *No, I* explain to him, *I don't play guitar anymore. No, I'm not writing poetry.* For reading material I carry issues of *Better Homes and Gardens* from the public library. My hair is coiffed and sprayed. I can think of nothing to talk about that I want to talk about save Madison. My new life, my life with Alex, is a subject to avoid. *How did I wander so far?* I ask myself, winding my way through the foothills of Mt. Shasta toward Red Bluff. I want desperately to go back.

◆

Next time I see Tom two years have passed. I have made my New Year's resolution in my mother's kitchen and left Alex. I am in a new place in every sense. Three months earlier I had started theological studies.

In November 1994, I go looking for Tom.

Eleven months had passed since my departure from Alex, and a few weeks since the finalization of our divorce. I do not have a phone number for Tom or an address, but I know he's still in Ashland. A friend of mine had recently attended the Shakespeare Festival and had brought back a playbill. Tom's name was listed among the season's actors.

Thus, I pack a small suitcase, my laptop computer, and a guitar. I head off blindly with money for a motel room I hope I will not need.

I arrive in Ashland at noon on a crystalline autumn day when each molecule of air seems heavy and charged with light. I ask around Tom's old apartment building, thinking someone from the festival might be there, someone who can tell me where to find him. Sure enough, after several hours of waiting in my car, drafting a term paper on my laptop, I encounter someone who knows where Tom lives. I write the address on a small scrap of paper and drive to a telephone booth to locate a map. By the time I park on the quiet residential street near Tom's house, night has lowered its veil.

My chest is full of hummingbirds as I finally step from my car and head toward the porch of his place, a tiny bungalow painted a deep shade of mustard. No one appears to be home, the house is dark, and I suspect Tom is at a rehearsal. The evening is brisk and the air redolent with humus and decaying leaves, the hovering immanence of earth's death and resurrection. Suddenly, just as I reach the walkway that leads to the front door, I hear someone up the street shout "Hello!" It is Tom. He is walking up the street, parallel with his next-door-neighbor's—arm in arm with a tall slender woman.

She is Tom's fiancé.

I am introduced to Jessamine as she fumbles for keys to open the front door, all of us standing on the porch in a dark knot of perplexity. She is exceedingly friendly. They have brought home a gourmet unbaked pizza and Jessamine insists I stay and share dinner with them. "I will make cooked carrots," she says, "there is too much pizza for two, *you must stay.*" Bereft of protocol for meetings of this nature, I consent, and Tom and I sit on the couch inwardly cringing while Jessamine takes care of preparations in the minuscule kitchen one room away.

Within five minutes I know all I need to know. Tom met Jessamine just three months prior, through the festival for which she works as a violinist. They have been engaged for a month.

Three months. One month. Though I had left Alex eleven months earlier, I had waited for the finalization of our divorce to find Tom, wanting to respect our five years of marriage.

I was three months late.

"You went back to college?" Jessamine asks from the kitchen. "What are you studying?" I explain my interest in theology, in ancient texts. She purrs like a kitten in a sliver of sunlight.

"I am *fascinated* with Hildegaard of Bingen," she exudes, tossing me remarks about Jüng. Clearly, the woman is intelligent, I note, in addition to musically gifted . . . kind . . . engaged to Tom Hendricks. I imagine her death by a freak choking accident.

My brain is an open drain. Just as I formulate a response to a comment, my incipient thoughts vanish. I struggle to swim for the light amid a powerful flood of distraction: the warmth I see all over Tom and Jessamine's newly shared apartment—cards perched on shelves that bear Tom's writing, snapshots of the two kissing, icons hung on the wall, a long shelf packed tight with integrated CD collections. Their cat, a recent acquisition from the Humane Society, jumps onto my lap and rolls over.

All said, the scene is disturbingly homey.

Just when I think I might pass out, Jessamine finishes dinner and calls Tom and me to the table. We take our seats. "We usually share a moment of silence before meals," Tom says, offering a hand to me and his soon-to-be wife. As I touch Tom's fingers they feel electric. Tom and my clasped hands slide under the table, forearms balanced on our legs, and Tom begins to squeeze. He squeezes my hand tighter and tighter—so tightly I can feel the impact for hours. As he grips my hand, I feel the blood throbbing in my fingers and the ache of rings pressed deeply into my flesh. My mind is lost at sea. Tom's hand-squeeze is loaded with meaning, with all that he cannot say, at least not out loud: *I am sorry. I know what you're feeling. I care about you. Thank you for coming.*

My hand remains silent.

Tension hovers between the three of us as we sit at that tiny table in that tiny kitchen. My memory lets go of each word as it drops, a conversation as transitory as breath. After the meal, Jessamine retreats to practice violin and change clothes in her and Tom's bedroom for a performance later that night. Tom and I make stilted conversation on the couch. We piece our sentences together like a puzzle, turning to look at them from different angles, struggling to make the picture come out right. I can see the words from Jessamine's perspective in the next room, from that of Tom seven years earlier when he was in love with a girl too young for him, in a relationship that wouldn't last. I see them from the perspective of Tom sitting next to me on the couch, and from the perspective of myself at thirteen and now twenty-four.

When Jessamine leaves, I let my eyes fill slowly with tears. Tom sits rigidly in place, with very little to say. "There is nothing I can offer you," he says. "I'm sorry." We both stroke the cat. "I was beginning to think I'd be single forever," he says. "Then I met Jessamine."

"She is lucky," I reply.

"I am lucky too."

We sit silently another minute before he adds, "You know, in theater we have the saying 'timing is everything.' With you and me, the timing has always been . . . *off.*"

Tom walks me to my car. "Next time it may be me showing up on your door step," he offers, a strange comment for someone about to get married. It is a glimpse behind the curtain. When Tom says goodbye and embraces me, I hold him like it's the last time we'll meet—tightly, with sounds escaping my throat. I cry and put my lips on his neck. I squeeze him, then squeeze him again. As we release, he says, "Drive safely, okay?" I turn my car toward Newberg and sob the five mid-night hours home, my seasoned heart as broken as a heart can be.

◆

Three weeks later, I discover the abbey.

I first visit Our Lady of Guadalupe in winter 1994 on a class field trip, the abbey being just fifteen minutes from Newberg. Our theology class attends lauds, visits with a gregarious monk named Mark, and stays the night, each student in his or her own "cell." Upon encountering the place, my spirit throws back her head and arms like she has finally, unexpectedly found home. Having been a spiritual peregrine most of my life, I stumble on the abbey like a pilgrim finding her destination after searching, no map in hand, no concrete image of what the destination will look like, knowing only in the hopeful memory of intuition that the place exists.

Our Lady of Guadalupe's old chapel first tells me. The combination of early evening light through vaulted, lavender-tinted windows, the room's simple, sorrel wood paneling, the vestiges of incense from morning mass, the candlelight on the altar and the haunting swell of the monks' chant, the swish of their draping white sleeves, draw me. The monks' plainsong harmonizes with a longing that is equally sensual and spiritual, awake to beauty, seemingly wordless, mysterious and quieting.

The cloister of Our Lady of Guadalupe stretches creamy and wide at the base of the monastery's wooded hills. An enormous garden runs the length of the cloister and in summer produces many of the vegetables consumed by monks and abbey guests, and long hallways in the cloister connect the monks' cells, library, dining hall, bathrooms, infirmary, and beyond the cloister, the abbey graveyard. Past this configuration are the book-bindery and bakery where the monks, in part, etch out their living. The abbey's property ascends upward into the forest, with walking trails crisscrossing acres in the hundreds, and the monks help steward the land. Adjacent to the cloister are a cluster of small retreat houses and ponds, the chapel where monks and guests celebrate mass and lauds, a zen-do and meeting house, a visitors' bookstore and kitchen, and a small dining room where guest meals are served family-style, most often in silence.

Most of the monks begin their morning at 4:30 a.m., at the first lauds of the day. After the 1994 field trip, I become a regular abbey guest and frequently visit the abbey to attend compline, the evening lauds at 7:00 p.m., the last lauds of the day. Compline takes place by candlelight, accompanied by the unadorned picking of a guitar, and ends as each person is blessed with holy water sprinkled by the abbot from what appears to be a giant, gothic rattle, as the monks shuffle out of the chapel to spend their last nickels of time before a day ends and another begins. Each one patterned after the last, as if midnight is a coda, and the monastic tune repeats itself day after day unto perfection.

Though I am curious about religion from an academic perspective and eager in theological studies, I have at the time no real spiritual practice. I've yet to find a public worship experience that fits my personality and evokes reverence in me. But sitting in that chapel at Our Lady of Guadalupe, bathed in lavender light and the simple strains of a guitar, I feel embraced by love. I experience an openness in that space that lets me breathe, experience transcendence, and pray, that allows my unique soul to rest and grow. It is the first step on a path that will lead me toward mysticism (a spirituality centered more in personal experience of the divine than in dogma). Sometimes I sit in that chapel and weep, my spirit utterly unguarded, utterly connected with God and with my own experience. It doesn't matter if I am alone or if one or two monks sits in the choir area praying. I feel completely at home.

The next best thing to lauds at the abbey is walking the trails. At Our Lady of Guadalupe, I can wander deep into a Pacific Northwest forest completely alone yet safe, something I had never experienced. At the abbey, I stumble onto a wonderland utterly available to me. I notice everything. From tiny clovers that festoon the trails to the evergreens that cut the sky into patterns of lace.

Saint Aelred's Trail is my first introduction. When I encounter her it is winter, the stream rimming the trail a downhill rushing torrent. The burble of water falling over rocks, heeding the pull of gravity, intones its own block-note plainsong. In the winter, glassy leaves blanket the path and cascading shards of light split the air through firs and naked towers of trees. Mammoth banana slugs inch across the trail. Deer tracks appear everywhere, chromosomal hatches in impressionable earth. Storm-felled branches litter the winter trail like abandoned crosses.

Saint Aelred's winds up a hill that features a small shrine and makeshift ball field at the top. One of the monks built a backstop on one side of a meadow, christening it "the field of dreams" as a gesture to his father who'd always hoped he'd play professional ball. The backstop spoke to others and evolved into a shrine, becoming a sort of pilgrimage. Visitors thread clutches of flowers, notes, flags, or bits of fabric into the wire mesh of the backstop. At the top of the field sprawls a picnic grounds where the monks celebrate Memorial Day and the Fourth of July. Beer flows, baseballs fly, and the monks take a vacation from vegetarianism to eat barbequed hamburgers.

Besides making short trips to the abbey to walk, I establish a new tradition: twice-yearly retreats. Each time I visit Guadalupe for retreat, I leave a doe's breath closer to release. I stay to myself at the abbey for years, not meeting any of the monks or interacting with fellow retreatants. The first gift of the abbey is solitude.

In the abbey's guest rooms, called "cells" in the tradition of monasticism, I feel more fully myself than I ever have. Those simple, small rooms, furnished with only a bed, desk, rocking chair, wardrobe, and icon on the wall, are a better getaway than any hotel suite. No television or radio, no scent of bleach and polyester and stale smoke, no distractions. The rooms sit one on top of the other with a shared bathroom in between, in small guesthouses clustered around the abbey's two ponds. Six structures in all. Looking out the guesthouse windows, retreatants can meditate on the still of the pond or the return of migratory birds that call the abbey home some portion of the year. The abbey and its small guest rooms became my ideal habitat. There, I slowly became who I am.

Abbey retreatants share meals around a large table surrounded by windows that look onto a compact strawberry tree, and beyond the tree, to the chapel. The food is simple. A main dish like pasta or a rice and bean concoction might be paired with salad, two or three different vegetables, and fried potatoes. And appearing fresh at every meal is the abbey's own wheat bread, a dense, nutty loaf that begs for butter and honey.

In springtime, Saint Aelred's becomes a carnival. White, three-fingered trilliums sneak into clearings and ferns brandish tight new question marks. Bleeding hearts bloom like new love, like tiny valentines. Buds, clenched like the hands of two strangers, appear on the branches of every deciduous tree, shrub, and vine. Small birds—finches, chickadees, sparrows—flit and quip, still visible through trees not garbed in summer foliage. Every rock and log around the stream sports a thick, bright smock of moss, and oxalis and epimedium, creeping ivy and blackberry, spring up everywhere.

On my second retreat to the abbey, I combine writing, reading, and resting in my room with walking the trails and attending the monks' chant in the chapel. I sleep and eat and look silently out my window. Again I throw off a thin layer of fear, shedding a few more defenses, almost by the hour. My shoulders loosen at the abbey. I stop leaning constantly forward, forward, and for once, consent to be right there. The focus of those early retreats is not spiritual seeking, per se, as I am not trying to discover something or reach some new level of faith. I try to pray. I acknowledge God's presence when and where I encounter it, but God still feels fairly remote to me at this time. I go to the abbey, rather, because it is healing, and I become more myself there. It will be years before I realize this is the truest kind of spiritual encounter.

With the exception of brief experiences at Our Lady of Guadalupe, I rarely feel loved by God at this time. I don't know that I had ever felt loved by God. I pray, and I believe that God is loving and present, but these are ideas shelved in my head. I recognize grace in my life, in the way paths have cleared for me when I was lost, yet I look back on these experiences from a position of removal, like a person watching a film or gazing into a fishbowl.

Grace and provision have happened to me. I see that. Yet I *feel* judged and watched and threatened, and I project these feelings onto God. I need to watch my step, to atone for the mistakes of my past, to earn love. If I experience love from God, it is always indirectly, through the natural world, or through snippets of poetry or song. But these expressions of love can be generalized: *a divine benevolence and love permeate the world.*

That spring I read Thomas Merton's *New Seeds of Contemplation*, then his book on contemplative prayer. The stirring I feel during lauds at the abbey piques my interest in contemplation and the monastic life, and Merton helps explain them. But Merton's way of looking at prayer and the spiritual life are relevant to a non-monastic life as well. They hold my interest. Merton's emphasis seems to be on effortlessness. Prayer, according to my interpretation of Merton, is an open-handed surrender to a spiritual connectedness happening at all times, in all places, forward and backward into eternity. To participate in this connectedness one needs to cultivate a readiness for prayer—a readiness that allows one to enter into the prayer that is already happening.

Since childhood I'd heard the injunction to "pray without ceasing," but it never made sense to me. *How can one say prayers all the time when there are other things to get done?* But Merton taught that the life of prayer is not about saying prayers or having thoughts. It is openness to God's presence. It is connectedness to the divine undercurrent running through all things. It is available to anyone at any time. Merton's emphasis on humility and emptiness as a path to true prayer rings true for me, as does his desert-language. The more I strip away, the more I rescind into silence and solitude, the more I feel ready for whatever is to come next, for whatever lies beyond the surface of my experience. For God, whomever and whatever God may be. Therefore, I stop trying to pray *correctly*. I stop *trying* to pray at all. Instead I try to notice divine presence and prayer inside of me and around me.

With the abbey, I arrive at summer. Clover and moss give way to purple and gold mountain irises, to wild roses and ripening crabapples. Lacy oaks and firs reflect in the azure depths of a quarry lake, in duck ponds just beyond the guesthouse. Ivy creeps up the trees for light. Blackberry briars extend barbed tentacles into every unoccupied space, and ferns burst open like the sky on a clear summer day. Fully leafed maples, towering cottonwoods, all shimmy and throw light like sequined dresses. The torpid, dusty air glitters. Bugs and butterflies, hummingbirds and salamanders, appear and disappear, and at night coyotes howl.

I begin to change my spiritual practice as a result of my reading. First I stop making words in prayer. Not entirely, but almost. Since I no longer see prayer as something that happens in the head, as thoughts, words, or requests, I set myself free from words. If prayer is tapping into God's presence and light, and if one can stay tapped in always through a posture of openness, humility, honesty, and love, then words are not important. If I do "say a prayer" for another person, it is not forced. I pray only as I am moved to pray, as compassion connects me to the love God has for someone I encounter. One of the most helpful things I learn from Merton is that prayer is not another thing to get done, another thing to be good at. Prayer is something that is done *in* me if I allow it to happen.

One summer while visiting the abbey, I bring along an old book by Evelyn Underhill, entitled *The Spiritual Life*,[1] and find Underhill writing about the same anti-effort type of spirituality as Merton. She says, "A spiritual life is simply a life in which all that we do comes from the center, where we are anchored in God" (p. 32).

If spiritual life is about letting God enter everything we do, as it seemed to be according to the writers I was reading, then, I suddenly realized, I didn't need to strive and *work* at it, something I had always failed at as a young person. All I had to do is receive it.

Receptivity is its own kind of effort, I suppose, but it seems to be the effort of letting go of all effort. If spiritual life is a constant opening up of our hands and letting go, or an awareness of when we are shutting God out and worrying what to do next, all we can do is begin again (and again and again . . .) in an "effort" to let go of effort and keep trusting.

Growing up, I'd felt like a miscreant according to the scales of "proper Christian behavior," especially those set aside for girls. I was too lustful, too opinionated and defiant of authority, too open-minded and questioning. As a child I had learned that rightness with God entailed stepping into a box, walking the straight line strung out by the church, being a good girl according to a fundamentalist definition of goodness, things I seemed incapable of doing. All my life I had been thirsty for the teachings on effortlessness I encountered in Merton and Underhill.

I drink them up. Maybe I am not a spiritual failure after all? I wonder. Maybe doing everything right has nothing to do with the spiritual life, and the nature of that life is a mystery to be unveiled. Both Merton and Underhill emphasize love as the outworking of the spiritual life, the fruits of what happens when we let God fill us. Not a sentimental love, but an unselfish, compassionate love. I don't fully understand what this means, and I wonder how we can both give up striving and yet love in a self-giving way, which sounds to me effortful. Yet something of this resounds in me.

I have experienced moments of aching love for people, of compassion, and those moments have been, in fact, effortless. I want to believe that this eagerness to love is in some way an expression of God. I have ached with love for my daughter; for a tormented mentally challenged boy named James I had known as a girl; for the wallflowers in high school whose hearts got mercilessly broken; for the lonely old man who came into the library almost daily for stacks of theology books; for the glue-sniffing, prostituting street kids I got to know at a Portland drop-in center where I volunteered; for the kid up the block whose father abused him; for Tom; even for Alex in his stubborn brokenness. I feel in my gut that God is in that love, and in all love, even when the lovers are bawdy and foul-mouthed and addicted. Somewhere deep in my soul I know it is this loving that matters, that through this kind of loving, God is found.

When I visit the abbey in autumn, I find a gleaming mystery, nature layering on the glam before death arrives—the way nursing home residents sport gold lamé and red lipstick. Trees explode with yellows, daubs of magenta, raining brilliantly hued leaves onto streaming waters. Grasses alongside paths grow tired, sag, and finally prostrate themselves into blankets of velvety green.

Crimson and white berries adorn tree branches like dainty earrings. The last great show.

◆

The college year begins anew. Sitting in class, I feel like a lost duck who has, at last, found a pond, a flock. The sure metamorphosis continues, a resurrection starting in my mind. Eventually it will reach my emotions and one day, my body. But in those days it is the incipient awakening of my intellect that stirs life in me. The classroom, like Fourth of July, such wondrous explosions of ideas in my head and all around!

If my mind is a Lazarus, my professors are Jesus. Not only do they coax my intellect and condition it, but more than anyone I have encountered in years, they begin to slowly rebuild my confidence—term paper by term paper, essay by essay.

During the first few months of my first year back to school, I trembled and nearly choked when I spoke up in class, though I forced myself to contribute, to vent the intellectual energy that would otherwise have overwhelmed me. But my professors pretended not to notice that I shook like a space shuttle being launched, that my voice abandoned me without warning. They looked at me like teachers should look at their students, like they loved me, like every miniscule gain I made brought them joy. My professors saw something in me that no one, to my knowledge, had recognized since I had withdrawn from college five years prior. They saw that I was actually (gasp) *smart*. They were not afraid to acknowledge it.

◆

My systematic theology professor reads aloud in class. One fall day he reads from an author named Frederick Buechner, his autobiographical trilogy.[2] Sitting at my desk, I hear the following words in which Buechner tells of his encounter with a surprisingly down-to-earth faith healer:

> More even than our bodies, she said, it was [our] hurtful memories that needed healing. For God, all time is one, and we were to invite Jesus into our past as into a house

111

that has been locked up for years—to open windows and doors for us so that light and life could enter at last, to sweep out the debris of decades, to drive back the shadows. The healing of memories was like the forgiveness of sins, she said. (p. 63)

As I hear these words, I stare at my desk and force back tears. Buechner's words seep deep beneath my layers of guardedness, behind the bulwark I had erected to keep from remembering the hurts of my past. The words stir in me a longing for something I hadn't even known I needed—the healing of memories.

The words linger with me all day: *The healing of memories is like the forgiveness of sins.* I picture God as an old woman, carefully working her way through dusty, stale rooms, humming, pulling back curtains and opening windows, whisking away the hurt and leaving rooms sunny and smelling of Murphy's Wood Soap, leaving the memories changed and hallowed.

In a few weeks I encounter Buechner again. At the time I am cataloging books for the university library where I hold a part-time work-study job. Almost every new book that enters the library passes through my hands. One day as I work through another monotonous MARC record, robotically filling in the necessary fields on my computer screen, I notice Buechner's name on the spine of a book halfway down my cart. The three short volumes of Buechner's autobiography sit there, waiting to be catalogued, waiting like a treasure in a field. Since I have the privilege of signing books out before they're processed, I take Buechner home.

I delve into those volumes of memoir the way I would relish good wine—*mmm*-ing over each sip, appreciating the richness—but in the case of Buechner, also weeping. Reading Buechner I feel as a child does, having done something careless or clumsy, and someone comes along to say, "Don't worry. It's going to be okay. *Everything* is okay." In Buechner's telling, that is like God. In his view, the only way we know God and see God is through the most ridiculous, painful, humiliating moments of our lives, because God is in those places embracing us and helping us along. God is there with the cursed more so than with the blessed. At first, I cannot read Buechner without sobbing.

Describing the way God speaks to people via the medium of everyday life, Buechner writes,[3]

> God speaks to us in such a way, presumably, not because he chooses to be obscure but because, unlike a dictionary word whose meaning is fixed, the meaning of an incarnate word is the meaning it has for the one it is spoken to, the meaning that becomes clear and effective in our lives only when we ferret it out for ourselves. (p. 4)

Buechner seems to *revere* human life, depicting everyone's life as undeniably sacred. Love and God are there if we look for them. And wherever love is, there is God; and wherever God is, there is sacredness. Embarrassed by the mistakes of the past several years, I had walked through life like a person with voluntary amnesia. I had refused to look back for fear I would crumble under the weight of regret. The mixed-up marriage, the loss of my self and the unheeded deterioration of my confidence, the seeming waste of those years—I had blamed myself for all of it.

Buechner urges me to look back on my life not with shame but with reverence and to let God heal the memories. Years will pass before I experience more reverence than repulsion, before I experience actual healing. But it is Buechner, more than anyone else, who turns me in the right direction.

Buechner walks with me that entire year. I read volume after volume of his writing.

Then I discover Thomas Kelly. At a reception for graduates in the Religion Department office in May 1996, a professor hands me a small square volume by the author. The book, called *A Testament of Devotion,* is no more than one hundred pages. Thomas Kelly was a Quaker educator who became known as a "Quaker mystic" for voicing the truths of mysticism from the perspective of Quaker theology.

One evening early that summer, I pull out Thomas Kelly. Madison is off to her dad's and I sit in a folding chair on my balcony, overlooking the hazelnut orchard abutting my father's flower garden. I watch the sun slip like a hand behind westward hills as the scatter of clouds in the sky flushes plum-pink. Once I start in to Kelly's book, I feel accompanied. Thomas Kelly, who did most of his writing during the Nazi advance on Europe before his young death in 1941 is, on a breezy, warm night, the best kind of company. Wide-minded and gentle, full of compassion, Kelly writes,

> For faith and hope and love for *all things* are engendered
> in the soul as we practice their submission and our own to
> the Light Within, as we humbly see *all* things, even darkly
> and as through a glass, yet through the eye of God [italics
> added][4]

I want this to be true. My spirit leans in close as I read. The current of my inner life had always moved toward this kind of unity, toward seeing things not through the divisions of good and bad, right and wrong, but through love. Yet the religion I had been exposed to throughout most of my life seemed to run counter to this unifying current. It seemed to be about boundaries and hoops to jump through, about pigeon-holing and deciding who was in or out.

My reading around this time opened a new world of spiritual thought to me, a world I was increasingly eager to explore. Every spiritual impulse I'd ever had was pulling me further in the direction of inclusive love, and further from the categories of religion that divided people into acceptable and unacceptable, lovable and unlovable.

I want to have hope and love for all things, to see everyone and everything as existing, somehow, in the presence of God, every last thing—as Kelly said, an opportunity for love. War-makers and bullies and rapists; friends and peacemakers and lovers. All of them. Everything.

I want to discover this "Light Within" Kelly wrote about, something Quakers frequently spoke of. I want to know where God is to be found in *me*. Thomas Kelly stirs my interests both in Quakerism and mysticism. He is also an academic, as I am at the time training to be, and has suffered humiliating failures.

Over the course of two and a half years, I have few friends but these: Buechner, Merton, Underhill, Kelly, and a few other writers. I encounter them like kindred souls.

Even before reading Thomas Kelly, I had developed affection for Quakers, who I was introduced to by professors at George Fox. I didn't know many *real* Quakers (whom I defined by their likeness to the earliest sect), but I had learned about their history and theological roots and admired many of the key figures of early Quakerism. I had Quaker professors I admired. Nevertheless, when I attended Quaker or "Friends" churches, they seemed little different from other churches.

Like all religious denominations, Quakerism has experienced splits and compromises. In the United States, these splits have become evident geographically, where Quaker churches on the East Coast and those on the west are vastly different, despite some exceptions on either side. Most West Coast Quaker churches, which prefer the term *Friends*, from the historic title "Society of Friends," to the term *Quaker*, are decidedly evangelical, meaning, among other things, that they teach a fairly literalistic interpretation of Scripture, believe salvation is found in a relationship with Jesus Christ, and tend to worship in ways highly influenced by American pop culture.

But on the East coast, Quaker meetings are more appreciative of Quaker distinctives (i.e., the belief that God is in everyone, the practice of nonviolence, the gathering in silence to attend "the Light") while often less comfortable with the Christian roots of Quakerism. Some Friends meetings in the middle of the country balance Quaker theology and Christian faith. On the western fringe where I live, many Friends churches are often less Quaker and more fundamentalist (rigidly literalistic in their interpretation of Scripture, politically conservative, committed to converting non-believers to conservative Christianity, and convinced that those who do not convert are unsaved). Of course, there are notable exceptions all around.

Despite the mind-boggling diversity in what is now called Quakerism, I adore the historic Quakers (surely all the more because I didn't know them!). The earliest Quakers worshipped in silence, emphasizing quiet meditation over wordiness and the unmediated availability of God to every soul; they adhered to nonviolence; they loved Jesus and did things he said to do like feed the hungry, help the sick, visit the prisoners, free the slaves, and actively make peace; they tried to live simply amid materialism; they let women minister as equals. I had yet to encounter the other historic peace church traditions: the Mennonites, the Brethren, who would also influence me.

For the time being, I became a convert, a Quaker.

Eye-Opening
The stepping back happened
somewhere across the Atlantic.
My king's-eye-view grew sharp
away from dulling billboards
of realtors, God-zilla-sized,
and 99¢ super-sized fries.
Now the outsider in that Wash-
n-Go operating theater,
America, where they dissect
and stroke and reconstruct,
with solemn, incessant
concentration, omnipotent
image of Image.
The manufacture of discontent.
From where these feet stand
I see vistas their best-kept-
secrets cannot touch.
And the resplendent truth
of what they don't see
makes me want to gush.

CHAPTER FOUR

Awakened Heart

At this point in my life, I liked to plan things, to schedule, to keep life as tidy as possible. When I graduated with my bachelor's degree in 1996, I was already registered to begin the MA program in theology at GFU. I viewed this as a necessary step in the direction of my PhD, which I would begin immediately following the one-year MA. I had applied to PhD programs in England and Scotland and was already corresponding with potential advisors at key universities. I was twenty-seven years old and Madison was four, and though I hadn't been on a single date since my split with Alex two and a half years prior, I was beginning to think this was for the best. I would be leaving the country soon. I didn't need the distraction of a relationship. How would dating someone in the U.S. help me get a PhD in Britain? *Maybe I'll meet a man overseas*, I thought.

Then, one sunny Sunday in July, I met Darryl. He was standing in church next to his parents, a charming, affectionate, older couple I had met several months earlier. They were the main reason Madison and I attended the church. We had taken to the Browns like monks to holy water. Darryl was thirty-five, living in Indianapolis, and had come to Newberg to visit.

I first noticed his eyes: clear-as-Wyoming-sky blue. He was also tall, thin, attractive. He wore Dr. Martin shoes, loose-fitting mustard-colored jeans, and a faded plum button-up. I knew the Browns' son was an illustrator and graphic designer and had seen his artwork. It was good—impressively good. I was pleased to find the artist equally appealing. That afternoon, I called and asked Darryl out to coffee. Since "coffee" is a way of making a date without making one, I was technically asking him, a total stranger, on a date. To balance the impression this gave, I suggested we walk at the abbey. If he thought I was overly assertive in asking him out, my taking him to a monastery might quell any suspicions about my character.

◆

At the abbey, Darryl and I walk Saint Aelred's trail. We sit by the pond admiring the finer qualities of the other's appearance. I notice Darryl's thin, fit legs, the legs of a runner, his lucid blue eyes. I notice the laid-back way he communicates, his genuine humility and gentle laughter; I admire how he talks about books, his favorite authors, Flannery O'Connor and Walker Percy. After coffee, Darryl and I make plans to see each other two days later.

For our second date, Darryl arrives barefoot, in long shorts. It is a hot July night. Because my apartment is a studio, the living room is Madison's bedroom and Madison's bedroom is the living room. Since she is tucked in bed but still awake when Darryl arrives, we sit on the sofa to visit while she falls asleep and have talked less than ten minutes when Madison sits up and asks in her most lyrical voice, "Are you two boyfriend and girlfriend?"

I abruptly take Darryl outside.

The sky is the siren blue of a stellar jay, stippled with stars. Darryl and I both look up, leaning against the railing of my small deck, standing side-by-side. I turn toward Darryl as he meets my eyes. Reaching his hand to my shoulder and brushing aside my hair, he says, "You look a little too . . . saintly." I see him glance at my shirt. I happen to be wearing my favorite tee, one from another monastery I'd visited. It reads: *Mount Angel Abbey Library.* I look down at the shirt then up, as Darryl hesitates, laying his hand on

the railing of the deck. "I am no saint," I laugh, "it is just a shirt."
I look straight into his eyes—one, two, three more moments.
Then finally, he leans forward and kisses me.

For five days, Darryl and I absorb all we can of each other, trying new restaurants, visiting the art museum, ignoring the movie
Emma while we kiss in the back row of the theater, talking about
past relationships, eating meals with both of our families. During
the meal at the Browns, Madison takes one bite of the meat set before her and announces matter-of-factly "*This tastes like rubber.*" It
is precisely the sort of candor that endears people to Darryl.

Darryl's manner is mild, but he is dotingly affectionate. He
touches me often, stroking my hair, covering me in quick showers
of kisses. It has been years since I felt so tenderly loved by a man—
since my first kiss with Tom when I was sixteen years old—and I
feel like a leper touched by the very hand of God. I am going away
to Scotland in a year and before bumping into Darryl in the foyer
of his parent's church had planned to continue my solitary state a
good while longer, at least long enough to land on the road to my
PhD. But Darryl flips the switch I had turned off inside; suddenly
I am *on*. I fall madly for Darryl, who is handsome and funny and
gifted and gentle and understanding. After those miraculous five
days, Darryl returns to Indianapolis.

Perhaps the time element—the fact that I am planning to be
on the other side of the globe in a year, adds a note of urgency to
the relationship. We both feel we have met someone extraordinary, perhaps our soul-mate, and don't want contingencies like
distance to prohibit a great partnership. If we are poised to end up
on separate continents in a year, we need to act. No time for
temerity and carefulness.

So we plunge.

Darryl and I talk every single day on the phone, usually an
hour or more, wanting to share our lives. At times we stumble
through a dense relational fog. Darryl has had many intimate relationships by the age of thirty-five and has never been married, and
I fear that no man, let alone one who has loved as many women as
he has, can be faithful to me. A year earlier he had been engaged to
a woman he dated for three years, only to have the relationship

disintegrate. He was still mildly in love with her when we met. At the time he met me, he'd been involved in a casual sexual relationship with a friend, not even a girlfriend, and tried, at first, to hide it from me.

Though I cannot see it at the time, I have been devastated by past disappointments with men, and am crippled with distrust and insecurity. The combination of our backgrounds proves, to understate the matter, problematic. I'm about as ready for the relationship as I am ready to have my teeth pried out with rusty tweezers.

"Sometimes I think I'll just be another woman to you," I sob over the phone lines. "I hate that you've loved so many women." I stop to blow my nose.

Darryl listens compassionately. He answers slowly, laying his words out with intention. "Tricia, you are special. I can't erase the past, but I don't hold you up to other women, I don't compare."

"How can you not compare?" I persist. I feel like everything about me: my body, my sense of humor, my knowledge of things that interest Darryl—art, design, architecture—will be scrutinized against the background of past loves, some of whom were gifted artists and designers. My latent insecurities about my intellect, my physical self, my abilities, ascend like bubbles to the surface. Suddenly I see nothing but flaws.

Darryl whispers reassurances to me over the phone. He sends me love letters and love faxes, many of them small works of art. He wakes up when I call in the middle of the night on one of my doubt-driven relational rampages. He sees me at my insane, ridiculous worst.

And he loves me.

During the remainder of 1996, Darryl makes two trips to Oregon, and I make one to Indianapolis. These reunions are charged with pent-up sexual energy and the rapture of having in the flesh the person who has walked so closely with us in prior weeks. On Darryl's first trip back to Oregon, we take a trip to Orcas Island, in the San Juan Islands off the coast of Washington.

On one indelible afternoon, we walk in the open woods of the decidedly rural Orcas, when we come upon a tiny, pristine chapel set in a meadow of wildflowers, smack dab in the middle of nowhere. The church, white and very old, has obviously been refurbished with care. It has a steeple with a bell and ornate trim, and inside smells of dust and wood and new paint. The place seems enchanted. There are no trails cut in the meadow to its door, and no roads in the immediate vicinity, just the surprise of a little church, plopped down like a symbol of God-knows-what. It is surrounded by wild bunnies—dozens of them, and tall, swaying grass, and to me it symbolizes the unexpected.

Darryl introduces me to Indian food and the world of graphic design, to modern '50s architecture and the music of Jonathan Richman. I introduce Darryl to the theology of nonviolence, to contemplative methods of prayer, and to Frederick Buechner, who soon becomes his favorite author. Darryl introduces me to A. A. Milne's *Winnie the Pooh* books, to the artful "Wallace and Gromit," and to the Coen Brothers. I introduce Darryl to radical politics and plangent folk music. While Darryl increases my levity, I cultivate his depths.

"So, do you want to marry me?" Darryl says on a September night during one of our daily phone calls. He throws out the question in his laid-back, light-hearted manner, so unceremoniously that I could easily have missed it as a proposal. But I do not miss it. "Yes," I tell him. The next day I send him a postcard with just one word written fifty times: *Yes.*

During our trips back and forth between Oregon and Indiana, Darryl and I spend a cumulative total of less than one month together. Yet we spend hundreds of hours on the phone. We email prolifically. Darryl and I talk far more than most dating couples do in a year. Thus we assume we know each other.

In a way, we do. We know each other *inside.* We know what the other one likes to think about when he/she sits waiting for a bus. We know what makes the other person cry or laugh. We know what the other person likes to order at a Chinese restaurant, and the books we choose to read twice. We know what the other person is most deeply ashamed of. We know what activates the other person's fears. We know, to some extent, why the other person's past relationships failed. We know one another's weaknesses and what people most like about the other. We know what the other person likes most about his/her closest friends. We share our creativity with each other—Darryl shares design, I share poetry. We *know* each other.

Just before Christmas, Darryl moves west to live in Newberg. He drives his belongings out in a moving van and sets up house in an apartment that will be our shared home for eight months. During his first two weeks in Newberg, between his arrival and our wedding, I observe him for the longest stretch of time before our marriage.

And I begin to notice things.

Darryl is alarmingly mellow. On a scale of 1 to 10, his enthusiasm peaks at 5. In the months of Darryl's absence, I have worked up a fervent appetite for *amor*, and I am dismayed to find our appetites out of sync. Darryl prefers to spend the majority of his free time reading books and during that time is more or less disengaged from his surroundings. Madison, either at her best or worst, rarely gets a rise out of him.

I reckon this a blessing. Madison's tempestuousness would lead most impassioned men to either hit her or run screaming away. And I am not, at this stage of life, even-tempered. Darryl seems the perfect antidote to Madison's and my intensity. Perhaps he is a bit *too* mellow, but he will compensate for our extremes. He will talk reassurance and sense to us when we are overreacting. He will answer the door when our eyes are swollen with tears. He will be reliable when we are capricious, and calm when we are enflamed. He is our perfect man, I reckon. His dry good humor will keep us laughing.

◆

Darryl and I married the January following the July we met, in a traditional Quaker wedding at a bed-and-breakfast in front of a large fireplace. Darryl designed my dress and I made it: a sleeveless, straight-skirted dress of shantung silk with a wide Venice lace trim at the hips. Darryl wore a sharp tux he had found by tremendous luck at a thrift store a few years back (he had it cleaned and tailored for the event), topped off with an old black bow tie.

The wedding was spare and beautiful, pools of silence interspersed with thoughtful words from our friends, vows we wrote ourselves, and no trace of wedding *schmaltz*. My friend Donna played Rachmaninoff's eerily lovely *Vocalise* on the violin, accompanied by my sister on piano, and Madison, in a big-skirted dress of chai-colored silk, served as our sole attendant. She spent most of the time sitting next to Grandma, staring behind her at the photographer, who took candid shots of the wedding and reception. During the service, Philippians 2:1-5 was read:

> If then there is any encouragement in Christ, any consolation from love, any sharing in the Spirit, any compassion and sympathy, make my joy complete: be of the same mind, having the same love, being in full accord and of one mind. Do nothing from selfish ambition or conceit, but in humility regard others as better than yourselves. Let each of you look not to your own interests, but to the interests of others.

Darryl and I married on January 4, 1998, at the turn of a new year. Another new year. Another resolution.

Over the next few years Darryl and I would learn an important, if woefully belated, lesson. There are things one comes to know about a person only by spending time with him or her over a long period: his or her quirks, one's chemistry with him or her, whether one appreciates his or her presence. At the time of our marriage, Darryl and I had yet to learn these things.

◆

Eight months after our wedding, the three of us stored most of our belongings, filled three crates to ship to Scotland, and stuffed our maximum allotment of suitcases full of essentials. We then boarded a plane for St. Andrews, where I would pursue a PhD.

Scottish towns and suburbs of more recent ascendance are generally edged in flats and strip-malls, the architecture bearing all the charm of a Dollar Tree.

Of St. Andrews, this cannot be said.

Driving into St. Andrews, either from the west or the south, I sensed what it must've been like to be an old-world pilgrim, to see one's long-awaited destination set off in the distance like a jewel. St. Andrews sparkles on approach. It is wreathed by sea to the north and east, and by miles of rolling countryside to the south and west. During springtime, the countryside shines with rape-seed, banners of bright gold. The town's jagged, chimney-potted skyline, punctuated by the tall spires of an ancient cathedral standing mostly in ruin, evokes a Scotland of storybooks. The city draws people like a crackling-warm fire in winter. I immediately fell in love with St. Andrews.

Of the twenty-hour journey to the village (by plane, bus, and taxi), Madison resisted sleep for nineteen and a half hours. Finally, she fell asleep in the cab just as we rolled into town. As with most children, Madison's weight doubled as she drifted off to sleep, and when she slept, she *slept*. A pack of wild boars could rage through her bedroom and the girl would not budge. Darryl carried her through town—up stairs and down corridors, from one office to the next—for most of two hours while we sorted out accommodations.

The postgraduate student apartments into which we would eventually move were unavailable for six weeks. We were thus placed temporarily in an old two-story cottage of stone. It adjoined other cottages in a townhouse layout and backed onto a garden shared with neighbors, most of who were renters on "summer holiday." Magenta hydrangeas and fragrant roses in full bloom adorned the garden. A clothesline stretched across the grass. Stone walls separated the garden from those of adjoining townhouses, each of which had a slate roof and multiple chimney pots (like every other house in town) and walls at least a foot and a half thick. Our apartment was sparsely furnished and tasteful, and it had a spacious bathtub Wilt Chamberlain would have loved.

Darryl had spent the first four years of his life in Burundi, where his parents were missionaries, and had lived six of his adolescent years in Tehran, Iran, where his father taught biology. As a result, perhaps, he is a reluctant traveler. Before our honeymoon to Mexico, Darryl hadn't left the U.S. for twenty years. But after our arrival in St. Andrews, Darryl began interviewing for graphic design positions in the region, interviews he'd set up before our arrival, and he soon secured a fulltime job in a town forty minutes from St. Andrews. Driving the various routes between the two towns, Darryl became more familiar with the county of Fife, and more of an explorer, than I.

Soon after landing in our new home, we were hit by a tornado of troubles: car troubles, housing delays, money transfer problems, missing shipments of luggage, and health woes in the form of relentless viruses that finally let up a year and a half later.

During the first two weeks we lived in St. Andrews, we bought a beast of a Volvo that broke down almost immediately—while parked in a *temporary*, fee parking slot in front of our cottage. The situation worsened immediately when a tow truck driver broke our one key in the lock of the driver's side door, and a cantankerous policeman decided we were going to make his day. He ticketed us from there to Toronto. We got to know the constabulary (police station) far too well far too soon, as we made multiple trips to plead our case with the authorities.

The challenges of living overseas bowled me over. It took almost a week to figure out where to buy towels (in the meantime sharing one hand towel among us) and how to adapt electronics, such as my laptop computer, to the high-voltage electrical outlets. Groceries seemed to cost twice as much as back home. Driving *anywhere* on the narrow, so-called "two-lane" roads in Scotland gave me a tension headache and evoked a rare longing for suburban America, with its wide, smooth streets and bold, well-enforced lines. Through all of this, Darryl's steadfastness and help got us through. *What would I have done without Darryl?* looped through my mind for weeks.

Throughout preparations for our move, I was able to fixate on the logistics of relocating a family and on concerns like housing, school for Madison, and pulling together passports. I avoided thinking about the PhD, the very reason we were moving to Scotland, thus avoiding the insecurity that was sure to descend in due time. It was easy to stand out as a scholar in a small pond like George Fox University. But at St. Andrews, I would have to earn my placement. I had won an Overseas Research Scholarship from the British government that allowed me to study at a U.K. university for resident tuition as opposed to the much higher tuition U.S. students pay. A scholarship from St. Marys College, the divinity school (religion department) of the university, would cover the remainder of the tuition bill. I would be studying at the university tuition-free because I had tricked somebody somewhere into believing I was a promising student. My old friend Insecurity slipped out of the cramped quarters of my suitcase and expanded to fill the space around me.

◆

Walking into St. Marys Quadrangle, I feel my gut plunge. Darryl, Madison, and I enter through towering wrought-iron gates set into a tall stone wall that offers the only entrance to the quadrangle, which is hidden from view of the cobble-stoned South Street. Sprawling before us is a grassy courtyard crisscrossed with paths and surrounded by buildings ancient by American standards: gray-stone structures with sculpted ledges and entryways, arched windows and massive wooden doors, slate-topped roofs, and at each entrance, a wide staircase. A circular flowerbed about ten yards in diameter stands between the divinity school and the science department and is home to a massive hemlock. To the right as one enters the quadrangle sits St. Marys College, the central portion of which dates to the 1500s—the oldest structure in the entire university, which is the oldest university in Scotland. The science department sits opposite the divinity school and stretches the full length of a block.

In front of St. Marys, we notice a gnarled, thorny tree. It looks hunched and shriveled with age, like a woman beset with osteoporosis. "I wonder if that's the famous tree?" Darryl asks. Madison skips ahead to investigate. We had heard of a tree planted by Mary Queen of Scots in the 1500s, We know it is near St. Marys. Sure enough, a plaque at the tree's base identifies it as the very one. I try to imagine the old section of St Marys, the ancient tree, standing there in the 1500s. I try to imagine the students in their scholar's robes and velvet hats, horse-drawn carriages on the cobbled street,

the ostentatious clergymen en route to the cathedral to discuss fo-
ment within the Church—the pre-Reformation church, the
church with a big "C" church. I try to imagine what the village of
St. Andrews would have looked like at that time, the ancient castle
and cathedral still intact, the compact downtown surrounded by
acres of farmland laid out in separate, diminutive plots.

Next to St. Marys College, on the other side of the wrought-
iron gate, is the divinity school library. We enter this library
through a featureless room housing a few computers, various refer-
ence books, and the circulation desk. From there, we pass through
a closet-sized hallway and ascend a creaky staircase. This hallway
opens onto the gaping old room where theology books are shelved.

The room appears little changed over the years. Entering it, I
feel a surge trace through me. Though no one is in the room, I
hush Madison, whose voice carries in the cavernous space. The
room is not elaborately appointed or even particularly quaint. But
the learning worn into the wood-grain, the centuries of ideas
volleyed back and forth within the walls, make it a sacred place.
The library is two stories high. It accommodates books from floor
to ceiling around its perimeter, with a narrow balcony lining the
upper level, providing access to the books on the second story.
Each tall bookshelf is covered by a wire-mesh door and fitted with
a brass latch, as if to protect the books from book-burners or brig-
ands. On top of weathered wood floors, scattered with antique
Asian rugs, sit desks with round-back wooden chairs that make
certain no student will nap there. Madison flits from one seat to
the next. She opens the latched doors and admires the books.

It is my first week in St. Andrews. Sneaking into St. Marys
Quadrangle with Darryl and Madison, I am a tourist. The thought
of actually studying in that place, of contributing something to the
auspicious academic environment, scares the living words out of
me. But school is not yet in session. I can avoid the subject a few
weeks more.

Within a few days, I run into my advisor, Professor Piper. I am
exiting the bank and there he is. He asks how I'm doing. Then he
tells me to set up a meeting with him the following week.

Reality sets in like gangrene.

Professor Piper is the main reason I have come to St. Andrews. When I'd written him almost two years prior inquiring about the university's New Testament Studies program, he had enthusiastically answered my inquiries, corresponding with me for several months about my academic interests. Then, at a Society of Biblical Literature conference in New Orleans a year later, we'd finally met. During the conference, he had treated me to a fine meal in a restaurant overlooking the lovely, pre-Katrina city, clearly hoping to woo me to the program.

He does. His attentiveness is impressive and seems a desirable quality in an advisor. Most of the potential advisors I've approached seem swamped with students. Piper, a somewhat awkward, bookish-yet-over-dressed American who had lived in Britain long enough to obtain an accent, will give me the attention I need. He is in every way an academic (excepting the snappy attire), in his fifties, and of raven-like appearance: sharp nose, thin face, dark hair. Despite his position and accomplishments, something about him, perhaps his shyness, reminds me of a grade-school boy.

The following week, I show up at his office.

Before coming to St. Andrews, I had carefully rehearsed my research plan and discussed it extensively with my New Testament professor back home. Still, my tongue has a habit of freezing up under pressure, and during the hour before the meeting I am a tangle of nerves. I am compelled to pee five times, my heart beats violently, and wide, wet rings form in the pits of my arms.

Piper's office is a stately, corniced, sun-filled room, strewn with dozens of stacks of books. Books everywhere—stacks of books on top of stacks of books. We make stiff small-talk for a few moments, and he politely asks how I'm settling in. Gradually, I begin to loosen up.

Then, just as I start to grow comfortable, Professor Esler, another St. Andrews professor I know, knocks on the door and expresses a hearty welcome. Esler had been my first introduction to St. Andrews when I met him at a Portland university where he was attending a conference. He is Australian, charming, and fun-loving. He sports baggy corduroy pants, worn tweed jackets, and shaggy gray hair with a mind of its own. His warm eyes and winning smile should put me at ease, but they don't. Despite the nerves, I greet him warmly. "Why haven't you come to say hello?" he badgers.

Then he sits down to join the meeting.

So there I am, suddenly faced with not one but two professors who've invested time in luring me to their school, and who are, oddly enough, curious as to what I plan to research. They both know I've won a full scholarship, dispelling all hopes of the department making money off of me, and naturally, ask me of my plans.

I open my mouth fully intending to wow them. I begin talking about Samaritan themes in the Gospel of John, and how I plan to explore a possible connection between the author and Samaria. Then, as I begin to explain *why* I have a notion to do this, my brain freezes like polar bear pee. I pause a moment too long—long enough to become distracted by the pause and the brain lull that has caused it, long enough to divert all of my cognitive energy away from the explanation I seek and toward mapping an escape.

The two men sit staring at me as the silence lengthens, and as a hot blush spreads, from top to bottom, across my face. The awkwardness of the moment is evident in the down-turned corners of their mouths, in the way they shift positions just slightly in their chairs. I am supposed to be one of the department's most promising students that year . . . and I completely and utterly *tank*.

I say something—something woefully short of glorious, but something. It gives the professors an opportunity to begin talking and thus to wrest control of the conversation before it devolves from disastrous to apocalyptic. I am grateful. They make suggestions, to which I somehow manage to respond. But I feel disgraced. The scene plays over and over in my head for weeks.

I preempt future advisor-meeting disasters by taking anxiety medication—prescribed to me by a Scottish doctor, bless her soul—and copious notes before every subsequent meeting.

After six weeks in the idyllic stone cottage on North Street, our family takes up residence in a rather hideous apartment complex. It is, as a concession for its ugliness, smack dab in the middle of downtown, carefully hidden behind a charming structure of nineteenth century ascendance. I can "pop out to the shops," as the Scottish say, on a moment's notice, for bread, milk, or fresh pastries. It is my first experience of village life. Though Darryl and I shop weekly at Safeway on the edge of town, I frequent the local downtown shops as much as possible.

Every storefront in those old stone buildings dons a hand-painted sign with meticulous serif letters. The wooden doors present a glossy confetti of blue, red, and green, with other shades tossed in. There is a dry-goods store directly across the street, a fish monger, a bakery with a broad display of picturesque pastries, a hardware store, a delicatessen, a Woolworths, and a candy shop. Many of the downtown stores cater to tourists, but the basics are covered as well, right down to spackling and nails. My favorite restaurant, Ma Brown's Tea Room, is located a few blocks east of our flat and one block north, near the castle ruins. It serves bacon rolls—plump flaky dinner rolls with strips of bacon sandwiched between them—and colorful pureed soups. A decidedly Scottish establishment.

The apartment complex in which we reside is designated for international postgraduate families, and houses families from around the world. In the building's eleven flats, nine countries are represented. Madison makes friends with neighbor children by cloyingly standing and watching them until they invite her to play, giving Darryl and me an in with the parents.

Madison's best friends include a vivacious girl from Kenya who pouts her lips and stomp-walks just like Oprah Winfrey's character in *The Color Purple*, and a boy from Japan who does a brilliant impression of Buzz Lightyear (with his accent, "To infinity and beyond!" sounds more like "To Kennedy fam-be-oh!"). Both children enter our flat without knocking, and Madison comes and goes freely from theirs. Madison also befriends a Muslim boy from Turkey whose favorite activity is undressing her Barbies.

Madison starts school in St. Andrews, in what would be kindergarten back home. P-1, as her grade is called, meets for a full school day, allowing me six to seven hours of uninterrupted work every weekday. It takes about one month for Madison to adopt a distinctively Scottish accent that grows more and more pronounced as weeks pass. That year we capture Madison on videotape doing a full-on Elvis show in "Scottish," wearing a bathing suit and tights, her glittery-red ruby slippers, and her blanket banded onto her head like a shepherd's headdress.

Our apartment complex bears an uncanny resemblance to a Soviet-era housing tract. It comes furnished with 1970s waiting-room-style chairs instead of a couch and slate-hard beds. The place is a fire trap. As such, it is equipped with an ultra-sensitive, blaring fire alarm whose ear-shattering siren sounds whenever a resident burns toast. It can't be disarmed until every member of the building has gathered outside and the lackadaisical firemen have checked the building for the latest culinary cause of commotion.

This often happens in the wee hours of the night, as some neighbors apparently like midnight snacks. All of us residents, freshly traumatized by waking to the siren, shuffle into our clothes and out the door. But as we stand in front of the building, watching children play on the blacktop in their nightclothes, intermittently laughing and moaning over our lot, poking fun at the hapless firemen who take twenty to thirty minutes to arrive, we create some of our best Scotland memories.

◆

During our first Christmas in St. Andrews, Madison's dad surprised her with a visit. Madison stood at the door with a shocked expression on her face as her dad shouted, "Maddie girl!" Speechless, she opened her arms in a bewildered hug. By the end of the evening, she had warmed. Alex and his brother, who had accompanied him on the trip, were holed up at an inn near the ancient golf course.

One day Alex and I went for a walk with Madison, our first outing as a threesome in years. We walked by the beach under a cloudy sky. We bought candy bars at a park-side stand. I answered dozens of questions about Scotland, and took turns jumping on a trampoline. That day Alex and I planted a seed of friendship that would grow by fits and starts over the next several years.

Alex visited again the following summer 1999; he and Madison occupied our flat while Darryl and I flew to Florence, Italy for a week. I'd dreamt of visiting Florence since watching *A Room with a View* at the age of sixteen. Some childhood dreams come true.

◆

On the drive through Tuscany to our destination, we pass acres of sunflowers, all craning their rapturous heads with the passing of the sun. The air is stirring, full of golden goddess dust, smelling like no air I had breathed before. Darryl and I choose to spend an entire week in Florence rather than travel around Tuscany, to relax and get to know the place, which we do. We spend long hours in museums and walking the pale roads traversing hilltop vistas and old-world gardens. Olive trees and grape vines appear everywhere, like a cliché, as too the statuesque human form.

Italy is a powerful aphrodisiac.

Our hotel room is the sort of diminutive, white-plaster-walled space I'd always associated with Italy, with long, gauzy curtains and wrought-iron railings on small ledges outside windows overlooking cobbled lanes, sconces over the bed and antique wardrobes in the corners. The *room* is an aphrodisiac.

In contrast, the coolness between Darryl and me bears down. We enjoy one another's company and friendship and the art of Florence, the sidewalk cafes and the pigeons in the plaza, but the energy in our bedroom is as unbalanced as Pisa's famous tower. I find Italy's food incomparable, so lathered in balmy olive oil it makes me close my eyes and moan. I devour plates of creamy gnocchi and pastas generously laced with scarlet tomatoes and pungent fresh basil. I devour bottles of chianti, the centuries of stories worn into the narrow streets, the amaryllis and flaming geraniums gracing window-sills amid a sea of terra cotta, the clotheslines waving a surrender on the sultry breeze.

Even the cathedrals evoke a connectedness to the body, so natural in a culture appreciative of God's creative impulse, so artful and awake to physical flow and form. If God is the Creator, the work of God's hands is good. And the work of God's hands is sensual; it feels, hears, sees, smells, and tastes. It swells with passion.

The worship spaces in Italy honor these aspects of God's creation. They are full of wonder and ageless beauty, as if the designers aimed to awaken the senses to God's presence the way they are awakened in a sunlit valley or fertile rain forest.

Like many drawn to Quakerism, I'm not especially partial to outward symbols of the sacred, especially symbols wrought by the forced labor of peasants, as were most cathedrals. Cathedrals always seemed to me wasteful, and the cathedrals I'd visited or viewed in photos looked like cold, ostentatious representations of power, like they were meant to scare people, to put subjects in their place. But I don't experience this aversion in Florence. Even the massively overwrought Duomo is humanized by the art of Michelangelo, who like much of the Bible, depicts peasants as children of God and kings as diabolical.

I experience two cathedrals in particular as holy places: San Miniato al Monte, built in the 1200s, and San Marco Convento. These cathedrals are much simpler, more striking in their bold lines than the Duomo, or the Santa Croce where the likes of Galileo and Leonardo da Vinci are buried. They are shadowy except for beams of slanted light through high windows, and they are imbued with an inherent stillness despite the tourists. As sightseers like us pass through, we notice people worshipping, kneeling at prayer benches, attending mass at altars, doing the things cathedrals were made for.

The San Marco Convento swarms with American teenagers when we enter. Clustered in small groups, they engage in the universal adolescent activities of teasing and/or flirting, running noisily between sections of the cathedral with the heckle and jive of teenagers, catching irritated glances around every corner. I, for one, exit the cathedral through a side door to explore the monastery adjoining the church, hoping to escape them. But it turns out they are everywhere, even rushing through the halls of the stark old monastery, up and down narrow stone steps. I am away from the cathedral about ten minutes before returning. Back in the church, I visit naves and alcoves, enjoying the famous paintings on the walls. The atmosphere has quieted, but I am not paying much attention.

And then an amazing thing occurs.

A sound rises through the church, a peaceful, soft music wafting from a choir of pristine voices. The sound is so beautiful and unexpected it is almost shocking. I turn to see the teenagers, the same rag-tag group that had been loosed on the place earlier, now seated in rows of pews, making the sound. Their singing fills the church with light and charges it with spirit I can feel to the ends of my fingertips and toes. I sit down in a pew behind them and close my eyes. The music, the resonance of it in that cold old cathedral, is as rich as good chianti, as harmonious and gentle as love. I surmise the teenagers are a traveling choir, returning the hospitality of Italy with surprise offerings of song in its cathedrals. The song, and the gift of it issuing from such an unlikely and off-putting source, is a sort of parable. Grace, the spaciousness of God, God's tendency to reveal beauty in the most unexpected of places, through the most unexpected of people—are all present metaphorically in that song, in the angelic notes of this traveling choir. The surprise is the most memorable of my life. It brings me to tears.

So does the violinist in the Piazza Della Signoria outside the Uffizi. He has staked his claim on the spot and plays most evenings Darryl and I are in Florence, filling that piazza with braided threads of longing and passion and joy. He plays with his eyes closed, his whole body drawn into the act. *Da, da, da, da, da*—an ecstacy of bow and wood and string, of elbow and neck. The violinist plays like nothing in the world could give him more pleasure than creating those notes, interpreting the composer's joy and pain, elevating the hearts of his listeners or drawing them into shadow.

He plays the way I want to feel about my life.

◆

As it turns out, the experience of living overseas proves more threatening than the program at St. Marys. My stressed-out body does not adapt well to the damp, windy climate of St. Andrews and its onslaught of new viruses. I am perpetually sick, in part a result of a fungus allergy I will not discover till years later. Each morning I walk Madison fifteen minutes to school, then return to our flat to spend five to six hours in my writing chair surrounded by books, forcing myself to work against every physical impulse. My head throbs. I am painfully tired. My chest rattles. I suffer yeast infections as a result of long courses of antibiotics for bronchitis and sinusitis. During Madison's school hours, I take a short nap in my chair and eat lunch. These are my only breaks. I am otherwise hellbent on writing a dissertation.[5]

What I need to do is sleep, to get well. I need a dry, warm climate where my body can heal. But I push myself forward. With my energy so low, the only thing that keeps me working is pure force of will; that, and the desire to leave Scotland soon and return to a familiar environment and a relative state of good health.

One Sunday, the weight of stress and fatigue is almost asphyxiating. We'd been attending Martyr's Church, of the Church of Scotland, since shortly after arriving in St. Andrews. It is an aged congregation that hosts "coffee mornings" to raise money for the homeless and to free slaves in Sudan. It meets in a grand old-stone building with stained-glass windows depicting John Knox, sundry saints, stories from the gospels. It is unlike any church Darryl or I have attended. We go for the minister's eloquent, left-leaning sermons, and for the hymns.

Church of Scotland hymnals are full of poetry—Christina Rossetti, John Greenleaf Whittier, Emily Dickinson, Gerard Manley Hopkins. A cantor pairs the verses with a tune from Scotland's folk repertoire, creating a whole new hymn-singing experience. He might say, "Hymn number 238, to the tune *Glengarry*," and the hymn begins.

That Sunday, I struggle to breathe, to quiet the mind-chatter. I am worried about a colleague who dislikes me, worried about teaching tutorials, worried I am too sickly to get a PhD, worried what my advisor thinks. I feel incapable of handling life.

The congregation begins a Whittier hymn while I fret and obsess, "Dear Lord and Father of mankind," they sing. My eyes stare at the hymnbook while my mind wanders. "Reclothe us in our rightful minds." The organ marches through the verses. I pull my long wool coat around me, buffeting myself against the building's inescapable winter chill.

Then suddenly the words of the fourth or fifth stanza wrest my attention:

Drop thy still dews of quietness
till all our strivings cease.
Take from our hearts the strain and stress,
and let our ordered lives confess,
the beauty of thy peace.

At once I am shaken into the present moment. Tears wet my eyes as I notice the words. *Dews of quietness. Strivings ceasing.* The words seem to be a prescription for my soul.

Yes, I want quietness. I sing along with a whisper, suddenly ready for conversion. I recite Whittier's hymn like it's the Drunkard's Prayer. If it had been a tent-revival I would have laid my worries at the altar, the demands volleying torturously about my head, my relentless insecurities. I would have laid them down like a bottle of 100-proof whiskey. I know the demands are self-imposed, words I put on the lips of colleagues and acquaintances. Still the chorus chants: "You are not good enough." *You can't, can't, can't, can't. . . .*

For the remainder of that church service I sit with the hymnbook open on my lap, repeating Whittier's lines again and again until they adhere to my memory. After the service, I don't stop. As I trudge through the Sabbath, cooking dinner and staring at a book, I chant the words in my head. I have never read Whittier's poem before or sung it as a hymn, but those five lines have, in one day, become my best friends. As I repeat "till all our strivings cease," the long fingers of ambition slowly loosen from around my neck. When my brain tires of the mantra, my heart takes over. During the coming months, I chant those lines hundreds, maybe thousands of times, like breathing. They change the way I pray, as I eventually adopt a hesychastic,[6] "mantra" style of prayer.

On that day at Martyrs Church, everything begins to change.

Over the course of the year, I gradually relax. I no longer need meds to get through meetings with my advisor, and I almost enjoy leading tutorials—small-group, discussion-oriented sessions with undergraduates. During my second year, illness becomes less frequent and I develop a solid topic of research and a good theory. I make friends. Still, I repeat Whittier's lines frequently. They are my reminder, my grounding. A beautiful life is not one of striving, they tell me, of copious published articles and long resumes. A beautiful life is one of balance and repose, and of passion and pleasure, they say. It includes nourished friendships, long, restorative silences, and senses awakened. It includes good health.

It is exactly the kind of life I desire.

Pre-Middle

If childhood is a cradle of universal arms
and middle age a turning back—needy
or humbly surrendered; if old age the return,
and death a womb of dust, "pre-middle"

is life's showdown with illusion.
We are discovering, my friends and I,
that we will never be as fearless or brilliant
or big as we thought you would be when

we grew up. We are acquainted with panic.
We know how it feels to betray others
in order to survive. We have faced our bodies'
first shattering, felt marriage plunge

like a canyon in the gut.
Pre-middle is watching the slow and stealthy
burial of our youth in fat and worried skin.
It is realizing our friends do not know us.

It is seeing our flaccid ambitions
as the ego-trips they are. It is watching
history repeat itself at least once, and
ourselves the mistakes of our forebears.

Pre-middle is discovering that the feet
we stand on are not our own.
It is seeing that the ground we stand on
is really nothing but grace.

CHAPTER FIVE

Broadening Light

By the time we left St. Andrews we'd amassed a cosmopolitan circle of friends. On the day we departed, they gathered on the gravel
in front of our soviet-block apartment complex to see us off.
Pamela and Nicole from Kenya cried and appeared forlorn; Masa,
Kaoru, and Mercy from Japan joked with Madison and wore the
same cheery smiles they always wore; Wagei, from Egypt, held his
young son, standing upright and stoic for the solemn occasion. In
a photo Darryl took of the group, I stand beaming amid a sea of
mostly somber faces, thrilled to be returning home, though also
moved by our neighbors' goodbyes.

Back in Newberg, Darryl, Madison, and I bought a house, a
modest, canary-yellow one-level at the back of a cul-de-sac in a
1970s development scattered with mammoth trees (on our lot
alone, I counted thirty). Darryl landed a job with a small but
growing design firm in Portland thirty miles away, and I hun-
kered-down in our home office to finish the last leg of my dissertation. Madison, for her part, entered private school, a choice we
assumed would lessen the transitional shock from the British
school system to the American. We plunged into a Quaker church
and began making friends. Everything, it seemed, was settled.

I concluded 1999 by submitting my PhD dissertation and began 2000 by teaching in my field: Literature of the New Testament to second-semester freshmen, and Writings of John to juniors and seniors. I would teach as an adjunct faculty member at George Fox University in Newberg.

It had been almost two years since I'd heard the Whittier hymn at Martyr's Church in St. Andrews. In the past six months, I had stopped reciting it as my mantra. Living back home in my own pond, away from the pressures of university life, finishing up my last year of doctoral work in absentia, I became complacent, comfortable. Darryl and I were personalizing our house, painting bold colors on the walls, and planting perennials in the garden. We reconnected with old friends and frequently hosted people for meals. My years of academic work were folding neatly into shape before my eyes like a colorful origami swan.

But then the start of classes approached. And my swan became a fretful old hen.

◆

Self-doubt descends. I am convinced I will choke, that my students will riddle me with questions I cannot answer, that I will instantly forget everything I know. My self-deprecating mind-voice chimes in, *Not one of your students will respect you. Come to think of it, they may actually hate you. How did you manage to get a PhD, anyway? A wrinkle in the fabric of academic logic, a fluke? You are an inexcusable fraud, my dear. And you . . . are . . . doomed.*

It is the first morning of classes. Though I have over-prepared, predicting every question a student can possibly ask and constructing a relevant answer, I am a wreck. I have packed my new leather briefcase with everything a professor might want: books, transparencies, red-ink pens, highlighters, Altoids. I wear a snappy black skirt and linen shirt ensemble that says "professional, yet comfortable." Fraud.

When I am nervous, my bladder shrinks to the size of a pecan. I pee twenty times before 10 a.m. *What made you think you could be a college professor?* my mind rattles on. Nothing scares me more than public speaking. My personality is well-suited to sitting hours at a computer writing, or with my nose buried in books—not to talking for hours a day in front of fifty slouching teenagers.

At home I review my notes for the eightieth time. I pick up my briefcase, lock the door, walk to the car, and drive my five-minute commute to the university. Garrison Keillor is on the radio: *The Writer's Almanac.* It is raining.

At the school, my heart quivers like a small tuft of down. I walk to the office of the Religion Department and ask the secretary for directions to the adjunct office, proceeding around the corner to my shared quarters, which (*blessed-be-the-Lord*) are empty. No one I know is in the halls and I release a quick sigh of relief. They would see through my feigned calmness to the white-knuckle terror of a mad woman.

After fumbling with the office key and opening the door to my broom-closet spread, I set my briefcase on an empty chair. No pictures hang on the walls, and nothing sits on the desk save a telephone and directory. Five textbooks lean on a small, lonely shelf. I proceed to work at my desk with the authority of a field mouse, taking out the book for my class, my notebook, setting them gently on the desk's surface. I look for a clock on which to count away the minutes, the full thirty-five minutes that stand between me and Judgment Day, the day I will be exposed. I think of the men on death row.

Just then I notice a small square of white paper taped to the corner of the otherwise barren desk. The Scotch tape on the edges is chipped and frayed. It has been there for some time. Words are printed on the paper in black ink, and phone numbers are scrawled on the edges in ball-point blue. As I glance at the words, I do a double-take. The name at the bottom of the paper says "John Greenleaf Whittier." *Cool,* I think, *I like John.* Then I glance at the poem itself, consisting of two stanzas. The first is unfamiliar to me. But when I reach the second, I read these words: *Drop thy still dews of quietness / till all our strivings cease. / Take from our hearts the strain and stress/ and let our ordered lives confess / the beauty of thy peace.*

. . . *My* words. How could it be? The words from the hymnal in St. Andrews. My heart mantra. Whittier.

I turn back to my book, so distracted and one-track-minded I almost miss the moment. Then I slowly, mechanically, turn back to the paper. I look at it, look to the corners of the small empty room as if I've entered the Twilight-Zone or been captured on a hidden camera.

The longer I look at the paper, the more it seems to be for me. A gift, maybe, a reminder.

A smile blooms across my face. Here, taped to my very desk, are the words that got me through my PhD, the words I need to read more than any others that morning, words that remind me what I believe: *Life is short. Breathe deeply. Stop striving. Everything is going to be okay.*

The words are taped to my desk.

That day I will begin an experiment. Maybe the outcome will be disastrous, maybe positive. Maybe I'll be humiliated, like the girl in my ballet class when I was five years old who wet herself in her little pink tutu. Maybe I'll be a pedagogical genius, like Robin Williams in *Dead Poet's Society*. Maybe, maybe not. Still, there is no such thing as a failed experiment.

And for a few brief moments sitting in that office, the outcome doesn't even seem to matter. Some sweet mystery has left me a note—taped to the faux-wood-grain of my shabby old desk. Something big. Something a lot like love. It is January, the new millennium, the ultimate fresh start. I have finished my PhD and am starting a new chapter. That morning I'd seen the first shoots of spring daffodils, the dew on my grass, lush as a broad swath of velvet. The birds of morning called to me, called like messengers, called like heralds of an ever-broadening light.

♦

I taught for a year, then quit.

The teaching was okay, considering I was teaching critical thinking about the Bible and theology to classes with a majority fundamentalist demographic. About half of my students had fully digested a Sunday-school flannel-graph worldview. These students didn't cotton to the idea that Moses may not have authored the Pentateuch, that the first five books of the Bible likely had a variety of authors over a variety of eras, or that the Scriptures are laden with factual inconsistencies.

One student took painful issue with me for suggesting that the earth was more than six thousand years old, as he had been taught by someone who'd calculated the precise age of the earth from the Bible. He found my willingness to believe scientists on such matters unbearable. *How can you be teaching at a Christian college?* he wanted to know.

Other progressive-minded professors tended to avoid these questions by not discussing them with freshman students. But I found this difficult to do. Shouldn't students have to face the uncomfortable questions? I wondered. Isn't that what a college education is about? The most intransigent students talked about me behind my back, called their youth pastors to grumble, and in one case, had parents complain to the department. According to this parent, I had told students that God was a woman—something I had certainly not said, since God is clearly not a man *or* a woman.

But the many exceptions to this lot were a calming breeze through my day. Some of my most accepting students were decidedly conservative. They had clung to the interpretation of Christianity they'd been raised to believe, one in which the Bible is literal, scientifically provable fact. But their conservatism did not prohibit their picking up new ideas, turning them over in their heads, and readjusting their preconceptions or laying them down. They were open-minded while still devoted to their core beliefs.

These students grew in love while slowly, bit by tender bit, banishing their fear of being wrong. Unlike the exclusivist types (who were more often intellectually lazy than religiously zealous), these students were interested in understanding people and coming to know God through other people's ideas. It was like they could see, almost despite themselves, that if Jesus wasn't here among us in our neighbors and our detractors, and revealed to us through the process of hearing people out, then Jesus was locked in a tomb somewhere, the tomb of prejudice and fear. These students were good listeners.

As much as I enjoyed these young people, I found teaching them exhausting. My temperament resisted public speaking and the dog-and-pony show great teaching required. As much as I wanted to be like Professor Keating in *Dead Poets Society*, I was no enchantress. I could arrange a lecture that presented ideas clearly and conveyed useful information, but I found no pleasure in and gleaned no energy from presenting it. Any spice I lent to the lectures was pure acting, and I cannot guess who was more bored, my students or I. Most likely I was, since at least the controversy of my lectures kept the room abuzz for listeners. By the end of each class, I needed intravenous espresso. Each day I walked to class silently humming to myself the rousing climax of Beethoven's Ninth ("Joyful, joyful, we adore thee . . . "), hoping to infuse myself with the enthusiasm I needed to get through class, with the drive and energy I lacked.

After a year of doing this, I realized my vocational trail had taken a colossal wrong turn.

Much of what I had done in my academic career was write. Write, write, write. It was what I loved most about academia. Yet here I was teaching, here I was a bona fide academic and the last thing I had time to do was write. Judging by the workload of my colleagues, the lack of writing time would not change as I progressed as a teacher of university. This, even more than my ineptitude in the classroom, gave me pause. I hungered to write in a way I had never hungered. I had honestly never known the feeling of *wanting* to work until I had *wanted* to be a scholar, and this not for laziness, since I'd inherited my father's propensity for hard work. Now I realized that much of what I desired about scholarship involved writing. Was it the pull of vocation I was feeling, a pull toward the writing life?

I wasn't sure. I only knew I was restless to learn and grow and find my voice as a writer. I'd done little creative writing outside of poetry, but I was restless to try. I hesitated to admit it, hesitated to say I was leaving the university to write. I had written almost solely in an academic vein. I had a sizable college debt to pay off, presumably by teaching. But I couldn't teach. I *knew* I couldn't teach.

So I held my breath and leapt.

For ten months I worked a ten-hour/week job at my Quaker church that paid the monthly student loan bill. Then I quit even that, finding I still had inadequate time to write. I was writing a book on ethics and global economics and each day had to compose something. I had to write, though I scarcely knew I could. But writing pulled so hard at me I couldn't resist. Nonetheless, I answered sheepishly when people asked why I'd quit teaching. I felt like an imposter saying I wanted to be a writer. I felt like a starry-eyed cab driver who had moved to Hollywood to "try to become" an actor, the sort of thing that makes everyone cringe. Yet I was "trying to become" a writer.

Darryl supported me through the vagaries of my academic and vocational life. He knew what vocation felt like. He loved his job as a graphic designer and felt gifted for it. He also loved books as much as anyone I knew, and recognized better than most the importance of writers. In addition to all this, he made a decent salary. With our preference for simple living, our family had little need for two incomes, and Darryl welcomed his bread-winner status since he went to work for fun. He would have done graphic design for half the money he made. Darryl also hugged me when I cried, listened compassionately as I slogged through confusion, helped with Madison, did the dishes every night, and tried, sometimes vigilantly, not to dismiss my changeability as flakiness.

♦

Who this woman was, this woman trying to become a writer, was still an open question. I had discovered a few things I definitely wasn't: an evangelical-fundamentalist, an obsequious wife, a celibate, a lay clergy-woman, a group leader, a teacher.

And I had spent so much of my life afraid. Now I was feeling a startling pull into risk-taking. In summer 2001, I became involved with Christian Peacemaker Teams (CPT), an organization founded by Quakers, Mennonites, and Brethren, that sends trained teams to conflict zones to do violence-reduction work, or nonviolent intervention. CPTers go where welcomed by local partners. They engage aggressors and accompany those threatened by violence, as well as monitor and report on human rights abuses. For several years I had followed CPT's work, reading reports from their projects and supporting them financially. But because of the risks involved, I could not see myself joining. I was, after all, the mother of a young child.

Yet I had been a convinced pacifist for six years by 2001. I understood pacifism to mean active peacemaking, or violence reduction, and wondered how much I was doing to help reduce violence. The first CPTers I had met, soon after my conversion to Quakerism, were a Mennonite couple who visited my undergraduate ethics class. They left an impression.

I asked the woman what it was like to engage in CPT work having young children as she did. We leaned toward each other across the arm-rests of two classroom desks. Her long graying hair was stretched into a braid that draped across a bony shoulder. "When I go to war zones," she said, "places like Haiti, I am always struck by the mothers. They don't get to choose whether or not to be there. They don't get to protect themselves and their children the way we do."

That was all she said on the matter, but the statement clung to my memory like a distinct scent. Over the years, I wove subtle meanings into her words: I get to choose safety over risk because of my white, middle-class American privilege, whereas mothers in places like Haiti don't have a choice. By choosing self-protection over reaching out, and by relaxing into the benefits of my privilege, I was, in my own way, furthering violence.

As this Mennonite couple described their lives to our class, I caught a vision of what a life of peacemaking might look like. Besides engaging in work with CPT, the couple adopted a lifestyle that was decidedly simple, which required far fewer resources than the typical American lifestyle. They chose to live below the federal tax line to avoid paying taxes that contribute to the military. Yet their simplicity came from a place even deeper than this. They didn't choose simple living merely because they were low-income. They *wanted* to live with less to challenge materialism and to consume only a fair share of the world's food, water, and energy resources, unlike the disproportionate share most Americans consume. The couple seemed humble and gentle rather than caustic or preachy. They simply told the story of their one shared life, and the story carried a universal message.

It would be a few years before I discovered more about Mennonites, through publications, through reading the website and watching the videos of the Mennonite Central Committee (MCC), and by getting to know a few Mennonites personally, but the impression this couple left was strong. When I was in Scotland, I became aware of the fair-trade movement and about fair-trade efforts supported by Mennonites, and I recalled the couple I had met while an undergraduate in college.

Not long after this, I began to probe for more information on Mennonites and into the development and peacemaking work of MCC. I soon learned that this diverse denomination, like all denominations, ran the gamut from conservative to far-left leaning. There were bonnet wearing Mennonites, and there were tie-dye shirt wearing Mennonites. The threads that held them all together, however, were connections to a tradition historically rooted in Christian peacemaking. Whatever the flavor of individual Mennonite churches in the twentieth century, those churches grew out of an Anabaptist struggle that was, at its core, about peacemaking. Though northwestern Oregon has few Mennonite churches and few Mennonites, I became friends with several Mennonites through CPT. These interactions went a long way in teaching me about peacemaking and in shaping my lifestyle over the coming years.

My interaction with the Mennonite CPT couple planted a seed in my life that would eventually sprout into CPT involvement. For years I assumed CPT work was something I would do when Madison reached adulthood. But I couldn't forget the commitment of the woman I'd met, who didn't use her children as an excuse to withdraw from risk-taking. As I began to learn about CPT, I realized there was a range of risk involved in their work. Perhaps the choice was not between withdrawal and absolute risk, but between willingness and unwillingness. I knew that some CPT projects were quite risky—for example Hebron (West Bank) and Colombia—while others were far less risky (for example, aboriginal justice projects among Native communities). Could I join CPT and serve only in the less risky projects while Madison was young?

Almost as soon as I posed the question, the answer was clear. I walked straight through the door I had just opened. I applied for a delegation, a two-week intensive introduction to a project, something every CPTer must complete before advancing to training. Then I was headed to Chiapas, Mexico.

◆

On the flight from Portland, I take in the view. My plane points toward Phoenix, passing over Utah. There the earth falls away from vast plateaus, forming jagged-edged canyons and a smattering of lakes. From a distance of miles the erosion looks sudden, like the earth is nothing but a cookie crumbling to bits. I think about distance and perspective, and how things might appear to God. I battle intense guilt for leaving Madison.

Madison and I are extraordinarily attached, and she had cried herself to sleep the night before I left, begging me not to go, and her tears in the airport washed over me in a quick sweep of panic. Whatever I am doing, it is no longer clear. Does God sometimes want us to do things so difficult for our children? Am I joining CPT because it is the right thing to do, or because it just seems right at this time? Is there always a right and a wrong?

When I meet up with the delegation I find a diverse mix of ages, occupations, and genders. There's the academic, the woman with her own gardening business, the retired postal worker, the student activists, the couple who are recent college graduates ready to train and join CPT full-time. Our group has ten members total, most of us checking out CPT and the situation in Chiapas with no intentions of joining.

By the time our bus weaves into the highlands of Chiapas after twenty hours of travel, all of my doubts about coming have dissipated like the mist hugging densely vegetated hills. I feel pulled into the present. I stay there the entire twelve days I am in Chiapas. From the bus I can see women and children with bulging mounds of firewood on their backs, disappearing into the bush along the hillsides like ghosts. I see few men. The women and girls wear colorful traditional smocks and satin ribbons woven into heavy braids. The women's bodies are sinewy and stout as totems. Our bus ascends past small houses with craft-works displayed out front for visitors and potential buyers: woven and embroidered clothing, wool blankets, metal works. Color and ecological abundance erupt. The air, rich with the scent of humus and flowering shrubs, is clear and breezy and smooth, crisp in the mornings and hot but not humid at mid-day.

And it is charged with a tension I have never before felt.

San Cristobal de las Casas, the city where CPT-Mexico's apartment is located, was the site of a stand-off between well-organized indigenous fighters and the Mexican government that occurred on the day NAFTA took effect, January 1, 1994. (NAFTA, the North American Free Trade Agreement, had nullified an important provision of the Mexican constitution protecting indigenous rights.) Though military checkpoints in the highlands had been dismantled some weeks before our arrival in Chiapas, guards and military personnel with machine guns were seen frequently in the city and surrounding regions. The indigenous fighters, or Zapatistas, had not used their arms since the brief insurrection over seven years prior, but the conflict in Chiapas has never been resolved.

As is widely recognized, the Mexican military trained indigenous paramilitaries to employ intimidation tactics and violence against Zapatistas and their sympathizers. Thus outbreaks of violence in the region mostly involve small-scale paramilitary attacks against unarmed civilians suspected of supporting the Zapatistas. This, and on a few occasions, massacres.

San Cristobal dates to the conquistadors. It sprawls with stately treed avenues and vivacious plazas heaving bougainvillea in shades of magenta and coral. Cobblestone streets traverse the entire downtown. Stone bridges arch over canals. Colonial architecture is preserved throughout the city, most prominently in the cathedrals looking down on the city's time traveling inhabitants.

Modernity tinged with antiquity is San Cristobal's dissonant chord, evident not only in the material culture of the place, but in the people. International and Mexican tourists and residents abound in the city, with their shopping bags, spotless white tennis shoes, and haltered dresses. But Mayans in traditional dress are ubiquitous as well, many as refugees from the highlands who live in stretches of cardboard shacks along the city's edge, and who work as street vendors in town, all of whom are controlled by middle-men who pilfer their earnings.

By 2001, the Zapatistas have established several autonomous communities throughout Chiapas, and our delegation visits three of them. "Autonomous" denotes independence, or the fact that these communities refuse to acknowledge the authority of the state, setting up their own schools, clinics, and leadership. On a trip to one such community, Magdalenas, we visit a women's weaving cooperative and a medical clinic with cleaner, brighter facilities, more medicine, and greater access to healthcare than the government clinics in other villages. Colorful *Papel picado* quiver along streets and balconies. Festively painted doors stand proud and tall behind layers of dust. The Magdalenas community seems hopeful, despite poverty, and I am struck by the young girls carrying infant siblings on their tiny backs, by the smiles on the faces of the elderly.

Autonomous communities are mostly Zapatista, but CPT had been invited to Chiapas by and is partnering with the Christian-pacifist *las Abejas* who are also autonomous. Las Abejas (meaning "the bees") are a large, highly organized society that struggles for indigenous rights in Mexico without aligning with either the Zapatistas or the government. They were the victims of the massacre at Acteal three and a half years before our delegation.

♦

We arrive in Acteal by bus on a monthly anniversary of the massacre, just in time for a commemorative mass at which many internationals are present. Perched on the edge of a hillside in the jungled Chiapas highlands, Acteal is a scatter of huts along a steep village trail. At the top of the hill, beside the road, stands a large memorial depicting people in travail that reads, "The old cannot kill the young forever." It is a grave monument for a community that, despite traumatic experiences, is surprisingly joyful.

Entering the village, I immediately notice the smiles on people's faces, the giggling children, the way every passerby greets CPT with overwhelming affection. CPT had been one of the first international groups to arrive in Acteal after the massacre, to provide accompaniment for the remaining families, and CPT's support for the community throughout subsequent months and years had met with abundant gratitude. As we arrive, the procession that begins each commemorative mass forms at the entrance to the village. Incense infuses the dusty air. Standing in the belaboring afternoon sun is a lively mish-mash of Mexican supporters, Abejas in traditional dress, and international *compañeros*, and at the front of the line, a man hammering a drum. Live music drifts up from the village chapel, and while a few from our group remain in the procession, the rest of us enter the village to greet our hosts.

We pass well-established huts as well as flimsy structures, sided with plastic sheeting, that typically belong to refugees. In front of one home young girls braid one another's shiny, ebony hair. They wear the shirts traditionally worn by Mayan women along with black skirts and layers of beaded necklaces and weave rainbows of ribbons into their braids. Many of their gorgeous smiles glitter with silver teeth.

At the bottom of the first incline, the ground widens. A clearing is edged by an open-air chapel and two plank-sided buildings: a kitchen and a workshop. Ushered to a bench in the chapel, we await the beginning of mass. I look around, glad for the shade of the thatched roof. The small chapel is packed with people, over 100, most sitting on wood plank benches, some standing around the chapel's periphery. As more people gather, the rectangle of swept-dirt floor before the altar begins to fill and the fringes of the chapel widen. Alongside the altar, a band of six men bounce and play instruments. Scents of toasted corn tortillas and beans, the aroma of village life, mingle with the cloud of incense as they float into the chapel.

After ten minutes, the procession enters the church and mass begins. Prayers, speeches, and songs spill forth, and letters from distant friends are read aloud. My head fills with the smoky air. My legs grow weak at the hours of prayer and singing, the litany—one name after another—of the dead. The losses of those around me slowly take shape in my head as stories are told and names read aloud, and the reality of what happened in that place begins to dawn. I look at sorrowful faces rimming the chapel and wonder who lost whom. I see a face and wonder if the name being read is a cousin, uncle, or mother of that face. The nearness of the loss, the weight of it hovering over that gathering is grievous, though the scope of it is almost impossible to conceive.

After the service, the entire crowd marches in procession to the nearby gravesite, a large cinder-blocked room with one door and two windows that is decorated by murals and photos of the dead. Buried in the floor are forty-five people, many of them children. We stand over them where they meld into the earth, sweating, crying, cramming into the space as we kneel to pray. The traditional manner of Abeja prayer surrounds me, building like a symphony, an eerie cacophony of separate whispered prayers that mingle in the air for ten whole minutes. My ears fill with the quiet supplications of the woman kneeling beside me. Like dead leaves, my defenses drop, and tears stream to the floor from my down-turned head. At the end of the ritual, a cantor says a prayer and people slowly depart.

A half hour later, visitors gather at the guest-kitchen to be fed. Picking up plastic plates and forks, we proceed in a line past the front, where young women hand out warm tortillas and spoon black beans onto our plates. The atmosphere is lively as people visit and laugh at the tables, but I feel emotionally exhausted from the day's events. I eat what I can, then find a place to lie down in a hut reserved for guests. I fall into a deep sleep.

I awaken in time for our group's next meeting, with the *Mesa Directiva*—the leaders of the Abejas—who recount how the Abejas were formed, telling us the full story of the massacre at Acteal. International accompaniment, they reiterate, is vital to the community. Someone asks the men if it is hard for them to repeat, again and again, the story of the deaths of their family members to foreign visitors, and one replies, "It is hard. But before the massacre, we thought we were alone. Now we know we have people all around the world standing in solidarity with us. These friends return to their countries and tell our story and it gives us hope."

The small *Mesa* office where we meet, a plank-sided building with a tin roof, also functions as a workshop. Throughout the talk a man with colorless hair and papyrus skin labors behind me on an early-model electric sewing machine that perches on a small table. The man is balding and has the soulful timeworn hands of the elderly but a steady posture. His eyes study his work. Our delegation forms a ring of chairs on the open wood floor at the center of the room, covered with political posters and pictures visitors have painted for the Abejas. A breeze drifts in through uncovered windows and doors bright with afternoon light. As the president and vice president of the Mesa describe the massacre at Acteal, the old man at the sewing machine pauses from his work, looks down at his lap, and silently sobs. His shoulders bend into a trembling arc of grief.

The leaders of the Abejas narrate what occurred in Acteal December 22, 1997, when, three days before Christmas, paramilitaries stormed the village chapel. Acteal families had gathered there that morning to fast and pray as a response to mounting threats of violence against them by the paramilitaries. As committed pacifists, the residents of Acteal refused to align with violent movements or government parties. It goes without saying that they refused to align with paramilitaries. As a result, the paramilitaries viewed them as co-conspirators with the Zapatista resistance, which the paramilitaries, and the government by whom they were trained, violently opposed.

When the guns burst in on the Acteal chapel, most of the men, women, and children ran out the back of the church and dispersed in all directions—down the hills and into the jungle. For seven to eight hours, they were literally hunted. In the end, paramilitaries had killed twenty-one women (five pregnant), fifteen children and infants, and nine men from the tiny community, and left many more seriously injured. After the massacre, the paramilitaries yelled "Long live the PRI!" (the ruling political party of Mexico at the time). Throughout the massacre police stationed 200 meters from the village responded to the Abejas' pleas saying, "What gunshots? We have heard nothing."

The Mesa ends their story with a prayer and we bow our heads. After the prayer, one of our delegation leaders reads Ezekiel 11:19: "I will give them one heart, and put a new spirit within them; I will remove the heart of stone from their flesh and give them a heart of flesh." As we gather in a circle to pray, I hold the warm, gentle hand of the man from the sewing machine. His tears mingle with mine.

◆

Later that evening, following nightly prayers in the open chapel, the Acteal band cranks up. They seem to play most hours of the day, no hour being too early or late, and Barbara, a fellow delegate, takes to dancing. With gray pixie hair and a T-shirt and jeans ensemble, Barbara glows. Her eyes glimmer like the stars. Stepping in the manner of traditional Mayan dance, a simple back-and-forth motion of the feet, she subtly sways, dancing just one or two minutes before a number of visitors trickle toward the center of the chapel and join her. The Abeja women sitting in the benches at the back of the church smile and chatter like starlings. Pretty soon, they too rise, one by one, and join the dance.

I remain seated on the end of a bench, observing. The high-elevation temperature has dropped and a velvety breeze drifts through the chapel. Bulbs hanging on the structures of the village provide the only light against a sea of monotonous dark. The jungle's scent has changed with the fall of the sun and becomes a smoke-tinged concoction of steamy air and dampening green. On the village periphery, lightening bugs jitter and flash.

My shell of shyness is still thick at the time, and I seldom wander far from it. The thought of dancing freely in the middle of the on-looking crowd intimidates me—no matter how simple the steps, and I hold back. I feel a sensation of shrinking. Challenging myself to be brave, I strike up a conversation with a friendly young woman sitting beside me, extracting the most necessary words from my thin store of Spanish. Then, after eight or nine minutes, a leathery-skinned Abeja woman, her wizened hair pulled back in a long braid, approaches me and takes my hand. She stands four-and-a-half feet tall and her eyes twinkle like Barbara's. I cannot refuse her. I follow, follow, follow her, and then I am there in that circle, moving my hesitant feet. I mimic the back-and-forth sway of Mayan movement, feeling absurdly insecure.

And then something begins to shift.

As I dance in that circle, holding the woman's tiny hand, feeling the press of her bones, something starts to build in me, an exhilaration, a mounting courage. I remember how it felt as a teenager to act on stage and to dance, to dance freely, with abandon—as a teenager, before so much happened to pull me into a shell of protection. There in that circle, my *body* begins to remember how it felt. The clutch of the old woman's hand, the quiet, beaming love on all of the group's faces amplifies steadily until, after a few short minutes, everything, including me, has been reborn. The music sounds incantatory, almost magical, and the indigo sky is charged with potency. The ring of women swells with laughter and affection and wordlessly communicates, *It is safe, you can come out now, welcome.* Out there in the center of that chapel, surrounded by a tangle of darkness, I sway in a dance of pure liberation. I watch the other women's feet as they carry me, inch-by-steady-inch, into that free and lucid night, changed.

◆

Later I sleep like a baby on the concrete floor of a guesthouse built for visitors to Acteal. The next day our group rides in the back of a pickup—the local taxi service—to the nearest town, then boards a bus back to San Cristobal. My body is carried from that tiny, animate village into the city. As the truck bumps along dirt roads and laces its way through the hills, my mind remains in Acteal, grieving and dancing. The details around me blur.

Then, as I am walking alone from the San Cristobal bus depot to the guesthouse where our delegation resides, the rain turns on suddenly, like a faucet. A terrible, beautiful onslaught of wet. It then revs up a dozen notches more. The sky lets loose a torrent, almost a flash flood, as I walk through the streets, water rising past my ankles and speeding down the guttered-deep edges of the road. Waterfalls leap off the awnings of shop after shop selling hammocks and woven bags, T-shirts and straw hats. Water cascades in heavy sheets down the plastered sides of buildings. The many trees of the city became glistening works of wax, and the summer air fills with the swell of humidity.

Soaked with water, my leather sandals stretch beyond holding until I finally take them off, kicking and splashing through the rainwater barefoot, holding my drenched skirt in one hand at my side. A smile drapes like a banner across my face. I pass a man standing at the waist-high door of a tortilla shop, the scent of browning tortilla paste meeting my nose. He laughs and shouts something to me in Spanish that I don't understand. I laugh out loud and keep laughing. The last vestiges of insecurity have been whisked away in the flood. Children hover safe and dry in doorways and point at me as I pass. They smile at the *gringa* soaked clear to her skin and grinning wide. I feel stunningly, joyfully, painfully alive. Inside me, a display of fireworks—the grand *finale*.

Inside me, it is dawn.

One Who Lived

A thousand baby maples dot my lawn,
a host of happy helicopter-seed landings—
two-hearted, single-minded and strong. Blood
red stems: lifelines. A maple now grows
in the crack of an old swing I ride
when evening light shines amber on the canopies
of trees, magical as a Marrakesh market. The gutters
of my house sprout maples, where seeds found
fecundity in the muck of home-neglect, in
rotting layers of leaves—each a tiny flag
twitching proudly on the wind. Last month
I carried home a tray of marigolds. Dug my
careful holes, placed each start in jet-black loam
(two bucks per cubic ft.), watered them by hand,
monitored their steady decline. I've failed
at marigolds before. Soil too clayish, chickens
too predatory, shade, too much. It's almost
a challenge: to make thrive the few that remain
shielded in pots on the patio. Prized and
preened. I want to be a maple, not a marigold.
Don't want to be Ophelia, Virginia, Sylvia.
No, make me an Eliot, a Walker, Lamott. I want
to grow, to sprout in adversity. Make
me a maple. Make me one who lived.

CHAPTER SIX

Whatever is True

*So much of who all of us are seems to go on [beneath the surface]—
the dreams we have, the impulses, the hunches, the changes of mood.
Often the decisions we think we make on the spur of the moment have
been years in the making, and plans that we suddenly change were
plans that we secretly abandoned long before.*
—Frederick Buechner[7]

I stomp my feet as the water rushes through the streets of San
Cristobal. I splash and laugh like a gale. The restive woman inside
of me takes possession for one joy-charged hour. I have never felt
more free. My body, my senses, have never been more awake. If I
could raise my head and look far up the road from where my feet
stand at that time, soaked to the soles and sun-tanned, about two
years into the future, I would watch myself make some abrupt
changes of plans. But those plans I suddenly change that distant
day in the future are secretly abandoned in that rapturous rain-
storm, so secretly that even I don't notice.

My first day home from Chiapas, I wake reluctantly. The
space I inhabit seems to pinch and bind like an outgrown pair of
jeans. I know the woman who possessed me in Chiapas cannot fit

that space. I carefully box up my restlessness and shove it into some interior crevice where it cannot be seen. It is a lead weight I bear with every step. As hard as I try to ignore it, I have become aware of its presence. It is now my secret.

My bedroom window stands open one inch, and I lay in bed a few moments listening to birds trill just beyond it. Sparrows have built a nest under the eaves, right outside the window. The small ones beg for food. Darryl has left for work and Madison sleeps, leaving the house quiet and eager for my return. The house—such a mixture of Darryl's hand and mine: my blue on the wall and Darryl's acid-yellow, my antique cobalt jars and his brushed-aluminum soap dispenser, my bird's nest and his Michael Graves salt and pepper shakers. Letting the dog loose in the yard, I check the chicken pen for eggs. The suburban air warms rapidly, smelling of dust and drying grass and hot pavement. I go inside to shower. My to-do list for the day: buy groceries, mop the floor, do laundry, water the garden and houseplants. . . . Soon, Madison wakes.

I feel unfamiliar.

Newberg had never felt entirely comfortable—the town of Alex's childhood I tried to make a home in, the town my parents moved to, the place where I tried desperately to recoup the losses of my past. Newberg can be churchy and parochial (at one point in the '80s it had the highest church-to-population ratio in the U.S.). Too many people I know had transgressed preordained boundaries only at grave expense to themselves and their relationships. I know my restlessness is dangerous in such a place. I feel both dangerous and endangered. I want to transcend my shyness. I feel sensual and fired up in a context where open sensuality is viewed as scandalous. I share a life with a man who inadvertently snuffs out my spark.

During those last days in Chiapas, I could say or do anything I had within me to do or say. I could cry or sing without restraint. I could splash and laugh in the street. I could be an attractive woman fully alive in my body and fully awake to its many sensations.

I could tell someone I wanted to leave my husband. My husband, such a good, good man.

During those days, I struggle to stay healthy. One of my ovaries had been surgically removed earlier that year after it gave in to tumors and endometriosis, falling like a lame duck. Without it, I am a storm of emotions. Darryl musters whatever support he can, but he remains remote. My depression and distinctly feminine illness put me beyond his reach, and besides, his nature is not one of reaching.

He doesn't begin to apprehend my general dissatisfaction, my despair at our relationship. He doesn't notice the half of it. At times over the prior few years I had tried to tell him my concerns about the relationship: about how I felt a stranger to him, about how we seemed not to share passions and interests, about his detachment from Madison, about our incompatibility sexually.

But since the conversations seemed futile, I stopped trying to explain. My instinct is to withdraw, so I withdrew. Darryl's and my disconnection, I believe, is the result of our vastly different personalities—personalities neither of us can change. I feel there is nothing we can do but to endure the disconnection, making the best of it.

Essentially, I shut him out. While we continue to share a house and a bed, and to some extent our friends, while we continue, to some extent, to share Madison, we do not share what is deep inside of us. Though Darryl would probably say he hadn't been listening throughout our marriage, hadn't been *seeing*, that his tendency has always been to sleepwalk through life, and though, to some extent, that is true, I had seen the disaster coming and I had withdrawn.

For all of my exposure, by this time in my life, to diverse understandings of spirituality, Christianity, and inter-connection with God, I still hold a gut belief that God's love is earned. Winning God's approval is the key to true spiritual connection, according to this gut belief I'd accrued in childhood. And God has pretty exacting standards. I subconsciously believe that leaving a marriage to a good man must definitely fall outside of these standards and that my contemplating such an action makes me unlovable. Yet it is, ironically, during this time that these deeply engrained assumptions about God begin to disintegrate.

I sink into my instinctual introversion. Speaking to no one of my feelings, I walk through my days absent-mindedly, turning thoughts over and over in the recesses of my mind.

As one of the most easygoing people I know, Darryl is easy to get along with, and we coexist peacefully during this time. But his easygoing nature can also be expressed as dispassion or coolness, to the point that he seems, to me, emotionally numbed. He is not apathetic, he simply cares for things in his own cool way. Darryl listens to NPR almost daily on his commute to and from work and reads prolifically from magazines like *Harpers*. He can dialogue with me about the Israel-Palestine conflict, or the demise of the environment and the necessity of sustainable technologies, about some new documentary. But political discussions go only so far to draw people together.

The things that hold us apart loom large. Experiences that stoke my heart to a white-heat cannot budge the temperature of his own: a film, a piece of music, an encounter with a friend. Sharing these experiences with him seems to render them powerless, like he is a dose of alkaline, neutralizing the poignancy, the intensity of such experiences. He seems generally unfamiliar with ecstasy. At times his tepid response to life seems to cast a wet blanket over mine, causing me to keep many experiences to myself. I experience passion, ascension and descension, fiery rage and heart-crushing adoration, and Darryl looks in on my life like an alien. Sometimes I feel he dismisses my extremes as immaturity, though he tries not to. I, for my part, find him at times catatonic. His tepid approach to life feeds my despair. As one who feels things strongly, I cannot help being stirred up. And much of what I experience in life, he can likewise not comprehend.

I am certain our mismatch results more from my capriciousness than from any lack of Darryl's. Darryl, so kind and constant and gentle. He may not experience passion, but he is reliable. Madison and I can depend on him. Yet being with him begins to make me feel, by comparison, unstable and eccentric. He views the relationship from the opposite angle; my intensity of feeling and my passion make him feel lazy and ineffectual. We try to affirm one another, "Yes, we are different, but your qualities are wonderful. You help people; people need you." We repeat to each other the same script.

Meanwhile, we range farther and farther from our small, shared patch of green.

◆

Upon returning from Mexico, a fog engulfs me. Then, after the 9-11 terrorist attacks less than two months after my return from Chiapas, and after they propel our nation on an insane jingoistic trajectory, my depression deepens. The depression of many people deepens. It is like I am part of a global state of despair. On top of all this, a beloved nephew is diagnosed, in October 2001, with spinal and brain cancer.

In the months leading up to this time, I had come to experience God's presence often. No matter the ennui or confusion, I sensed God with me, a comforting spirit. I sensed I was not alone. But after September 2001, God seems absolutely silent, absolutely *absent* to me. When I settle into prayer or participate in silent worship at Quaker meeting, it is dark. It had been years since I felt so bereft of a spiritual presence around me, alongside me. The void I feel at this time is worse than a lack of presence. It feels like a black hole threatening to swallow me.

Two years earlier, Darryl had built me a tiny prayer room (7' x 7') behind our house. It has walls the color of maize and soft, sable carpeting, and a comfortable chair for sitting in. Whenever I can carve out time—an hour one afternoon, a half-hour two days later, I sit in the silence of that room. I sit waiting and hoping for spiritual connection. I want direction. I want comfort for my soul. I want assurance that God is with me, helping me see things more clearly, showing me the way forward. But I seem to inhabit a sliver of the universe devoid of spirit. Where before I'd felt draped in spirit and led by an unseen light, I am now, it seems, abandoned. I embrace the silence nonetheless. It allows me time to think, to acknowledge my restlessness and loneliness.

I do continue to pray. I continue *believing* God is there. I have read accounts of spiritual journeys that include periods of divine absence—the "dark night of the soul," as I'd heard the phenomenon described. Though I don't presume I am experiencing a dark night of the soul, I know experiences of God's absence have marked the spiritual journeys of others. This lends a measure of comfort.

During these desolate months, Madison at age eleven is my deepest well of joy. She spends most of her free hours concocting *schemes*. She spends most of a day painting tiny watercolor pictures and constructing labels and price tags for an art sale in the front room. She organizes her own library in her bedroom, equipped with library cards, pretend book scanners, and labels for her book shelves. She and her neighbor-friends cull flowers from people's gardens then sell them door-to-door around the neighborhood.

Whatever the scheme, no detail is overlooked. Madison cares far more about the details than actually carrying the scheme through to its conclusion. She loves creating a grown-up universe in her own small world, a universe where people need ID cards, and filing systems, and signs made of poster board. Even if she doesn't get around to inviting a customer or patron into the scheme she is happily consumed with the details.

Madison is also fine tuning the quick humor and stage presence she inherited from her dad. She stages magnificent shows, like the one she staged at age five singing Elvis favorites in a shepherd's head-dress. By eleven, her performances have become a bit more refined. She and two friends will spend one day writing, blocking, costuming, rehearsing, and performing a play in the theater that is her friends' back yard. By the end of their version of *A Little Princess,* the girls (not to mention the parents) are crippled with laughter. In one scene, Madison's friend Anna stops mid-sentence to gaze past the audience. "Is that a raccoon?" she exclaims, as the furtive creature sidles across the lawn. No matter what, actors struggle to regain focus when a raccoon appears.

Madison still has a rampant temper that can bring down the house. She opposes change militantly, sometimes hurling herself onto her bed and screaming for hours to protest my moving a piece of furniture from one room to another. One two-hour tirade originates when I trade-out the rugs in the office and front room. I don't need a degree in child psychology to recognize deeper issues hidden beneath those rugs. Madison herself understands. "Why can't everything just stay the same?" she howls. "I hate growing up! . . . I hate you!" *How could this be my child?* I wonder. Me: so fluid, an ever-moving stream traversing the hard-edged ruts. Madison is a 5,000 ton boulder, the kind you see in photos of Bryce National Park. Madison is prehistoric.

I pray and wait. Madison continues to entertain. Somehow the year offers another summer, and CPT calls again.

Madison accompanies me this time, for a month-long training for CPT in Chicago. A sitter is available for the sessions, a college-aged woman with Mennonite Voluntary Services who takes Madison and another girl to the zoo, the beach, the natural history museum. Madison lives with me in dilapidated tenement housing above an inner-city church that CPT very recently acquired, intending to fix it up for use as office space. Not a square foot has been touched when we arrive. Wearing various shreds of wallpaper, the walls don gaping holes where plaster has crumbled away. Everything in the place has the thick smear of wear. The house smells of dust and mildew and the grimy, rotten aroma of the streets that drift through the constantly open windows. In July, Chicago is sweltering. Relief comes only by sitting directly in the path of an electric fan, so Madison and I sleep on air mattresses on the floor in front of the ever-buzzing box-fan variety. One night while we are sleeping, I am wakened by gunshots in the park across the street.

During Madison's month in Chicago she runs through fire-hydrant fountains, cavorts with CPTers, participates in protests both in downtown Chicago and in the backwoods of Wisconsin at a communication center for nuclear submarines on Nagasaki Day. In each new context, Madison, ironically, *thrives*. This is odd, considering her immobility at home. But once out of her element, Madison seems to enjoy fresh experiences and new people. She can suspend her need for predictability and enter the flow of unfamiliar waters. In completely new territory, there *is* no predictability. This allows her to open her hands and receive what is new.

My CPT training group includes a psych nurse, two college students, two elementary school teachers, a Franciscan sister in her sixties, two people of the "hippie-activist" variety, a grandmother from rural Iowa, a retired jewelry-shop owner from England, and a peace studies post-graduate from Pakistan. For all the variety, our group fits together like an old wooden jigsaw puzzle. Our weeks of training drift by with raucous laughter. Again, CPT companionship is levitating. It is the magic wand that lifts my depression. Maybe it is the like-mindedness of the companions. Maybe the friendly, accepting spiritual environment.

Darryl comes to visit during the training, taking Madison on a side-excursion to Indianapolis to visit old friends, and he witnesses the dynamic amongst our group. He gets to know some of the participants. In a cursory way, he comes to understand my kinship with CPT.

By the end of a month I am exhausted by the grueling training schedule and weary of the ramshackle living quarters, yet a part of me doesn't want to leave.

◆

Oregon is a long way from Chicago. I return that fall to the routines of my suburban, West Coast life not realizing how soon those routines will change.

At eight years old, Madison had been rigorously tested for and diagnosed with attention-deficit, hyperactivity disorder (ADHD), upon the recommendation of her teachers. The diagnosis did much to explain her emotional vagaries, her occasional out-of-control-ness, her preference for predictability and order. As I learned more about ADHD, I was able, to some extent, to help her. But two years later, in autumn 2002, Madison starts to fall farther and farther behind in school. She cannot focus in a bustling classroom well enough to do schoolwork—which in fifth grade becomes demanding. And she cannot do homework at the end of an exhausting day when her concentration is shot.

As a sensitive kid, she notices her teachers' frustrations. Her teachers constantly hush her. They repeatedly call her back to task, while Madison spends most of the school day distracted and restless. "Mom," she tells me one day, in tears, "Mrs. Taylor treats me like one of the bad kids." Madison's grades sink to the bottom of a shallow pool.

My sister and a close friend had both homeschooled their children for several years, and the thought of homeschooling Madison had occasionally crossed my mind. Whenever it did, I resisted. The hours Madison spent at school were sacred and solitary hours for me. Any writing that got done, got done during those hours. By this time I am well into writing a book entitled *Free People: A Christian Response to Global Economics*, and feel a strong pull toward creative writing. I want *more* time for writing, not less.

But Madison needs help. She needs a quiet, low-stimulus environment in which to read and work. As a work-at-home mom, I can provide this. *Not* homeschooling Madison begins to feel like neglect, like I will be denying her what she needs to thrive. So after Christmas break 2002, Madison and I take up homeschooling. It is a choice I make without feeling I have a real choice. And it is one of the best choices I ever make.

I start small: Howard Zinn's *People's History of the United States*. I read it aloud to her for weeks till she groans at the very mention of the book. Then I back off. I still teach her the important stuff—women's history, poetry-writing, early Quaker history, the history of significant social-change movements. After a few years of homeschooling, Madison can read articles from *Smithsonian* magazine and excerpts of books from Darryl's and my collection, material some college students cannot handle. She can write better than most adults and do math at a level above her grade. She gets to travel with me to locations where education becomes a thing that is lived.

The same winter Madison and I begin homeschooling, CPT opens a project in a Native community in northwestern Ontario, Canada. The reserve is called Asubpeeschoseewagong, or Grassy Narrows. It is home to a community that has opposed clear-cutting of trees on their treaty-protected, traditional-land-use area for years, by every legal means available and to no avail.

So in the grip of winter's most relentless temperatures, young people from the community set up a blockade of a major logging road. They literally sit in the middle of the icy road and wait. They are soon joined by others, bringing logging in the area to a halt, while Grassy Narrows becomes a rallying point for Native people and their supporters across Canada. CPT is invited to accompany the blockaders and to help ensure the safety of the parties involved, and begins work in Grassy Narrows in winter 2002. About four months after the start of the blockade, Madison and I pack up our school books and thermal underwear. We join the CPT team for three weeks.

Almost the minute we roll into town in early March 2003, the spring thaw appears. After months of biting cold, people walk through the streets of Kenora, the town nearest Grassy Narrows, in T-shirts, reveling in the bright suggestion of spring. Roads soften in response to the thaw and logging comes to a virtual, temporary stand-still. For five to six weeks, there will be no trucks confronting the blockade. Not one. Though blockade leaders still desire CPT's presence at the encampment to lessen chances of dismantlement by authorities, CPTers will have little accompaniment work to do. Madison and I are in for some very quiet days.

So we help build an A-frame cabin for the team, which had been staying in a small, rented trailer with gas heat. We try not to freeze, since spring-like temperatures lasted only one day. We spend hours visiting with CPTers and Native partners around the fire in the roundhouse.

Most of the area is still draped in white when we arrive, though the snow is fading. The region's myriad lakes don heavy strata of ice. In the forests of northwestern Ontario, so unlike the forests of the northwestern U.S., white and red pines share space equitably with the prolific white-barked birches, aspens, and poplars, and a bird called the whiskey jack, a medium-sized gray bird with white and black markings, has the sky practically to himself. At times a low rumbling swells from the earth, almost a hair-raising moan, as thick sheets of ice slowly thaw and shift. Dense stars obliterate the stone-still blackness of night.

Five CPTers . . . and Madison. She and I do school work for two hours each morning during the first weeks of the trip, then take the last week off for Spring Break. We study Zinn's chapter on the colonization of Native people. Madison writes of her experiences in Grassy Narrows—of befriending a husky dog on the reservation, of soft-stepping onto the lake's icy facade—and composes a poem about the blockade. She attends every team meeting. Hours and hours of adult conversations waft around her, conversations about Native experiences, about Canada's logging policies, about CPT's role in Grassy Narrows. The hours cluster around the wood stoves in the roundhouse or cabin, staying warm, fending off boredom. Though the team members joke with Madison and ask questions about her violin playing, or Oregon, or her dog, no one caters to her and no one talks down to her. She is treated as an equal. At times when the team works on the A-frame, Madison wanders to the empty roundhouse for warmth, and at times the space and quiet, the loneliness, threaten to bury her. I wish I could say I was always sensitive to this, to her, fully tuned-in as a mother and present to her feelings, but I would be lying. Madison was extraordinarily patient with me, with the discomforts of the trip, and I was not as appreciative as I wish I had been.

A week into our stay, the team completes the A-frame. We roll up our sleeping bags and carry our belongings down the hill to the place where the cabin overlooks the snowy lake. We inhabit the drafty, chilled space between its walls that includes two sleeping spaces on stilts, two spaces on the floor beneath the elevated beds, and one space beside the stove. One morning we awake to find ice in our water bottles. Because she is small, Madison uses one of the elevated beds, passing each night buried in a heap of wool blankets. She doesn't change clothes for days to avoid exposing her body to the frigid fingers of Ontario's winter. I sleep by the stove, feeding it with logs throughout the night, struggling to maintain a room-temperature fit for human habitation.

Most days we drive to the reserve at least once, to eat moose-meat stew at someone's house or to take showers and do laundry at the home of a close friend or at the school. As we drive into the reserve the first time, I am struck by the windows. Every other house seems fronted with a broken one. The broken windows are card-boarded and duct-taped so the houses appear to be winking as I pass. The window coverings are barely a nod to the sub-zero temperatures of the area. Smoke billows from chimneys everywhere.

Some houses are relatively new and well built, while many are shacks falling apart in thin pieces. Many stand far apart, with broad strips of white at the margins. Others are clustered together on side streets, their yards a tic-tac-toe of fresh boot tracks through the snow. Some sit on the lakeside. Others are tucked down lonely drives. The government, I learn, builds houses on the reserve but does not repair them. Therefore, houses deteriorate in the keeping of residents with little money for home maintenance. If a family on the reserve finds a job away from home, its members might return to the reserve and build a house with money they've earned in town (a house to which they will hold no title). But the nearest town and nearest jobs are, in winter, almost two hours drive from Grassy Narrows.

Thus reserve residents are forced to choose between connection to community, land, and culture on one hand, and economic sustenance on the other. Either stay on the reserve and have the former, or leave and find work in town, where racial tensions wind everyone up tight, and where Natives are routinely mistreated in grocery stores, doctors' offices, banks, government buildings, restaurants, hospitals. . . .

The blockade is a ten-minute drive from the reserve up a graveled logging road, pot-holed like the surface of the moon. It sits beside the road on a wide strip of land that backs onto a wooded hillside and lake. Though several structures dot the site, such as "trapper's cabins" and trailers, the most important structures mark opposite ends of the camp's periphery—the roundhouse and the teepee set apart for the sacred fire.

Sided with plywood and plastic tarps, the empty roundhouse looks like the quotidian hub of a campsite. It is built using a traditional structure of logs, but is full of tables strewn with food items—bags of powdered milk, peanut butter, loaves of bread—and large tubs of water for washing dishes. Camping chairs and metal folding chairs scatter across the room's center, and colorful posters, banners reading "We Believe in Traditional Land" and "Stop Clear-Cutting," decorate the walls. Nestled on opposite sides of the circle are two wood stoves, and next to them, fire-blackened pots for cooking.

The room suggests little by way of uniqueness. But when people congregate there, one can sense a dynamism. The roundhouse is a gathering place for the energy that seems to touch every friend who visits the blockade, one that is, above all, hopeful. At times community members and CPTers sit together around a woodstove in silence, at other times, laughing and telling jokes. Blockaders hold potlucks in the space, with moose and beaver, apple crisp, and stacks of golden bannock (fry bread). We play games, with Madison holding her own at checkers. Sometimes we listen to songs sung and played by musicians, and in especially brave moments, I join the players.

The roundhouse is the site of occasional sharing circles, in which members of the community pass a feather, each taking a turn at speaking and respecting the speaking-space of others. On one occasion, our team is invited to attend a circle. The topic is the blockade and its significance, and I listen without speaking though my words would have been welcomed—an honor.

During our time in Grassy Narrows, Madison and I listen to Native women drumming and singing plaintively into the night. One sunny morning we watch a trapper-friend of the team skin a handsome beaver. For the first time in our lives, we see the northern lights prance across the sky like ribbon-dancers, the spectral hues like the color of freedom, the color of laughter. Madison makes two friends from the reserve, both the daughters of women close to the team and blockade, and she plays at their homes or joins them for games at the blockade. The girls slide across the ice on the soles of their boots. During a potluck attended by several families from the reserve, Madison and a dozen other kids play hide-and-seek across the shadowy sprawl of the camp.

The opening inside of me widens inch by inch. The drawing open is like the parting of a curtain, and I begin to see what stands waiting behind. It is a life rooted in the body and the earth and the heart. It is a life that turns and responds, like the ice mass moaning and shifting on top of the lake against the caress of the sun.

While we are in Grassy Narrows, Bush starts a war in Iraq. That night our team huddles together around the roundhouse fire with candles burning, praying for peace and wondering what grievous domino trail has been tipped this time. We pray for Iraqis, pray for soldiers, pray for the CPTers living and working for peace amid the bombing in Baghdad. I feel very far from home, far from the Western media, far from government spin. I feel surrounded by a kindred body of souls I do not wish to leave.

By this trip, I notice a pattern, one that involves eagerness to be away from home and reticence to return. Is this simply a covetousness of adventure? Do I feel happier away because I experience an emotionally jolting thrill? Am I that shallow? Or am I profoundly discontented with my life?

◆

This is spring. Then comes summer and I collide head-on with that discontent. I have just returned from another few weeks in Canada. My life as an in-every-way-respectable wife, mother, churchgoer, and friend has come to feel like a prison. I am, in fact, not "respectable." I fantasize leaving my husband every day and have for months. Unbeknownst to my friends and family, I am a volcano threatening to erupt in recklessness. My marriage feels fragmented, with Darryl and me passing our time withdrawn from one another, spending few of our hours in the same room, touching each other little. The impulse to run tugs harder than ever. Resisting it has made me tired, as has the charade of satisfaction. I have maintained such a careful garden of illusions! Through careful custodianship, I have made everyone comfortable with my life, except me.

One Sunday afternoon, I sit Darryl down on our bed. Sun filters into the room through our north-facing windows, and we lean our backs on the wall next to one another, our legs outstretched. I explain that I want to separate. I still remember what I was wearing, the same clothes I had worn to church that morning, when we stood in the pews together sharing a hymnal, still living in a world that was about to end.

My words that afternoon are like a grenade lobbed into the comfortable fortress of our lives, which are never to be the same.

We do not look at each other's faces as we talk. I tell Darryl I am confused, tired of pretending. I tell him I have been mildly depressed for two years and think the marriage is a cause. In that one sentence: "I want to separate," I threaten everything in our lives.

Though I had to some extent explained my feelings to Darryl, I had never stated matters so baldly: *I cannot live with this marriage.*

Darryl's reaction is one of shock.

When I let my true feelings move from my heart and mind into my mouth and past my lips, I touch off a crisis that has been brewing inside of me for many months. Now it belongs to others, to Darryl and Madison, to my parents and Darryl's parents, to our extended families and closest friends. My decision precipitates a certain hysteria. I know the gravity of what I am doing, but I have no idea how shaken I will be by what unfolds.

The best word to describe the months leading up to my decision is "confusion," profound confusion. The time I had spent in Canada only heightened the confusion as, in my time away from home, I wrestled with what I wanted and didn't want. I had always considered it unthinkable to leave my marriage. Leaving a situation that is blatantly dysfunctional is one thing; leaving my marriage with Darryl was another.

Darryl is a good man, and it is unthinkable to leave a good man. Yet in that deep underground well of truth, I *had* thought about it. I thought about it often. Distance from home had created the space to admit it to myself. Somehow, away from my home environment, it had become easier for that underground truth to surface. The more I told myself the truth about my longing, the more dissonance I experienced, the more incongruity between expectation and longing.

Almost everyone back home *expected* me to stand by Darryl, and that is what I had, until recently, expected of myself. I knew that if I moved in the direction of my longing to leave the marriage, I would upset a colossal fruit basket of expectations. Could I survive it? Could Darryl survive? More than anything, I feared Darryl's pain.

But during the trip that preceded my summer conversation with Darryl, then shortly after my return and before talking with him, I heard something that tapped the spring inside of me. Two separate occasions. One common message. Once the ground was broken, I could no longer hold back my dangerous feelings. The truth came gushing out like a geyser.

In the first instance, I was at an Episcopal church in Canada. None of my CPT teammates cared for formal liturgy, so I visited the church alone one sunny Sunday morning. Among the hymns was the John Greenleaf Whittier verse I had become so well acquainted with, the one I had sung in St. Andrews, chanted for months, and found on my desk that first fretful day of teaching university. But the words I once memorized and chanted as a mantra were not the words that leapt out at me this time. This Sunday, as I stood in front of my spit-shone wooden pew at the Episcopal church in Kenora, Ontario, I was struck by the following:

Breathe through the heats of our desire
thy coolness and thy balm;
let sense be dumb, let flesh retire;
speak through the earthquake, wind, and fire,
O still, small voice of calm.

The lines were strange to me. I don't know that I had ever listened to them before. Whatever the case, the words were laden with fresh meaning that Sunday morning. They spoke profoundly to my condition. I encountered them, somewhat ironically, as a resounding affirmation of the *sensual*.

Yes, God often speaks beyond flesh, outside of the language of desire and *after* the rumble of the earthquake and the crackle of the fire have died down. But as I heard those words, I was struck by the earthiness of "earthquake, wind, and fire," by the flesh-ness of our sense and desire—and how, before anything else, these are creations of God.

Sitting in the refracted light of that sanctuary, I felt an in-rush of spirit like I had not felt in years, since the absence descended that fall of 2001. I absorbed the words into my consciousness. I let their affirmation sink deep into hidden parts of my heart. And I became filled. Spirit whisked through me, blowing open closed windows. I felt somehow filled to overflowing. I felt bathed in love. My flesh-ness, I felt, was *hallowed*. From this day on, a sense of my belovedness to God began to build within me.

All I remember of the sermon that day was a simplistic illustration of a cracked water jug. It vexed its poor owner, who couldn't reach his destination before water had all but leaked out of his cracked pot. It vexed him for days and weeks until one day he finally took notice of something. Along one side of his route tiny wildflowers had sprung up from seeds watered through the crack in that old, supposedly worthless jug.

On that glaring morning, heavens parting with luminosity, I felt as cracked-up and leaky as I had ever felt. Yet the illustration, the rushing in of God's presence told me: *This is okay, I will give birth through you to beautiful things. You are loved.*

Then, not long after returning to Newberg, I heard something in the course of open worship at Quaker meeting. For months, almost *years*, I had heard nothing but silence in that intentional circle of listening. I had "attended the void" as I described in a poem. I "lent silence my ear." And just when my ear was least expecting it, I heard this: *Whatever is true, whatever is real—act out of that.*

What? I wanted to ask out loud, wishing the voice would repeat itself though I had heard exactly what it said. Was it spirit whispering to me? Was it my own voice articulating a subconscious longing? Was it self-serving gibberish? All I know is that I experienced it, clear as day, as *coming to me*. A message from who knows where. A simple phrase to hold close as I struggled to find my way through a muddle. *Whatever is true. . . . Act out of that.*

After that day, I open the door, the door that will lead me out of my marriage. The door to light and clarity opens simultaneously, and I begin to tell the truth. It will take years for the sun to fully rise, but it is during this chaotic time it begins to ascend. Its broadening light casts many things in sharp relief, at times in a very unflattering light. Lies I have told myself, relationships I have with family members and friends that will buckle in the flood, insecurities I have about myself and about God that I have not faced. But it also brings treasures to light, little gems buried in the surface of my life that need to catch those widening rays to be noticed.

My friendship with Brother Martin is such a gem.

Martin began writing to me regularly when I went to Canada the first time in 2001, and I, far less faithfully, wrote letters to him.

By summer 2003, when I am ready to make public my discontent with my marriage, our friendship has established itself as a patch of *terra firma* in my life. I tell Martin I want to separate from my husband, and he writes me the following:

> Sept 18, 2003
> Muy querida Tricia,
> You are truly a heart reader. Yes, you have been in my mind and heart the past weeks since I last saw you and you told me about your marriage to Darryl coming to an end.
> I have prayed for you & Darryl & Madison, that the Great Spirit bless you with God's healing powers as there is always pain in separation, and in searching [for] God's way in new changes in our lives. As I read & reread your note, I thought of my departure from home over 51 years ago. Yes, God keeps God's word, he/she never lets us down. God leads us way beyond our dreams and we forget the painful parts of our journey.
> Here I am, all my life leading to this moment when I am writing a letter of LOVE and encouragement to *mi amiga* Tricia Brown. It makes the communion of saints that we pray in the Apostles' Creed become real.
> . . . My schedule is pretty flexible, so I can make time to share with you at times. . . . If I can do anything for you please let me know! I am grateful I share your journey.
> Love, Martin

Martin often says he and I experience the "communion of saints." At first, I bristle at this. *How could he include me in this phrase?* I figure I must have deceived him into believing I am righteous, that I am a saint, and my displeasure at this turns me confessional. I want to tell Martin everything, about my lust, my wandering, my disconnection from God.

And I do. I tell him God had become absent from me and I am only beginning to sense a change, I tell him I am unable to stick with my marriage, I let Martin see my depression, my peevishness.

But the more I let him see, the more he says it—"communion of saints"—as if he measures sainthood by a wholly different yardstick than other people. He sees God in me. He almost refuses to see anything else.

As soon as I tell people I will be separating from Darryl, that I plan to do so after finding a way to support myself and Madison, the proverbial shit hits the fan. I receive sermonizing letters from my mother and sisters, one of which is blatantly hellfire-and-brimstone in tone, stating I will be "outside of God's grace" if I proceed with my plans. Several of Darryl's and my mutual friends become tight-lipped and awkward around me, as if I am walking around unclothed. Their children stare at me strangely, and I wonder if they've heard me discussed in a compromising way. In group situations certain friends talk *around* me to the person sitting behind or beside me, as if I've become invisible. Others are passive-aggressive, like the friend who "makes fun" of a part-time job I've taken: "so it's like low-level computer grunt-work?"

I don't believe any of these people intend harm. They simply don't know what to say or do, or how to reconcile themselves to the vulnerability of their own marriages. My mother, for her part, reacts to the loss of her last threads of control.

All in all, I watch the leaves of my friendship tree grow very thin. I have always known that if I left Darryl the price would be high indeed. In that sense, I have seen it coming: the set jaw and cold eye of disapproval, the attempts, some respectful, some not, to talk me out of my decision. After those first months since my announcement, only a few stalwart leaves remain firmly attached to my tree—Martin, an acquaintance named Sue I approached for spiritual and emotional support, and three other close friends. Those five, and oddly, Darryl. He and I continue to rely on the best aspects of our friendship—listening, compassion, admiration—even as we watch our marriage crumble to dust. Darryl's parents, true friends, true saints, offer me kindness, but I see them less and less.

◆

A man seldom prone to tears, Darryl frequently sobs. My decision, my honesty with him about my feelings, and the hopelessness they imply, devastate him. Since he does not tend to feel things strongly, his grief over our marriage is unimaginably intense. He feels nauseous and cannot eat. Some days he takes Vicodin left over from a skateboard injury, letting it whisk him off to a safe sleep. On good days, he drifts into denial, working out hard at the gym, sweeping leaves off the roof and cleaning out the garage, thinking he can win me back by displaying greater "motivation," as he puts it. But while he genuinely believes he can transform himself into a different kind of person, I am skeptical and believe it is, in any case, a terrible idea. He is a marvelous person already. We simply do not fit together.

Darryl's pain and striving brings me to the verge of panic. Hurting him has always been what I feared most about leaving, and I have hurt him grievously. As he sits next to me on our couch or bed and cries, I hold him and sob. I stroke his head and neck and question whether there is any way I can commit to the marriage. My questioning always ends with a "no."

Yet I have never seen Darryl feel so strongly about something. His pain disorients me. Repeatedly I try to explain myself, but when he reflects back what I've said, the words appear as distorted as images in a carnival mirror, not at all what I've tried to convey. It seems impossible for Darryl and I to understand one another. One day I tell him I want to live with greater integrity, that I want the inside and outside of my life to match. "Integrity?!" he huffs angrily. "Don't talk to me about integrity. . . . That makes me sick."

At times I long to step in front of a wayward bus and abruptly end the matter. The counselor I am seeing says I am "passively suicidal," that the stress of the situation has become too much to bear.

♦

I am driving to a car-maintenance appointment in a town thirty minutes from my house. It is mid-day and the dulling sunlight hitting the windshield accentuates my lethargy. I have exhausted myself with crying. My mind is a swirl of conflict and accusation and aimlessness. A traffic light turns green and I begin to accelerate. Then all of a sudden, like I've been knocked off the road by a semi and plunged into a lake, I feel I am sinking. Anxiety grips my throat, steals my breath. A ton of weight settles onto my chest, and the phrase *panic attack* flashes across my mind. I have never before experienced a panic attack. I am surrounded by a bustling flow of traffic and wonder if I can control my car. Will I suffocate? Will I lose control of my limbs? I am falling, falling, helpless, like I am being chased. It is like a nightmare, where I cannot move or scream or run.

It lasts a fraction of a minute.

The experience leaves an indelible impression. Never before have I teetered so close to the crumbling edge of my emotional reserves. Never have I understood what it is like to have a breakdown. I immediately drive to a nearby health-food store and buy a homeopathic formula for anxiety. I take a dose much stronger than the recommended one and continue taking it for the next three hours. I repeat the mantra I'd been praying frequently in the previous days: "Jesus, have mercy" or "Jesus, please show me the way." That afternoon I pray, "God, help me," and I feel God near. Eventually, I calm. I don't experience a panic attack again.

A few days later, after telling Sue about the experience, she asks, "What would happen if you focused only on taking care of yourself right now?" She strings her words together with a long thread of silence. I ponder her question, the idea of taking care of myself. "Stop worrying about everyone else for a bit," she continues. "Don't think about what Darryl needs. Don't think about what your family needs. Ask yourself, what do I need to take care of myself?"

Before the panic attack, I don't think I could have considered it. I wanted to minimize and heal the damage even as I created it. I wanted to take care of everything. *Clean up your mess. Be a good girl.* But the picture shifted. I now know that I can be lost, that I can sink into an emotional quicksand from which I might not ascend.

"Take care of yourself," Sue says. "That is okay. Let everything else go."

So I do.

◆

I go to see Martin at the abbey. We walk toward two plastic Adirondack chairs facing the larger abbey pond. It is a late August afternoon, warm, and we sit in the dappled shade of a hawthorn tree, next to fat bunches of grass rimming the water. Sunlight casts golden coins all over the surface of the pond, shining through the oak trees and firs towering around three sides. The water reflects the brilliant blue of the sky, the trees in their swaying form.

I wear a tank top, a knee-length skirt and sandals, and Martin remarks, "you look sun-kissed!" Through a broad smile he says, "You have a real *Latina* tan." As he reaches his chair, he steadies himself, gripping the back as I then he sits down. I am exhausted. I smile through teary red iguana eyes.

"Tricia, tell me how it's going . . . your journey of loving?" His look embraces me.

"I am overwhelmed by Darryl's pain," I tell him, "by every-one's reactions to my decision. . . . I haven't been doing so well." I go on, "No one seems to believe me, that I might know what is best for me. Everyone thinks I am doing something unthinkable. It's like I've suddenly transformed in everyone's eyes. But I'm the same person I've always been. That's what people don't realize. I'm just trying to be honest about what I feel."

Stress bears down on my shoulders. I feel a hundred years old. "Everyone just wants me to *stop*. But I can't stop. I can't go back to pretending. It's impossible now."

Martin tells me a story about a friend who had left her marriage to eventually become a contemplative. He tells of his own struggles to stay committed, through the years, to the community of monks at the abbey. Martin's voice soothes me as he talks, though my mind wanders. "I can see in your eyes that you love Jesus," Martin emphasizes. "You just have to keep loving Jesus and trying to tell the truth." He adds, "Jesus will show you the way." He reaches his hand over and quickly touches my hand. "I will pray that Darryl and your parents will see that love in you."

Not long after this, in late October 2003, I have a dream I re-member so vividly I record it in a notebook upon waking. In the dream, I'm on an outing to the ocean with an older man I recognize upon waking as my family doctor, someone I admired a great deal. In the dream, he is a close family friend. We stand on the sand overlooking the surf. He is about to leave and, before turning to go, gives me a deep, caring hug, a hug that conveys absolute acceptance and love. He says, "Never settle for anything that doesn't feel this good," then walks away. As he leaves, I feel surrounded by love and compassion.

A few moments later, in the dream, up walks a peer of mine from college, someone I seldom interact with but who inevitably makes me feel judged. He sneers as he passes me. He says, "So, I see you are very close with the doctor." And I feel ashamed.

I remember my dreams often in those weeks and continue writing them down. Frequent appearances are made in dreams of men I've felt shamed or patronized by. There are also profound experiences of love in my dreams, like the dream just described, or the one in which I baby-sit someone else's child, and the baby loves me like I am her mother. I also destroy things in my dreams—like when I burn a bundle of electrical wires bunched in a cubby-hole in a wall of our house, until the house bursts into flames. And I have my things destroyed—like when someone takes pots I've just thrown on my wheel, and smashes them to bits on the floor.

Within days, I come to recognize the doctor/friend in my ocean-side dream as Jesus, a representation of God. The embrace that man gave me in the dream was an embrace of absolute acceptance and appreciation of who I am. It was a picture of what I was slowly coming to understand in my wakened, conscious mind: a picture of infinite divine love, a love that did not ask for perfection but only acceptance and a willingness to confront the truth. The love and embrace illustrated in the dream stand juxtaposed to the disappointment and judgment I feel from those in my family and community, and in a different sense from Darryl, who wishes I would go back to pretending, who wants the Tricia who makes him comfortable. Though the reactions of my community blast me in enervating gusts, I experience in prayer something different, something just like the doctor's ocean-side embrace.

This experience begins to transform me. The love I start to glimpse at this time begins to change everything. It changes the way I see myself, the way I see life. It changes how I view the force at the center of all things.

If it had not been for Martin's love, and for the love of Sue and my few close friends, I may never have been able to recognize it.

I Wake Happy Here

I wake happy here.
The light outside my window,
waves' grandmotherly hum, the ample
luxury of this sane-soft bed. I smooth
the quilt as I rise.
Each window-blind a magician's scarf
stripped away. Light crests the hills, hint
of sun on the sea, bleached breakers
an elysian white. Daughter asleep,
house steeped in milky quietness—
holy *casa del mar*,
as my monk friend says.
Birds of morning fly
into my tree, turn breasts
to wakening day.
Once
from my window I saw the word
WELCOME spelled out in foam
on the beach. Swift sagging message
returned to sea. Back to mystery,
second-guessing. Back to who-
knows-where. It didn't matter.
All of life a flash of messages:
who we are, where our hearts belong,
where the deep welcome of time
will not be lost. Birds fly
into our trees, then ascend, mere
quivers of light, and come back again.

CHAPTER SEVEN

Oceanside

The first time I enter the house I will eventually inhabit in Ocean-side, Oregon, I experience something like hunger, a raw, gnawing, down-to-the-bowels pang. At the time, it is to be the home of my friend Karah, who is giving me the tour before moving in. The place boasts all of 400 square feet, yet feels endless. Perched on a hillside overlooking a wide stretch of the Pacific, the house is all porch and windows spreading across the front like an enormous smile. When Karah and I walk down the steep hill that leads from the house to the beach, she leaves me to go use a pay-phone. As she disappears from sight, I sit on a driftwood log and bury my face in my hands.

Why, for heaven's sake, are you crying? an inner voice demands, hoping to stop up the tears. I kick myself for not celebrating a friend's good fortune, wondering if I am jealous, maybe reacting to Karah's freedom and space—the freedom and space I long for. Whatever the cause of the tears, seeing that tiny beach cottage screws my heart into a shriveled knot of longing.

Karah resides in the house for eleven months. When she leaves town, she invites me to house-sit (Oceanside being an hour and three quarters from Newberg), and I take five retreats to the beach cottage in all, sometimes to visit Karah, sometimes for solitude and house-sitting. Each time I feel pleasantly removed from my life. I experience rest and release. One night, I sleep on the grass in front of the house, letting the hum of the waves fill my dreams. On another occasion, I splash in the surf in a wetsuit. Always, I laugh and cry. In Oceanside, I feel wholly and compassionately myself, like I can be whatever I need to be.

Around New Years, Karah and I sit together and compose two lists each: What I Want to Hold Onto in the New Year, and What I Want to Let Go. We fold the "letting go" lists into our pockets and walk them down the moonlit hillside to the beach, crumpling the papers into tiny balls and hurling them out to sea. I throw out "my concern for what others think of me," and "the retributive God of my youth." I hold onto ecstasy and passion and hope.

On a last retreat to Karah's, after she's announced she's moving to Colorado, giving notice to her landlords, I take a long, doleful walk on the beach. My feet are bare. I wear a gauzy skirt I hold wadded in a fist at my side. I walk through the wide shallow surf that seeps across the flat beach after waves have broken. Warm and windless, the day is a glistening, sapphire-sky miracle. With the red face and swollen eyes of a Muppet, I ignore the people I pass on the beach, staring straight ahead, toward the sea, at my feet. Lately, exhaustion has threatened to overwhelm me. How I appear to passersby is the least of my concerns.

During the previous year I have struggled to find a way to change my life. I have tried on ideas, chased down opportunities for jobs and house mates, mustered my creativity like an organizer with a political action committee. Every escape I've attempted has failed. Over the prior couple of months, I've become more and more convinced I can do nothing to change my circumstances. If they are to change, the change will come from outside of my self. I am filled with a sense of helplessness, not helplessness in the sense of being without help, but in the sense of being entirely unable to effect my own rescue. All I can do is tread water, float, and wait.

Yet I am at this time, and by nature, a do-er. I like to *get things done*. I am not the type to float around and wait for help. I make calls and check the ads. I craft lists. I act. I am willing to make sacrifices, if necessary, to move forward, but I want to move forward, to get out of a situation that has come to feel claustrophobic. To open my hands and let go of everything, to float, seems too much to ask.

However, during the weeks leading up to that walk on the beach, I started to recognize a dangerous futility in my struggle. I had become so tired I feared for my emotional health. If I continued to struggle, I could drown in depression and anxiety. Several weeks earlier I'd been boogie-boarding in the surf and had floated too far from shore. I found myself caught in a rip tide, as the strong current carried me farther and farther down the shoreline, very far from where Darryl and Madison sat like ants on the beach. I almost panicked. The episode lasted only a few moments, but it struck me with a feeling I will never forget. I knew that if I panicked, I would lose control of my body and my breathing, and I would drown.

So I calmed down. I held tightly to my board and stopped struggling against the tide. I listened to the quiet and noticed the warmth of sunlight on my back. Eventually, the current carried me out of danger.

Over the previous year, I had experienced moments of pronounced anxiety. Like a child who wanders too close to the edge of an imposing cliff and looks over, I knew, for the first time in my life, I could actually fall off. I could reach the end of my emotional and physical reserves and careen downward.

That afternoon, walking the beach with sea lapping at my heels, I suddenly realize what I am doing. Once again, I am struggling, striving, trying to rally my determined nature to rescue myself. I'd been thinking over job prospects as I walked: *Should I follow up on this or that? Why hasn't X or Y worked out?* My tears come from frustration, like the tears of a child trying to untie a knot with clumsy fingers. And here the knot isn't even mine to untie.

Recognizing what I am doing, I continue to step forward, eyes still leaking tears. But more and more, they are tears of surrender. I know I must let go and stop trying so hard. I see it now. I must let the current take me. And with each movement down that broad expanse of glassy beach, I slowly experience release. I envision my hands opening, opening, till they are splayed out as flat as a hospital gurney. I pray that God will take over. *Help me, please help me.*

I have walked perhaps five minutes in this stance, meditating on this posture of surrender, of letting go, when something flashes across my mind—almost like a heard voice. It is an idea, though, but not of my origin as far as I can tell. It is a flash from the middle of nowhere. I call it an epiphany.

The idea or epiphany says, "Come here."

Never in my weeks of brainstorming escapes have I envisioned leaving Newberg. This was not possible, in my thinking, because I needed to keep Madison in the same town as her father, extended family, and friends. And never in the weeks since Karah announced she was moving have I considered taking over Karah's apartment. The thought hadn't even crossed my mind.

The experience shocks me. *Come here? To Oceanside? Leave Newberg?*

I walk two minutes more in this state of surprise, then look down to find a full sand dollar directly in my path. In my many walks on that beach, I had found broken sand dollars, hundreds of them, but never one intact. Picking up the perfect, whole sand dollar, I start to smile. I put it in my pocket.

♦

Where the prior year had been a series of frustrated attempts at transition, the way to Oceanside rolls out before me like a red carpet. Not only do obstacles not arise, but astounding provisions fall into my lap. Karah needs someone to store her furnishings, so I can use them while gradually collecting my own. Out of the blue, I am offered a very part-time editing/formatting job I can do from Oceanside. Alex cooperates with my decision to move and my proposal for visits from Madison. Darryl is willing to live apart from me while maintaining our marriage, to participate in a sort of marital experiment. After so many months of struggle, I am almost incredulous. I partially hold my breath, expecting the whole arrangement to collapse like a sand cave on my head.

But it doesn't. Not only has a way opened, a way completely unexpected and apart from my conniving, but it is a way more attractive than my most indulgent hopes. It is a way that leads to the place I'd longed for from the moment I laid eyes on it, so intensely, in fact, that it stung. The pang I'd felt at that time had not been jealousy but homesickness.

◆

The town of Oceanside is far enough removed from Highway 101 that it remains docile year-round, at times eerily quiet. "Downtown," which comprises all of a half-block, includes a post office and fire station, two restaurants (one espresso shop; one fine dining), a tavern, and an inn. Oceanside is flung across a steep hillside just north of Netarts Bay. As you round the cliff that girds Oceanside to the south, the town opens before you like a silk fan, ocean and towering rockscapes on one side, cliff-side town on the other. The town is bordered to the north by a massive headland. Every other week Madison and I drive to Newberg for two days. Madison stays at her dad's while I stay at Darryl's (Darryl comes to us on alternate weekends). Each time I drive back into Oceanside, reverence and gratitude boil up in me. I am floored by the beauty of the place, by the baffling grace that allows me to live there.

That fall the area is granted idyllic weather, unusual weather, days upon days of sunny, warm climate, mild and dry, and on a sunny day, Oceanside is spellbinding. Sitting with Madison on our porch, writing or crocheting, playing guitar or lying on the diminutive plot of grass astride our ocean-prone house, I am precisely where I want to be. Light prances on the water. Cloudscapes part and converge, billowing gradations of white and basalt-gray with gossamer sideburns, layers of steely blue. The movement of the clouds and position of the sun constantly arouse new shades on the water, purples, hundreds of shades of blue and lemon-yellow. Occasionally the sea looks like an endless vat of milk. The diamond-dance of light and unfurling of color make the ocean, on a warm day, mesmerizing. It hushes and dazzles me all day long, only to climax in a passionate flush of amber and rose at dusk, the colors of a child's Popsicle.

At sunset I set aside my doings, perch on the porch with Madison (or, if it is cold, in the chair by my window) and simply take it all in. Sunset sometimes comes at supper-time. Sitting at the table we scooted into a front bay window, Madison and I stare out and eat, few words to say, resting amid the sight and rumble of the sea.

The beach apartment is the bottom story of a small cottage and consists mostly of one room, about 12 x 16 feet. (Every month, the owners arrive for a weekend to use the upstairs.) Furnishing our tiny space is a futon-bed where I sleep, a desk and computer, an eating table and easy chair, and two bookshelves—leaving a narrow path for walking. Madison uses the one bedroom, equipped with an ocean-facing window alongside her bed. Rounding off the apartment are a coat-closet-sized bathroom, a cracker-box kitchen, and a laundry room/mud room, all walled in a combination of cedar-panel and white cinderblock.

The front room of the cottage features a rusted-out fireplace skirted by a rainbow of hearth tiles, deep navy to saffron, copper-red to burgundy-red to pink. The colored tiles, as well as the glass-block windows in the kitchen and bathroom are my favorite elements of the house. Less desirable is the leaky ceiling. That winter we occasionally place pots and pans strategically around the apartment to catch water that seeps through our storm-battered shingles and into the house. Because this reminds Madison of cartoons she has seen on television, with some character sitting amid a sea of pots and pans, up to his ankles in water, she barely minds. Such a good companion, she is.

About once a week, Madison and I venture out of town, to Newberg or to run errands in Tillamook. Other than that, we share our small "hermitage," as Martin calls it. We subsist on the child support I get from Madison's dad and the small amount I earn from various odd jobs. We eat a good deal of rice.

Since Karah's departure date and the day I started paying rent were three weeks apart, I had moved into the apartment gradually. When my official move-in date arrived, I was already unpacked—plants on the hearth, pictures on the wall, dishes in neat stacks on the cupboard.

♦

The weekend I move in happens to coincide with the abbey's "old-timers'" retreat to the Oregon coast, when the eldest monks stay at a beach house in Neskowin to watch football and videos, drink beer, and generally satisfy their year-long cravings for junk food.

On Saturday morning I drive to Neskowin to pick up Martin, having asked him to pronounce a blessing on my house. He is happy for a reprieve from the other monks who, though his dear brothers, can be tiresome. When Brother Joel, an old monk who turns into a rollicking fool in a woman's presence, sees me at the door, he says, "Oh, glad to see a woman around. We need someone to do the dishes!" I try not to glower.

When Martin walks into our little beach apartment, he beams. I direct him to an easy chair in a front bay window and serve him a cup of mint tea. "I haven't felt so at home in decades!" he gushes. The place reminds him of his family's two-room abode along the railroad line in La Mesa, California, where he grew up, simple and cozy, and full of "holy light."

My friend Shonna has spent the night and she and Madison sit on the futon laughing and crocheting. With all four of us congregated in the main room, the house seems to shrink like a tilting room at a carnival. But we sit and chat, eating salsa and chips and drinking tea. Martin quizzes Shonna about her childhood (it turns out the two of them had lived, as older kids, in the same San Diego *barrio*—Shonna over fifty years later than Martin). She serves us from an exquisite pecan pie she's baked as a housewarming, pie being Shonna's preferred art form.

Though the morning's weather is cold and blustery, the sky as thick as an old wool blanket, we carry chairs onto the porch for the blessing. Shonna and I drape ourselves in quilts and Martin dons a wind-breaker, while Madison opts to watch from inside where it is warm. For several minutes, we sit in silent prayer, observing the crashing of waves and the jostling of trees. Seagulls rise on gusts of wind, their wings unflinching and broad. They dive and then rise, dive and rise again. Shonna cries. Martin, in the end, says simply "Bless this house."

Around four, the sun comes out and paints things golden. On our way back to the monk's gathering in Neskowin, Martin takes me to a Franciscan retreat house set amid velvety hills that remind me of Scotland. He's had the best day in years, he says. When I drop him off at the beach-house retreat, he loads my back seat with food like I'm taking off to deliver Meals-on-Wheels. "The brothers bring too much food to these retreats!" he proclaims, shaking his head in feigned frustration. "We can't be hauling this stuff back to the abbey!" He piles in a box of tomatoes from the abbey garden and an assortment of other vegetables, a huge block of cheese, bread, tortillas, crackers, juice, and some donuts for good measure. He gives me a hug and a peck on the cheek and tells me, "This day was a real blessing to my heart. . . . You've made an old monk's heart *sing*."

◆

Around the time I move to Oceanside I am reading *Everything Belongs*,[8] by Franciscan priest Richard Rohr, the book becoming a stalwart favorite. But it isn't until settling into the solitude and quiet of Oceanside that its message starts to sink in. I read it through, then start over at page one. Then I read the entire book a third time.

Everything Belongs is about entering liminal, dark, transforming spaces. It is a reminder that God is there, in those places, and that our openness to transformation swells when we are in them. When the way opened to Oceanside, I felt elated. At times I flitted through my preparations for the move. But after it came and I settled into the quiet, I knew I was in for something hard, for wrestling. Not wrestling like I'd done over the prior couple of years, which had largely been a struggle with the perimeters and shape of my external life, but an inner wrestling. I would undergo this struggle in a settled, peaceful place of exquisite beauty I was happy to be in, but it would unsettle my foundational assumptions about life and who I am, about my future.

I had experienced bouts of prolonged depression for three or four years. First I associated it with my marital unhappiness, then the upheaval and stress of marital crisis. But as life changes in

Oceanside and I enter a more placid state, the depression becomes conspicuously cyclical. Though I no longer feel persistently depressed, each month around the same time I descend into emotional sludge—like the joy-train has up and left the station without me. I become listless as a street dog in the Deep South and caught in an undertow of sadness. I cry much of the day at these times. This can take the form of soul-wrenching sobs or a heart-crushing leakiness that lasts for hours.

As it turns out, a good deal of my depression is related to hormones, to the female monthly fluctuations that have, in my body, raged out of control. A year later, I am diagnosed with Premenstrual Dysphoric Disorder—perhaps a consequence of my one-ovaried state—and promptly put on medication to balance my chemistry. This resolves the cyclical depression immediately. But in the meantime, over the course of about a year, I experiment with natural remedies for hormonal imbalance and spend about half of each month in the depressive depths.

My hormonal/emotional state, the solitude of my life in Oceanside, the silence allotted to me for reflection, my acute career frustrations, and the losses I have incurred over the prior two years of marital crisis, combine to create a crucible.

Just the sort of liminal space Rohr wrote of in *Everything Belongs*.

After Shonna and Martin leave the beach house, the gravity of my changed life pulls me into a hollow, expansive place. I have walked away from the community I'd lived in for seventeen years to a place where I know not a soul; walked away from a traditional marriage to a precarious marital experiment; turned a quiet shoulder to family and friends who think I've made a horrible mistake; and entered a life of stillness and retreat that looks to many like career suicide.

To help pay for groceries, I clean house every two weeks for an elderly neighbor. As I vacuum her floor and scrub her toilet, I think about my years of work on a PhD, about the high expectations my professors had placed on me. I feel torn down the middle. On one side, I question my judgment for letting my professional potential languish. On the other, I feel irresistibly free, freer than I have ever felt before. I have defied the societal norms that dictate life, family, career, and love. I have straightened my back and walked away. But no matter what side I lean toward, I find myself in a solitary place. Only I can hear the drummer. Only I can see that what I am doing is the sanest thing I have ever done.

Once my friends have left, my emotions plummet. I sit in my window feeling the air leak out of me. A hang-glider swoops in front of my house and drifts back and forth along the wide stretch of mountain before settling blithely on the shore. The day has opened to a glistening display of sunlight, clear sky, and sparse cumulus clouds. The ocean flaunts her gleaming breakers like a brazen showgirl whisking a white feather boa. I take it all in feeling a compression of dull, aching perceptiveness.

Madison asks to play in the surf with the boogie board. I help her into my wetsuit, grabbing a folding chair, and we head to the beach.

That afternoon offers perfect boogie-boarding waves, big enough for speed, but not powerful enough to overwhelm a novice. Every few minutes Madison works up more courage, venturing farther out. Wearing a huge grin, she rides the waves for an hour and a half until she can barely walk. As I sit in a chair on the beach watching her, my mind registers a sort of delight while my emotions remain numb. I am pleased to see her playing, enjoying the grandeur of the sea on that stunning day. But I cannot describe the feeling as happiness. Later that day I write to a friend, "I know I will be sad here, probably a lot. I am prepared to feel sad. It is good to be in a place where I don't have to maintain appearances."

Two days later Madison's closest friend comes for a two-night sleepover, and on the first evening the girls ask to build a bonfire on the beach. They want to cook bread-on-a-stick, they tell me. Since they insist on going alone, I mix up a batch of bread dough and allow it to rise while we eat an early supper. Then I pack a bag of campfire supplies and send the girls off to the beach with instructions to return before sundown.

Around 7:45, I decide to see how the girls' fire has progressed. I pull on a sweater and descend the steep hill between our house and the beach. As I near the sand, I catch the scent of campfire and swell with pride. *My girl can build a fire!* But as I walk onto the beach, I don't see flames. The girls' giggling voices bounce in the distance. As I approach, Madison relays that the burning smell is newspaper, copious amounts of which have been burned to no avail. Apparently fire-building skills need developing. Nonetheless, we sit for a spell just laughing, enjoying the scene. Then we pack up the dough, now gritty with sand, and head home.

Despite my blunted emotions, I already love our life in Oceanside. The orientation to the sea, the relaxed pace, the almost overwhelming beauty—it suits me marvelously. Even when I feel depressed, the ocean soothes me, and its sprawling stillness and raging power remind me of God. I think about the mysterious universe that lies beneath the surface, behind a curtain of reflected light. *Whales* live there. And fish so colorful they appear electric. I cannot wrap my head around it. I cannot imagine anything beyond the surface, beyond what I can see.

I love that Madison is turning her face toward the ocean every day. At age twelve, she is far less nature-loving than I am and less inclined to venture outdoors. Yet the magic right outside our windows gets her attention. Sometimes late afternoons or evenings, Madison plays in the lot just below our house. Most of it is overgrown with grass, fireweed, nasturtiums, and wild cucumber. But she creates a fort-like space at the top of the lot, just below the stone wall lining our small patch of grass. Sometimes she sits in that space for an hour, looking out toward the deepening azure of sea and sky. At times I watch her talking to herself, or singing.

I settle into a routine in Oceanside. Each day I wake up slowly, lying in bed for several minutes before rising. I stand up and open the blinds to a sight that never ceases to amaze me. I make coffee and drink it in my chair, watching the first movement of day outside my window. In the morning, light from the east casts coppery shadows on the mountains. It slowly burns away pockets of mist and fog that cling to the sides of cliffs nearing the bay. Early in the day birds chirp and flirt with morning, descending in small flocks on the one wind-battered tree in our yard. These delicate birds, mostly finches, sparrows, and chickadees, make exquisite company. Sometimes a crow joins them, or a red-shafted flicker.

Madison awakens during this time and walks to the kitchen to forage for breakfast. Since Madison is decidedly not a morning person, I promptly vacate the premises to take a shower, dress, and leave for my morning walk.

It takes about ten minutes to descend from our house to the bottom of our steep hill. At the bottom, I stroll onto the beach, proceeding southward about fifteen minutes before turning around. Sometimes I pray and chant a mantra, sometimes I ponder, sometimes I listen to a book on CD as I take in the sights and smells of beach. The planetary knots of sea grass, the wispy sandscapes, the outcroppings of basalt that rise out of the sand like the backs of giants, the bleached out sculptures of driftwood, the salty, fishy detritus, and the lively seabirds. Of course, the mesmerizing sea. The stretch of land between Oceanside and Netarts Bay is lined with cliffs covered in salal, grasses, and wind-swept manzanita. It is sparsely dotted with houses.

Before ascending our hill I stop at the tiny Oceanside post office to pick up our mail. If I receive a letter from Brother Martin, as I often do, I sit on the bench just outside the post office and read it. After returning from my walk, I eat.

The hours between my walking and supper fill with a combination of writing, letter-writing, editing/formatting (which I do rarely, as the work is sporadic), and sitting outside or by the front window reading, playing guitar, or visiting with Madison. Madison does her schoolwork and whatever activities strike her daily fancy. Occasionally I run to town for groceries or to the bank. And almost every day, I nap.

In the evening I cook supper to share with Madison, then we pass the day's last hours on my futon-bed, crocheting or knitting together, watching a movie or reading side-by-side. Sometimes I read aloud to Madison from a novel. And often, we laugh.

The predictable, relaxed flow of our Oceanside days is soul-healing. I sometimes feel I've been whisked away to a spirit-hospital where I am slowly being mended, brought back to life on a steady diet of nature, rest, and reflection. I had no idea when I moved to Oceanside how badly I needed these things. But the force that brought me there did know. It is a force I am experiencing more and more as benevolent, full of beautiful, boundless grace.

Shortly after moving, I see my first seals in the water below Oceanside. From my window, I glimpse their shiny black heads bobbing in and out of the surf. At first sight, Madison and I mistake them for surfers. Then we pull out the faithful binoculars to find four seals clustered together in the farthest breakers, stopped in one area where they appear to be playing, leaping out of the water, diving into waves, and circling back to the group. Over the course of several days we observe that many seals make a daily trek between Netarts Bay and Cape Meares, at least during that season of the year. At the same time each morning and evening we watch them on their frolicking commute past our hillside.

Some mornings I notice a seal as I walk along the beach. Seals are friendly creatures when not on land and fascinated by people. I experience this on three occasions as seals swim adjacent to my position for several minutes, only twenty yards away from me, as I walk. They bob in the shallow surf alongside me, looking at me until I glance their way. When I turn my head toward them, they shyly duck under water or shift their gaze forward, like boys caught staring at pretty girls in school.

During the months I live in Oceanside, I put forth no effort to make friends. For company I have Madison, the seals and birds, the enchanting sea. When I try to forge connections for Madison with girls her age, she resists, so that neither of us have close friends in the area the entire ten months we live there. I have her and she has me. By the end of our stay, loneliness has afflicted Madison, growing over her like a thin mold. But for the first few months, she seems content to play alone.

On the first weekends after our move to Oceanside, when Darryl comes to me or I go to him, we're physically affectionate. We take walks and catch up on small and large details of our lives. We cook meals together and trade backrubs. The new relational format temporarily suffuses the relationship with connection, as if the air is charged with a magnetism that rubs off on us. Whereas Darryl and I are generally, by default of our personalities, withdrawn from one another, we are during these early visits present.

Darryl had been skeptical about my move to Oceanside, as he was skeptical about most of my decisions from the time I told him, months earlier, I wanted to separate. He finds it unbearable to accept I could be right about the marriage, so he holds to a stubborn certainty I am wrong. From this perspective, all actions and judgments that move toward separation are misguided. From my first admission I was contemplating a split, Darryl distrusted my character, my judgments, and my intentions, and the perpetual distrust I sensed in him caused me to withdraw further.

But as Darryl observes me in Oceanside, he sees me breathing more deeply, stretching loose of the bounds that constrained me in Newberg. He knows I relish the wide-openness of my life in Oceanside, and his reservations about my move seem to soften. As our geographical distance draws us emotionally closer, he even views it positively. Still, he sees the distance as temporary. Naturally, he wants us back together, in the same house—at least the same town—in due time.

◆

There are periods in one's life that have a faint, hazy glow of miracle about them. It is difficult to look back and describe them on the level of language and reason. They are times we walk into as one person, as though entering a tunnel, and walk out of as another. From the bird's-eye view of memory, we see ourselves entering the tunnel, and we see ourselves exiting, changed, but we no longer have a real-time vision of the tunnel's interior. It is a vague, otherworldly memory we struggle to outline, like a dream.

My months in Oceanside are that tunnel.

I first become aware I am entering it as I walk the beach each day contemplating what I am reading and rereading in Rohr's book *Everything Belongs*. In the early months, I spend a good deal of thought on the experience of failure, on the fruits of failure—what failure has to teach. For some time, several months, I have felt like a colossal failure, and resisted the feeling with every slice of my being. At the time, few realities seemed more painful to embrace. But as I settle in to Oceanside, my hours of reflection quietly lead me back to failure, coaxing me to face it bravely, to let myself see the failure in all its distressing forms, and to admit the dimming hopes of success that spawned them. I want to know what I am striving for, what impulses keep me reaching for praise and falling short. I want to touch the holes in my spirit I try to fill. And I want to let go of the striving because I am tired, and it isn't working.

Central to Rohr's teaching is this: success and praise often— *usually*—distort our perceptions. They make us resistant to the letting-go, the emptying of ego, so important for spiritual growth and maturity. Awareness and compassion are almost always birthed in the dark times, in the flailing and the questions, when our false scaffoldings of security fail us. It is during those times of darkness that, ironically, our vision of ourselves and our lives, of the world, becomes clearer. It is during those times we see what is really holding us up.

When we cling to things, whether money, or righteousness, or career advancement and professional accolades, or relationships, or good deeds that prop up the ego, we become convinced we're self-reliant, that maintaining our hold on these things is true security. We are afraid to lose the things that create our security, so we cling. We resist the emptiness that, according to every mystical tradition, is what allows us to be filled with eternity, wooed by eternal, true things. Our clinging convinces us we already have what we need, our ego is secure. But the reliability of the ego is our greatest illusion. Our clinging and our sense of self-reliance actually distort our vision of the world and ourselves, making wisdom impossible, making compassion impossible because of our need to defend our security at all costs.

So in a sense, freedom really is having nothing left to lose. Losing everything makes us perfectly free to see things as they truly are. We no longer resist such seeing for fear of what we'll lose in the process, and we become available to God; nothing else is competing for our attention, not our ambitions, not our relationships or our self-congratulatory preening, not our judgments of others. Awareness then can enter.

Great spiritual teachers say that freedom cannot exist apart from awareness. When we cannot see things as they are, we remain caught in cycles of illusion, fantasy, and reactivity. We may think we are free, but as long as we don't clear our vision, we are captives, constantly whisked away by false realities that won't let us rest and be and savor—simply enjoying the present—because of all we must do to defend the security we think we have.

Some of us won't experience devastating failures and losses. In this case, we do the spiritual work of undoing illusions without the help of these guides. But when we realize the gifts failure and loss can bring, we are free from the constant fear of them. Generally, the more we have, the more worry we schlep around. Our worries are illusion-stories we tell ourselves, dark tales of all the terrible things that will happen to loot our security. Our worries are relentless captors.

But our successes lie behind these worries. Successes cause us to cling to our illusions of worthiness, our superiority over others, with a quivery death grip. We think our deservedness will be a bulwark against loss and devastating failure. We think we are loved and secure because we deserve to be, because of all we do to earn love and praise. We are loved for our beauty, our helpful service, our humor or brilliance, our purity and righteousness, our talent.

Success, then, is a captor even more oppressive than worry because it blinds us to the love people and God truly have for us. Rather than seeing clearly God's provision and grace to us—or in the Christian tradition, seeing that Jesus simply *loves* us, and rather than acknowledging in a compassionate way how we benefit from privilege, we attribute our secure place in the world to our hard work, inventiveness, and charm. Rather than viewing the daily pleasures of life as gifts of a benevolent creator, we see ourselves enjoying what we have created. But it is a crippling illusion. Somewhere deep in the gut we know we aren't perfect and more deserving than others, and we see that the true revelries in life are free to everyone: love, family, wild flowers, and stars. Sooner or later, clingy success makes us resist awareness at all costs, or makes us hate ourselves and our lives.

Mystics tell us to wake up each day fully aware of who we are, the good and the bad, and deeply grateful we are loved through it all. In awareness, they tell us, we see that God and others love us despite our failures, and we finally understand love. *We stop work-*

ing so hard to earn love and become reflections of the love we can fi-nally, clearly see. This is true freedom.

In Oceanside, I begin pondering failure out of frustration. I seem unable to write something publishable and have self-pub-lished a book few people at the time are reading; I have twice failed to keep my marriage vows; I am unable to find a steady, paying job I enjoy; I am, up to this time, prone to physical illness (though as I experience spiritual release, this changes to a large extent); and many of my former friends are no longer friends. In these and other respects, I am, indisputably, a failure. I am led to wrestle with failure because I cannot seem to escape it. I have succeeded brilliantly at failure!

But as I consider failure from Rohr's perspective, which is the perspective of the great religious paths, I open my arms to it, to ponder what it offers, and to accept it. Perhaps God wants to be present to me in failure, to usher me to greater awareness and transformation through it.

The more I wrestle with failure and the pain on its heels, the more clearly I see the source of that pain. All of my life, I've been trying to earn love by impressing people. I started young, when I strove to excel in school, to keep my room tidy. When I did these things, I won praise, and praise seemed like the elixir of love.

This pattern continued into pre-adolescence, when I would clean house for my mother, who by then had four kids and would sigh "Oh, me" with withering regularity. My quest for love was why I worked so hard to win the speech contest, to become stu-dent body president and head cheerleader in eighth grade. In mid-dle school, I was elected "Most Likely to Succeed" two consecutive years, and it was toward the end of middle school that all of these shelters of praise came crashing down on me.

After middle school, I sought love-via-success in new ways, by impressing people with my creativity or by singing well. When I won a role in the school play, I tried to steal the show. With steeper competition, I no longer stood out academically but was an above-average student. And though I no longer fit my parents' churchy perimeters for the perfect young lady, it didn't matter. I had dis-covered something more potent than parent-love—boy-love.

For many years, boy-love was the primary arena in which I worked out the success-brings-love equation. I would impress boys with my beauty, my art, my allure. This worked okay until I ended up eighteen, married, and devastated by a colossal failure of a marriage.

Not surprising, then, that after the end of this marriage, I set out to demonstrate success in such bold new ways. I would pursue a PhD, as a single mother of a small child, no less. I would prove a phenomenal student and a phenomenal mother in the process. I can now see it was a desperate scramble for love. But when my academic successes had little impact on the people I most wanted to squeeze love out of—my parents—I was, again, bereft.

At about that time, I remarried.

Walking the beach in Oceanside each day and sitting quiet hours staring at the sea, my life plays before my eyes like a movie, a long litany of love-seeking successes and failures. And throughout most of my life, I had not even felt loved or successful. I had merely felt tired.

Really, I had been successful in many things. But because these successes hadn't earned me love, I had disregarded them, one after another, a dull parade. They were like drinks that don't work to numb the pain, so they are followed by another, and another. . . . Often my successes had won me admiration or praise, but these dissipate like smoke. In the vacuum they left behind, I experienced love's opposite, a frustrated emptiness.

As I take stock of the few friends I do have who, I know, love me, I realize they do not love me for impressive things I have done. They love me because I am kind to them and loving. They love me because I reflect their love back and help them to better understand God. They love me, in other words, for the same reasons I love them.

But the radical shift really comes when I see failure as a good thing. I have become a success-and-admiration junkie. I know that as long as I view success as an avenue to love, getting success will throw me off kilter. It makes me hunger for more of the drug. I need a clean break from the high, a cold-turkey descent into obscurity.

As this awareness dawns, I find it hard to write. Poetry comes more freely, but prose drips from my tap. Out of stubborn discipline, I force myself, for a spell, to write two paragraphs a day on a young adult novel I've started, and which I soon put down. Eventually I stop writing altogether, aside from occasional poetry and journaling. And though I have just finished recording, with the help of several musician friends, a CD of songs I wrote, I resist those who encourage me to perform.

Then, just as I've started to let go my clingy ambition, I receive an e-mail from *Sojourners Magazine*—a progressive, Christian, political magazine—saying they are reviewing my book. I had self-published *Free People: A Christian Response to Global Economics* six months prior, after a year of unsuccessful publisher-seeking. Because it is so difficult to get self-published books reviewed, and because *Sojourners*-types are precisely the audience for the book, I am thrilled.

The book review editor, in her e-mail, calls the book "wonderful." *Great!* I think, *It will be a good review!* (but *Sojourners* rarely publishes bad reviews, so I am not seriously worried). I wait four weeks for the outcome, even subscribing to the magazine. I want to read the review as soon as it comes out, basking as I am in the prospect of a good review, a small boost for my book. Though I've been embracing failure, the very whiff of a small success has made me as high as Keith Richards.

Well, *Sojourners* breaks tradition to publish a bad review. Because *Sojourners* is widely read among progressive Christian readers, and because *Sojourners* would likely be the only weighty magazine to review the book, the overall effect is not good. If *Sojourners* had published a favorable review, it might have helped the book substantially. Who knows the effect of a bad review?

What is worse, they not only break tradition to print a bad review, but they review the book *badly*. I know the book has weak spots, weak spots reviewers will pick up on, and I am not surprised *Sojourners* points these out. But the reviewer makes several misleading statements about the book as well. Friends who are familiar with *Free People* are, along with me, scratching their heads upon reading the review. We have to wonder how carefully the reviewer had read my book. She actually implies I am calling people to an Amish-like existence, saying that to live ethically in the global economy one needs to grind one's own corn and sew one's own clothes. She has overlooked key points of the book to pull out and highlight such minutiae. The overall effect is distorting. It is also strange, considering I am rather ideologically on-track with the magazine. *Why would they diss my book?* I plead. I cannot understand. The review, at the time, feels devastating.

I cry about it for days, whenever it enters my mind. I rage. I have not felt so frustrated for months. It is like I've tasted a drop of my drug-of-choice, then had it whisked away by a friend. The withdrawal effects make me writhe and spit. I had almost curled my fingers around a coveted price, an ounce of public acclaim, then heard it shattering to bits at my feet.

And *nothing* could have worked better to wake me up.

The humiliation of the experience smarts. I know many people will read the review, people whose opinion matters to me at the time, and I have to slowly accept the chagrin. But as difficult as this is, it casts in sharp relief my maniacal attachment to praise and to other people's opinions. You would have thought a dear friend had died, for all my sobbing. *Yet it was just a bad review, and in a relatively small magazine.* So my book might be set even further back! So I might look stupid to the thousands of people who would read the review but never read the book! So I wouldn't get to bask in the glory of a small success! At the time, though, these points make no sense. The disappointment feels huge. The perceived loss stings like a gash.

In the end, the review helps me to see how off-balance I have become. But months will pass before I can finally make out the illusions. I had thought a good review would bring me love. I had hoped it would give my book a boost toward success, and that a successful book would bring me love. I had thought that if the review was positive, I would be, somehow, important. And important people are loved.

The review of my book takes me farther down a path to awareness than any other single experience, exposing many illusions. It coincides with the unveiling of other misconceptions precipitated by other losses, making this period a time of profound dis-illusionment. I am seeing myself more as I truly am, becoming conscious.

And I feel, like never before, *surrounded* by love.

◆

One afternoon I sit on my porch in a camping chair and read the following from *Everything Belongs*:

> True religion is always about love. Love is the ultimate reality. We can probably see this only through real prayer. For love can be hidden. We don't see it unless we learn how to see, unless we clean the lens. The Zen masters call it wiping the mirror. In a wiped mirror, we can see exactly what's there without distortion. In a perfect mirror I see what's there, not what I'm afraid of, nor what I need to be there, but what is really there.

As Rohr points out, many people in places of power and influence have not undergone this practice of self-observation. He urges us to do it without judgment or accusation, to observe ourselves with compassion. And when we do this practice, he says, we will begin to see how much we are loved. "When the veil parts and we see *love*," Rohr writes, "the self-conscious watcher, preoccupied with doing it right, just forgets the self" (p. 103).

◆

The dawning of awareness in me at this time, the disillusionment, is essential to my experiencing divine love, to my coming to believe the Jesus who graced my dreams as a representation of that love. I have spent my entire life trying to earn love by being well-behaved, or clever, or artistically and intellectually gifted, or beautiful. But in my head I know I cannot earn God's love. Who can? I believed God loves everyone, that God is infinitely benevolent and merciful. In my head, I even believed God loved me. But my gut felt otherwise, and had since childhood. At my core, I felt threatened and judged. My first assumption was not of a benevolent force protecting me, a force I could call love. Regardless of what I believed in my head, I felt alone, like the only thing saving me was my own striving.

From my earliest memories up to those healing Oceanside months, I had felt debilitating shame. Shame followed me around like a stalker, making me feel watched and scrutinized always. I could not throw off the notion that I was inherently bad. Though my parents loved me deeply, I never felt convinced of their love. I believe my thirty-four year struggle with shame stemmed from this perceived lack of parental love. But it was a matter of *perception*, rather than reality. I have *loving, generous* parents. They are flawed perhaps, and have often been judgmental, but they love me. What had skewed my perception from such a young age?

Developmental psychologists believe that a child's earliest bonding with his or her mother teaches him/her security and love, that he/she is taken care of, that he/she is good. During my early months in Oceanside, as I become aware of the shame at my center and my perceived lack of security, I spend more time pondering my mom's struggles during my infancy, as mentioned earlier. Whether my mother's circumstances during my first two years impacted my psychological development, I will never know for sure. But I do know that as a child I felt a strong need to earn her love, even if it was freely given. My *perception* was always that it cost. Though I knew she loved me, even as she struggled at times to understand me, I *felt* shamed, I *felt* unloved. This is not because she did wrong as a mother. She was a wonderful mother. I simply picked up a misperception of the world during my earliest days, an inevitable consequence of the insecurity I was born into.

Becoming aware of this dynamic, of the circumstances of my mother's life which may have shaped mine in infancy, jimmies open a long-closed door in my heart. Suddenly I feel free of my parents' opinion of me. I feel free to let them wrestle with their own shame, their own hang-ups, and free to forgive them. To forgive them the little and big ways they have failed as parents, because we *all* fail, in our own ways, as parents. I am able to look at my parents, for the first time, from a place of freedom and security.

All of my life I had projected insecurities and experiences of threat and judgment onto God. I did not *feel* that God could be trusted or that God was taking care of me. I felt that no one was really taking care of me but me. In a sense I had long suspected these feelings were projections but had been unable to break the pattern. I knew in my head God was love, but my gut said otherwise. I knew the point of breakdown was inside of me, yet I could not make out the origin of the breakdown.

Exposing the root of the insecurities, pinpointing them in my earliest life, helped me to see clearly what I was doing. God had always loved me, but I had somehow missed the experiences that enable a child to know security and love from God. Whereas, as I child, I was supposed to learn that a loving force of kindness and benevolence moved the universe, and that I could rest in that kindness and love *no matter what*, I had stood fear-struck on the cusp of my life, feeling existentially alone. This loneliness and lack of security had been my ever-present shadow for thirty-four years.

And as I become aware of this, the shadow slowly disappears.

A haze parts across my horizon. Walking at the edge of the ghost-lit Pacific, or sitting on my porch listening to the hush and roll of waves, I suddenly feel embraced by an endless, grand *love*. Sometimes I just sit, basking in it, eyes dampening. I suddenly know nothing I have ever done can alter that love. It is trustworthy. It is there for me and always will be. I can count on it like a baby counts on her parent to catch her as she is tossed, giggling, into the still air. In the eyes of this love, failure and success do not exist. There is no contest. There is only awareness of the love and lack of awareness, but the love is always there. The love is *always* there.

As I experience this love, I am changed. I am no longer under threat, no longer ashamed, and can rest in that absolute security. Everything will be okay. Everything is *radically* okay, as Rohr says.

Naturally, Martin's refrain of "Jesus loves women," begins to take on new meaning for me at this time. I begin to see how perceptions of female worth I had accrued in my earliest life had melded with experiences of shame and incredulousness about divine love for *me* to create a substantial mental block, a block that made a phrase like "Jesus loves women" ring incoherent to my ears. And I begin to wonder how many women with backgrounds similar to mine hear "Jesus loves women" with the same ring of incoherence—or for that matter, "Yahweh loves women," "Mohammed loves women," "Krishna loves women.". . .

As I begin to experience the love at the center of all things, to feel bathed in it, surrounded by it, I imagine a knowing smile on Jesus' face, a look that says "She's got it!" I also imagine God symbolized in different forms, some anthropomorphic, some not, greeting me always with an endless embrace, with celebration. And suddenly, as if a lifetime's worth of heart encoding has been erased practically overnight, I know that that divine love is indelible. Nothing can earn it and nothing can take it away.

◆

It was after this dawning that I began the very intentional practice of letting go, slowly loosening the grip I had maintained on every aspect of my life, my work, my relationships, my beliefs. My letting go had been, at first, a survival strategy, a reaction to enervating frustration. Lacking the energy to make things work in my marriage and career, I gave them up. Not gave up on them—but gave them up to God, whom I was learning to trust. But now I knew that marriage or no marriage, friends or no friends, publishing or no publishing, everything was going to be okay.

I'd been trying for about a year to find an agent for a young adult novel I'd written, my first work of fiction. The process had taken great effort over the past several months, and then I wasn't sure the book was even ready for publication. In keeping with the loosening inside of me, I decided to put the project on the shelf until later, to let go of the persistent, fruitless effort I was investing in agent-seeking, and to come back to the novel when I felt inspired to improve it. This is an example of letting go—one of many from my life at this time.

I still have a deeply ingrained tendency to cling. But when I notice myself clinging to *anything*, such as hopes for a certain friendship or written piece, dearly held viewpoints about politics or God, opinions people have of me, I close my eyes and carefully picture my fingers opening like anemone petals.

And gradually, as I let go, I experience greater and greater loosening in my spirit. I still *hold* things: opinions, thoughts, dreams, but as I practice letting go, I become more and more detached from them. They no longer hold me. I can stand apart from them and look at them objectively, so that when a hope or belief is threatened, I am no longer convinced *I* am threatened. And more and more I can articulate to others what I believe or hope without a compulsion to control or convince them. As I encounter people with a strong need to be right, I can more easily walk away, without a need to defend or convince.

Around this time I read books by Natalie Goldberg, a writer and Zen practitioner, and listen to tapes by Thich Nhat Hahn as I walk the beach. I begin to practice meditation, using Buddhist techniques for guidance—particularly *mindfulness*, as taught by Thich Nhat Hahn. What I pick up from this practice is transforming. Goldberg and Hahn, along with Rohr, midwife me into a new relationship to the world, a relationship in stark contrast to the controlling evangelical-fundamentalism of my upbringing. It also stands in stark contrast to the self-righteous zeal of the progressive movement, with which I've more recently been aligned. It issues from awareness and compassion, not right-ness and determination, and it offers a freedom I relish.

Whereas both evangelical-fundamentalism and political progressivism tend to be divisive, the principles I am learning from these teachers are essentially unifying. If lives lived out of awareness and compassion effect change (which I believe they do), they do so not by humiliating or destroying anything or anyone, or by overpowering one ideology with another. They bring about change through the power of focused, persistent, inclusive love.

◆

I really do not know where I am going as I sit on my Oceanside porch, waiting and watching. But the more I sit, the more I become convinced I am taken care of, that all I have to do is receive. This is an assurance I have never felt before. While most of my life I'd spent suffocating in the clutches of insecurity, I suddenly feel sprung from those clutches. I worry far less about money, or jobs, or books, or what people think of me, or what will become of my relationship with Darryl, or what will come after

Oceanside, or how Madison will make friends, or what I am doing with my life. I imagine myself like a leaf on the wind, trusting spirit to land me exactly where I need to be. Yet adopting this posture of waiting is not effortful. It is a sort of anti-effort, like even the empowerment to do it is received. Trust fills the vacuum that forms as I abandon my striving, as I sit down and get still. As it turns out, this is all I needed to do to enter the transformative tunnel.

Richard Rohr says, "There is a necessary light that is only available in darkness . . . that can be known only if we are sufficiently emptied." This "necessary light" that comes in darkness is the unifying love at the core of all being. When our cups are full, we cannot receive it. When our cups are full, we become convinced we are loved for what we offer. But as long as we think this way, we don't experience the depth of God's love for us; we don't even scratch the surface.

Letting go strips everything away so that we are naked as mole rats in the world's eyes and in our own. And then, *then*, when we have little around us to cloud our vision of it, we get a glimpse of the love. And I am telling you, it is good. It says everything about you is okay. Even your "failings" are teaching you. It says you are *absurdly* loved.

Enter wonder, ecstasy, compassion, and wisdom. Enter joy.

Oceanside is the beginning of a grand unraveling. Knots inside of me begin to loosen during those lengthening seaside days where little much happens. In my early practice at meditation, I try to embrace the emptiness of those hours, to let it move into my body, so I can become more spacious within myself, more free of attachments.

One attachment I worked at releasing was to that place. I had never loved a place the way I loved that *casa del mar*. But as our months in the Oceanside house increased, so did Madison's loneliness and boredom. Furthermore, I'd been unable to find a good home for our dog, who was still in Darryl's care, and needed a place where Madison and I could keep a pet. I begin to think about moving. And as I think about moving, I think about places teenagers might reside.

Within days of beginning our search for a rental, Madison and I find a pet-friendly duplex farther up the coast of Oregon, in a town called Cannon Beach.

◆

I visit Martin just days before our move. We sit on the porch that skirts the front of the abbey's guesthouse.

"I have had a hard week," he explains, describing how the liturgical hours feel empty to him. "Tricia," he says, "I can watch a little bird hopping along the railing outside of Bethany House, and it brings me more into God's presence than the Mass." He knows I understand. He knows my church is the chair at my front window.

"The saints people go on about here—Bernard, or Saint Benedict, they just don't speak to me, you know? I feel more connection with Cesar Chavez, or with that tree over there!" Martin spent a weekend once with Chavez, whose daughter had married a close friend of Martin's family.

"Last night after compline," he tells me, grinning, "I sat and meditated on friendship." He laughs quietly, and the laugher makes fireworks go off in his eyes. "It is a special grace for me," he says, leaning close, "a real moment of mystery."

That afternoon as I'd walked toward the guesthouse from the parking lot, I had crossed paths with Brother Matt, a young monk with whom I am not acquainted. Matt is in his thirties, close to my age. "Hello," I said, as our paths met. He returned the greeting. After a moment he added, "Are you here on retreat?"

"No, but I visit often."

He nodded as we went a few more steps. "Do you live nearby?"

"I used to, but now I live on the coast. Brother Martin and I are close."

A smile flashed across his face. "Yes," he laughed, "who isn't close with Brother Martin!"

Visiting with Martin on the porch, I tell him about the exchange. He grips my forearm, his eyes spritely. "Ah, don't believe him!" he gushes. "My friendship with you, it is a special grace."

Martin continues, "You know, to have someone who understands things, like the communion of saints, or silent music . . . just to have someone to share my pains with—it is a special grace."

He looks into my eyes and I realize I don't want to be one of his five hundred friends. I feel Martin understands my soul better than anyone, ever, and I want this to be the result of a unique friendship. But I also stand back and observe my clinging, my old hunger to stand out and be special. I bring it into awareness.

Then Martin says, "At night, like at 10:30, I can go just blank. I feel too tired to do anything. Too tried to read. Too tired to pray. I don't want any more words. So I just sit and listen to Tricia's silent music. . . . You are a real lifesaver!"

Tricia's silent music. It is something Martin has started saying. Though I don't understand all that it means, I know it denotes a deep soul communion. And while I see the clinging in my satisfaction upon hearing the words, I am also deeply grateful for the experience of friendship I've been given with Martin.

I had been reading a book he loaned me, *Burro Genius* by Victor Villaseñor, and I ask Martin about Villaseñor's experiences, how he hears trees talking to him, and how he encounters the spirits of animals. I ask if this is part of Mexican culture. The thought of souls communing across time and space seems to mesh well with Villaseñor's experiences.

"When I read Villaseñor's book *Rain of Gold*," he replies, "it was just like hearing my mother talk." Martin's mother, Carmen, had been profoundly spiritual. Years ago, Martin told me about her, how she and his dad had opened their cracker-box home to every passerby in need, adding more to the soup pot to feed them, whatever she could find to accommodate surprise guests. The family home was a two-room structure along the rail lines outside San Diego, with a pump out front, a toilet in an out-building down the way, one tree in the dusty yard.

"It was like when I saw part of *The Exorcist*," Martin continues. "My mom could have dictated that movie . . . the way she experienced spirits!" he explains. "We have gotten so technical. We miss so much of what's going on around us . . . a lot of spirit, a lot of *mystery*."

"The other night, I could swear I felt my grandma's presence in the moonlight," I tell him. My paternal grandmother, my penny-pinching, fruit-leather-making grandma with whom I was very close, had died just a few weeks prior, while I was in Canada serving again with CPT. "It was a full moon, and around midnight it shone directly into my room. I left all the blinds open and lay on my bed in the light. Out my windows, I could see the moon reflecting on the ocean. I felt like the moon was bathing me in protection and that my grandmother was watching over me, somehow, in that moonlight."

I change the subject. "Martin, I am a little nervous about this move." My eyes wander to the tall oak trees in front of the abbey, then back to Martin's gaze. "I don't know if I'll be able to make it, with the higher rent and all. What if I can't find a good job in Cannon Beach?"

Martin tells me how anxious he feels when he goes to the city, or into a big, new store. "I feel so out of place," he says, braiding his insecurity into mine. I take in the tranquility of the trees, dozens of varieties within immediate view, and think about living in a place like the abbey. "But, Tricia," Martin continues, "it is a real faith journey. . . . I know you are going to be okay."

◆

And we are.

During the next week, Madison and I move. Just a month later, I land a part-time job—a good job, as Curator/Program Director/Grant Writer for the Cannon Beach History Center and Museum. The job is a block from my house (which is five minutes walk from the beach), tailor-fit to my skills, and leaves time and energy for writing. Once again, opportunities open before my eyes like poppies in afternoon sunlight.

Late that summer I decide, once and for all, to leave my marriage. I had recognized with a new certainty that it would not last when I fantasized ways for the marriage to end: Darryl could move far away; he could meet and fall in love with someone else; he could die. When I found myself hoping again for a split, I knew it was time.

During that summer I'd written a poem about Darryl, the death of his beloved cat, and the demise of our marriage. At the time, I didn't realize what the poem implied and neither did Darryl. But within weeks of writing it, I tell Darryl what I have been trying to tell him for two years. I tell him, with a clarity that devastates us both, that our marriage is over.

Sleep and Waking

I love how you looked,
stepping from the car with your cat
dead in a veterinarian's box. All your
beauty in pained eyes and bent

lips. Long hug on the driveway, next to
where she lay on the hood, rigid in her
cardboard casket. Your sobs released
like the scent of lavender in fresh fists
or unearthed tales buried in the droll

silt of genocide. How it feels to feel.
The tears I would replace with joy
or passion. But I'd keep the tenderness,
the soul's deep hammock of longing.
This is how it feels, can you see?

Months later, into surgery with you.
Skateboard injury. One more round
of anesthesia, you—a stone rolled
blissfully away. I imagine you before

the traumas that folded your heart
like a fan. A boy alert to nightmare
and dream, crawling to mother's bed
full of ghosts. The tinseled autumn
before numbness set in and overtook

you. Your doctors, so gentle,
ushering you to the velvet state
I can never attain. The drugs you
save for rainy days when my wild
heart and blunt-truth ax strike deep

beneath the layers of sleep. The bed
of my love, no comfort. Slow tearing
asunder, the one dry wound
that somehow you manage to feel.

Mothers & Daughters

I watch how you watch me
while you pretend not to notice—
a mother's life like a nature program
depicting embarrassing things.
Two animals having sex, perhaps,
or a female giving birth. Someday
will you say: *What a wonder!*
The delicate workings, the grace
in it all, seeing how I struggle
toward life? You, the cautious one,
who will hold a steady job when time
comes, keep one husband, a sensible match
you will choose by ticks on a page.
Not altogether fair you have me—
a puff of air, and not a family home
in the country you can work and save
for, buy one day for your own child,
a daughter who will long for alien
lands, exotic people, the jolting
twist at the end of every tale.

CHAPTER EIGHT

Healing Voice

That night I choose a sexy shirt—close-fitting, light pink, and revealing of cleavage. I sweep my hair into one style, then another. I hopelessly loofah the calluses on my big toes before applying lotion and paint my toenails for the first time in ten years. Sheer light pink, like the shirt.

Ten days earlier I had met two Mexican guys who were re-roofing my house. Though neither was bad looking, I was drawn to Miguel. He had stunning sweet eyes and muscular arms on a stocky frame. He caught me looking at him through the window, and started glancing my direction as he worked. When Miguel returned from his lunch break, I mustered the courage to say hello. I peeked out the door and asked where he was from. Despite my cursory Spanish, a conversation ensued, and when his co-worker Sebastian returned, he joined in. Before long they'd offered to teach me Spanish—at least to hone skills I already had. They wanted more than a student, I was sure, but they seemed polite. I liked them. I invited both to dinner, ten days from that date, 6:30 p.m, at my house. We would speak only Spanish. Maybe even sing.

When I look back on what was to happen, what would follow, I wonder at the things in my head those ten days: the thoughts and anxieties about the future, the reaching out for connection, the gnawing physical neediness, the lust. The loneliness and fear. The vagueness of my memories mean I will never really know.

♦

Ten days pass.

For dinner I cook chicken enchiladas with sautéed onions, topped with fresh cilantro. I crumble cotija cheese into a small bowl and slice iceberg lettuce and cucumbers onto a plate. I sprinkle the cucumbers with dill.

Sebastian phones at 6:08 to ask if I need anything, announcing "we've stopped at the store, but we're on our way." Plopped into a chair with my legs crossed, I raise a glass of wine, my heel swinging. Tracy Grammer sings softly in the background. For the first time in ten days, I feel beautiful.

Miguel and Sebastian pull up in a white '64 Ford Mustang. When I see them, I descend the stairs of my second-story apartment and traipse onto the porch to say hello as Sebastian hands me a dozen white roses and shakes my hand. "*Como estas?*" Miguel greets me, carrying a six-pack of Corona. He is as handsome as I'd remembered, though I notice the weathered-ness of his face at close range. "*Bien,*" I reply to Miguel then thank Sebastian for the roses.

It takes ten minutes and moving to the dinner table for our edges to soften, but once they do, they are velvet. I speak mostly Spanish, with a bit of translation assistance from Sebastian, and conversation flows. Immigration. Family. Financial woes. Big subjects right off.

Sebastian had immigrated to the U.S. in the early '90s from Mexico City. His father was a U.S. citizen of Spanish decent, his mother Mexican, and he'd moved with them. He was legal. By 2003, when Miguel made the leap, the process had become very difficult and dangerous for undocumented immigrants. Accompanied by ten others, Miguel journeyed through the desert for two days. He explains that as hard as this was, getting into the U.S. is now far more difficult than it was in 2003. "People can work strenuously their entire lives," Sebastian says, describing life in Mexico, "and not reach financial security." A smile breaks the seriousness of his face. "Mexicans who think they can make it will come north," he says. "I'm sorry—they just will!"

We continue talking at the table long after supper, after the sun has set and our only light is a dying candle and a glowing paper star in the corner of the room. "*Mucho gusto,*" I tell them. I am glad to meet you. They are glad too.

The rest of the evening we sing—songs in Spanish they teach me, and my own songs I play for them on guitar. When I finish a song, Miguel claps and shakes his head. When I glance his way, he appears focused and soft, and I sing to him. He is so nice to sing to.

Afterward Madison, having arrived home from a day at a friend's, joins us for a walk to the beach. The sky is a circus tent of stars, the air warm and still. We stand at the water's edge, gazing up at the sky, then around at each other, our bodies silhouetted in the dim light. Miguel's eyes and mine, moths to flame all evening. My mind sinking, sinking, then gone.

A week and a half later I receive a long "love note" message on my answering machine from Miguel, in Spanish. "I cannot stop thinking of you," he says, his voice cracking just slightly. He goes on about my green eyes, how interesting and intelligent I am, how much he wants to see me again. "I like you very much, Teresa," he finishes, "I like you very much." I save the message and replay it several times.

Miguel calls again two weeks later, this time leaving a number. I call him back and we set up a date. I have recently told Darryl our marriage is over, and in a way I cannot detect, I am reeling, careening downward in a manner that feels like ascension but is actually a dive, the way it feels when you've had too much to drink. I am stumbling, but in my imagination, my gait is steady, my judgment unhindered.

On that first date Miguel and I walk to the beach from my house, grabbing a large blanket on the way out. We sit by Haystack Rock as the sun slips below the horizon. Under the cover of dark, we make out. We talk about past romantic relationships, about our families and our dreams. Miguel had been married once and has three children in Mexico, and he tells me how he misses them.

Though I haven't been drinking, I feel wild and a little inebriated. On the way home, I ask Miguel about spirituality—whether he cares about it. "No," he says, "I am not a spiritual person." Then he grows quiet, as if my question has disturbed him.

Before he parts with me at my door he asks, "Can I say *I love you?*" I hesitantly nod yes. "I love you. I love you, Teresa," he says. "I like you even more than before this night. This is the best night of my life." He kisses me again and again before climbing into his car, waving as he drives away.

Twice that week, Miguel visits my house. On one occasion we go walking with Madison at Oswald West State Park. As we pass enormous evergreens, Miguel tells me of a forest in Mexico, trees over 1,000 years old. I tell him of the redwoods in northern California, about the 2,000-year-old trees I had seen there. "Wow," he exclaims, "I would love to see that." He seems earnestly appreciative of nature.

My dog trails alongside us on a leash, and he plays with her shouting "Fiona! Fiona!" He jogs ahead to excite her. He tells me about the dog he'd had for sixteen years at his parents' house in Mexico, how much he'd loved her. On a wobbly, wood-slat bridge crossing a creek, he reaches out to me and holds my arm. "Don't worry," he insists, "I will catch you."

"*O-kay,*" I offer hesitantly, "I will trust you then."

"What is that word," he asks, "'trust'?" I explain it to him. "Trust," he repeats, the word misshapen and awkward on his tongue, "trust. . . . You can trust me."

On another occasion, Miguel eats dinner with Madison and me at our house. We watch half of *The Color Purple,* my favorite film and one of the few I own with subtitles. He perches in a chair behind the spot where I'm propped against it. He leans over my shoulders, his arms folded around me, touching me or kissing my neck the entire time, running his fingers through my hair.

I am losing my head. I like the feeling *immensely.*

Before coming to my house, he calls to say he's on his way. I watch for him from my window, then skip down the stairs to greet him from my porch as he pulls up. Each time he steps from his car, it is the same: surprise at how much I adore him, surprise I get to spend time with someone so nice to hug. He is five-seven and of muscular build. He has neat, thick, gelled hair, and Mayan-esque features: a flattish nose and almond-shaped eyes. His eyes are mesmerizing, like the rising, full moon. He has a marvelous backside.

About a week later, he arrives looking particularly handsome in a white long-sleeved soccer jersey and khaki cargo pants. It is Saturday evening and Madison is out of town. As we walk through the front door, I turn to kiss him, and he puts his hands on my face, pulls me into him. Our bodies, close and ready.

We are headed to the beach with a wool blanket and down sleeping bag when he suggests we drive to Humboldt Beach. "Too many people at Cannon Beach," he says, and I know what he is thinking. We take his car, an old BMW he's borrowed from a friend. Slouching into the seat with my head back, I smile at him. I feel more alive than I've felt in years.

As I step out of the car at Humboldt, Miguel hugs me big and long and kisses me again, then turns to retrieve the keys he's absent-mindedly left in the ignition. He is brimming with nervous energy. Silently, we walk toward the beach. "How was work today?" he finally asks, breaking the silence.

"Fine," I say. "Nothing exciting to report, really." Again, we are quiet.

Continuing until we've reached an unpopulated, secluded section of open sand, we spread out our blanket and climb under the unzipped down bag. Slowly we proceed, whispering to each other, instructing. The sun hovers on the horizon. Waves fold onto the widening shore like hands.

We lay and talk for three hours. Miguel starts out serious and confessional, telling how he missed his kids and mother, about his gambling problem (he'd lost $300 the previous weekend). "I spend everything I make," he divulges, sounding embarrassed, "other than what I send for my kids. . . . I should be saving for the future." He lies on his back, me in the crook of his arm, and his hands move over me constantly.

Turning his head, he looks into my eyes. "I feel lonely, I guess. . . . So I go spend money." He turns back to the sky. "That's what I have here, a good job and paycheck. Nothing else." He wants to open a savings account the following week, he contends, to stop blowing his money, start putting it away. He won't gamble anymore.

"At work I am impatient," he continues in his confessional tone. "When I can't get things done, I get frustrated and angry. . . . I work too hard," he adds. It is clear he needs to tell me these things, to get them off his chest and into the middle of our room.

When the conversation turns to me, it lightens. I toss in Spanish words as I'm able. "So I got all this education, and now I'm a poor writer!" I explain with a laugh. He laughs along. I tell him about my projects and how I like to create things. Sliding his hand over me, he tells of his dark past as a teenager in Mexico City—gangs, drugs, recklessness. He pulls me into him, into a tight embrace, and kisses my face. He asks for words in English when he's stumped. "I could stay here all night," he says, "I will never forget this memory."

We talk until the sun fully sets and the air begins to cool. On the way home Miguel plays Spanish love songs—the words about him and me, he explains. In my driveway, he sings to me, translating the words as he goes. *Only you know who I am . . . only you know the way I feel—you, changing the way I think.* "I love you, love you," he says again. At my door: "Dream of me."

I see Miguel for about six weeks beyond that. After the first two weeks, which were blissful and surreal, the relationship begins a fast downward spiral. Half-blind, I struggle to see as far as I can through the muddle. I try to let loving action dictate my behavior without allowing infatuated feelings to distort my mind, all while trying to heed my gut, which tells me something is *terribly* wrong.

I try hard not to react. I try not to distrust Miguel for his differences from me. Struggling to sift through cultural perceptions and misunderstandings, I try not to mistake certain actions, such as lateness and unreliability, for disrespect. I try to communicate clearly and to understand Miguel though he and I are both unskilled in the other's language. I try to give Miguel a chance, instead of reacting to bad experiences I've had in the distant past. *It is like walking a high-wire with my feet tied together after downing a full bottle of wine.*

On two occasions during our two months our dating, I tell Miguel I need a break for a week, I need space. I ask him many questions. His answers seem sincere.

◆

Readers may wonder at my sexual ethics at that point in time, and with good cause. I offer no excuses. I was experimenting, for sure—having sex with someone I barely knew and could not say that I loved, who was undeniably risky. I had no illusions of commitment or a long future with him. It was a relationship inconsistent with earlier beliefs I'd held about sexuality and with beliefs I hold now. It was inconsistent with what I tell my teenaged daughter. It was inconsistent in so many ways. Period. It was a mistake.

But it was a mistake I needed to make.

From the start of the relationship, I am honest with Miguel. Early on, he asks if I will ever marry him. I doubt I will ever marry again, I explain (a self-defensive illusion I hold at this time). Though I hope to find someone to be with for a very long time, I add, I do not plan to marry. Still, I worry Miguel will misinterpret my resolve as personal rejection, that I will hurt him.

One morning, a month after I've started seeing Miguel, Brother Martin calls. I am in the shower when the phone rings. I run to the phone dripping-wet, wrapped in a towel. I am happy to hear Martin on the line.

"How is your heart?" he asks with his husky, earnest voice.

"I am confused . . . and scared," I tell him. "I can't seem to think clearly." Martin recommends I back off, take it easy for a time. "You are a person of great depth," Martin says. "It will take a very unique person to appreciate you. Miguel is probably just focused on making a living." I don't want to believe this. Despite our different backgrounds and lives, I like to think Miguel and I can appreciate one another. Almost reading my mind, Martin adds, "It would be very hard for Miguel to appreciate you.

"But it is all part of the journey of loving," he continues. "And I still think it is better to love."

Before hanging up, I tell Martin, "I love you." I decide to keep my heart open, but I know I need to be smarter. I think about

Martin's phrase "the journey of loving." I'm so confused at this time, so unsure of what interpersonal love is, especially how it relates to my experiences with Miguel. But it is a prescient phrase. Martin can see, in ways I cannot, how I am groping my way on the path to real love.

Until Miguel, I had never been with someone as expressive of affection and warmth as I am. However insane the relationship, it carries this blessing. Miguel's way of *physically* expressing adoration, and the experience of meeting that in another, is a gift. Sitting together watching a movie or studying English, touching and kissing, being physically awake and alive to one another, Miguel and I are an extraordinary physical match. I absorb his affection like a sponge left in the sun an entire drought-ridden summer. When we eat together, talk, or sit and drink coffee, his eyes fix on mine unflinchingly. He walks up behind me as I cook and slips his arms around my waist, pulls me into him, and kisses my neck. I feel it *every*where. He meets my passion perfectly and holds back nothing. Our lovemaking plays out many wishes I have had for a "lover."

Except that it lacks the presence of true love.

In the midst of my last marriage, I had begun to think it impossible to find a man expressive of physical affection the way I am. Maybe there was no such person. Maybe I was *too* physically expressive, my need for touch too great, my sexual passion too expansive. Darryl once jokingly compared me to our cat who liked to get in your face, butting her head against you repeatedly, demanding affection. She'd work herself into such a frenzy one wanted to hurl her across the room like a basketball. Spittle would drip from the corners of her mouth onto one's hands.

I may be amorous . . . but not like that. Having my dispassionate husband insinuate I was did not go over well. Still, even if I am not like Velvet the cat, maybe my passion *is* too much to match. *Maybe*, I thought, *I am destined for celibacy, or a life of unreciprocated affection and physical love. Forget it,* I say, *shoot me now.*

Being with Miguel assures me it is possible to have my expressions of affection reciprocated. If that assurance had been all I took from the experience, it would have been enough.

But even though Miguel and I are a tremendous match in some respects, we are in other areas, as Martin gently reminds me, incongruous. His differences render him intriguing to me, though, and me to him. I am eager to learn about his life, and he seems genuinely interested in mine. He tells me stories of growing up in Mexico City, about his enormous family who live all together, to this day, in one neighborhood. He tells me of his travels to reach this country, and of the process by which he got to the Oregon Coast.

Many unsavory details about himself and his life surface in these talks, about his troubled youth when he was a prolific street brawler, about his hard drug use in Mexico, about his neglect of his children as he traveled around Mexico as an electrician (he had married in his early twenties). He tells me how his wife left him for a more stable man after he'd moved to Juarez to find work. Though he doesn't express much compassion for her, neither does he glorify himself. Shortly after their split, he came to the U.S.

Miguel tells me of problems he's had in the States: gambling, repeated traffic tickets, irresponsibility with money, involvement with two different unsavory women, both white and American. At times my gut tells me not to believe Miguel, but he throws in so many unflattering details, I figure he must be telling the truth. *If a man is going to lie, wouldn't he at least try to make himself look good?!* I ask myself. I keep ignoring my gut.

Still, Miguel is perpetually undependable. At times I buckle under the frustration. He often doesn't call when he says he will call, or come by when I am expecting him. At times I glimpse an intense need to control, a need he usually represses with me, knowing I dislike controlling men. A *"feminista,"* is what I'm called in his language.

At one point he tells me he wants to change my hair, to have it cut to the chin and permed. "Absolutely not," is my prompt reply. My hair is stubbornly straight and does not keep a curl. It is long and straight. That is how it is; that is how I like it. End of discussion. He acts mildly hurt by my reaction, and I suspect he reads my resistance as indifference, as though he assumes a woman who likes a man will naturally change her hair for him.

The times I request time apart, I sense a cooling in Miguel, an insecure withdrawing, as if he takes my request as an indication I do not like him. "It's not that I don't care about you," I reassure, "or that I don't like being with you. . . . I *really* like being with you. It is just that I need time to think." Still, my assurances do not penetrate his insecurity. He probably hasn't heard this request from a woman, his past relationships having been with women who were emotionally needy or who had acute *financial* need of him.

At the time, I don't think of this. Later I know that Miguel read my reserve, my need for space, as rejection. And the hurt this caused him is my deepest regret.

Sometimes Miguel says things that unveil his intransigent insecurity. "Tricia," he said on one occasion, "you can show me your books, your paintings, your poems, but I have nothing to show you." He laughs a bit, but it is a laugh that masks sadness. "I have nothing to show you," he says again. Once, when he visits my house after a day of hard work, he lightheartedly quips, "Don't touch me, I'm a dirty Mexican." On two occasions when we are sitting at the dinner table, he remarks out of the blue, "I have just never lived this way before." He says it with hesitancy in his voice, like a kid, uncertain whether he can live up to imagined expectations placed on him.

A twinge of guilt squeezes through me. It makes me resent what my gut keeps chanting: *You are not being respected. You are being used. You are being lied to.* I ignore it some more.

Miguel needn't be insecure. He has much to give: his expressiveness, his good-natured sense of humor, his intuitive sense of how people feel, his sweetness, his natural intelligence, his affection, and his commitment to doing good work, his beauty and ability as a lover. Miguel possesses many admirable qualities, though he seems blind to them all.

Despite my need to draw back, I come to care deeply for Miguel. I want his best. I express this to him repeatedly, though I am not sure he believes me. I am gentle toward him, even when I feel confused or frustrated. Miguel brings out gentleness. He is atypically *adore*-able. Expressions on his face, the way his hands always reach out to express affection or comfort, his bear-hugging arms—he is nearly *irresistible*. He knows I pray for him. Still, he continually asks if I will someday marry him. "No," I contend, "I won't." The last time we spend together, he asks about marriage *three* times. He is trying to be charming, to soften me. He pulls out all the stops, putting his head on my shoulder, telling me how nice I look, saying he wants to change his life and he needs me to help him. In his desperation, he has become sloppy.

He has become obvious.

The last days of the relationship are an unfurling, a devolution that includes my receiving repeated hang-up calls and mild threats from his drug-addicted, obsessive, emotionally unstable ex-girl-friend (an American), who I find out, in the end, was never an ex.

I discover this on the day she calls and leaves a message on my machine threatening to kill me (fortunately, this was a week Madison was out of town). When I hear the message, I immediately walk the two blocks to the police station, answering machine clutched under my arm. I turn in the recording. I file a report of phone harassment and the woman never calls me again.

Miguel, it turns out, had lied to me repeatedly and ingeniously about the girlfriend, and about other aspects of his life, such as where he lived. I was led to believe he lived with his brother's family, when he was actually living with the girlfriend. He had lied about his occasional hard drug use, something the police also clued me in to. All of the lies rested on elaborate, convincing stories Miguel had told.

Miguel had told me about his "ex"-girlfriend, and I knew she hounded him. She sounded like a racist, abusive, crack mom with a low IQ. She was not attractive. I couldn't comprehend why Miguel had been with her, but when he described the situation he emphasized his compassion. He felt sorry for her; she had no one; she needed a friend. Still, I could not understand why he had gotten together with her in the first place. Perhaps he just needed *someone* and she was the someone who came along. Whatever the case, Miguel was, in a sense, the best thing that had happened to her. Naturally she was holding on for dear life.

The more the scene unravels, the more unspeakable it becomes—the way I had been treated, the way I had treated Miguel's girlfriend. What is likewise unspeakable is how my gut saw it coming, and my mind refused, repeatedly, to listen.

While Miguel's affection for me had almost always seemed real, he had not learned to care for a person ingenuously. While he possessed a great *potential* for love and friendship, he had chosen to live by love's opposite: a calculating deceitfulness. On the day of my discovery, I feel as if the warm, caring Miguel I knew had never existed. . . . Or perhaps I had glimpsed the real Miguel, his essential goodness, a goodness he nevertheless allowed his shadow to overtake. The Miguel I glimpsed *did* recognize love. Part of him even longed for it, and for its source, which I call God.

One evening Miguel and I talked about Brother Martin. "He prays for you," I'd told him. Miguel smiled and nodded his head slowly. "That is good," he'd said, "I need that." His voice was thoughtful and serious.

"My mother prays for me a lot," he divulged, "and sometimes, when I talk to my kids on the phone, they tell me God loves me." He was obviously moved by their expressions of love.

"When will I get to meet Martin?" Miguel asked that night. "Soon, I hope."

"I want to learn how to pray," Miguel offered. "*Quiero paz en mi alma* (I want peace in my soul)," he continued, in a voice that was sincere and pensive. Miguel told me he never prayed, though he understood it was important.

At times, I'd told Miguel God loved him. He became very quiet when I told him this. He looked at me a moment, then said, with deep feeling, "Thank you, Tricia. Thank you very much."

◆

I run into Miguel just after learning about the girlfriend, a few hours later. I am on my bike, headed to the post office, and Miguel is literally standing in the road as I pedal by—a miracle of timing.

I brake abruptly and dismount my bike. "What are you doing, Tricia?" he asks with a quizzical grin.

"Do you enjoy lying to people?" I ask him. He shrugs and averts his eyes from my stare, looking up the road. It is obvious he knows what I mean.

I motion for him to follow me down a quiet, desolate side street where we can talk. He follows. When I stop, he stops. He leans his back to the wall of a building abutting the sidewalk. Defensiveness has cast his sweet face in dull steel.

"You know, all you are interested in is using someone," I say, my voice sharp and insistent. "You want someone to take care of you. . . . That's it."

As I make these accusations, he turns his head from the right to the left, right, then left, unable to look in my eyes. In his sagging, averted eyes and the droop of his shoulders, I can see that my accusations are correct. "I'm right, aren't I?" I insist.

He begins to shake his head "no," but stops.

"How could you lie to me all this time, about so many things," I shake my head, my eyes narrowing. "It is unbelievable. . . I just can't believe it."

Miguel shrugs his shoulders as he looks up the road and down at the sidewalk. When he looks up I see his eyes redden and grow damp.

"Well, I really cared about you . . . really *care* about you," I continue, forcing him to meet my gaze. "I will *always* care about you, Miguel. I am not sorry that I met you."

He reaches out and takes my hand, which is limp, non-responsive. My hands are freezing cold. He slowly takes the soft, cotton work-gloves off his hands and threads them onto my own with no assistance from me.

"I want you to find happiness," I tell him, struggling to steady my voice. "I think you have a good heart . . . deep down."

As I say these things, Miguel looks in my eyes. His gaze has softened and he reaches up and strokes my face as I speak, runs his fingers through the ends of my hair. I will not touch him back. He takes one of my cold hands in his two hands and tries to warm it. Then he does the other.

"I've changed my phone number," I say, my voice steadied. "I won't be giving it to you." He lowers his gaze, then looks away. When he looks up at me he appears sad, even heartbroken. Throughout the exchange he's said less than fifteen words. He continues to hold my gimpy hand.

Finally I take hold of my bike and turn to leave. "I need to be going," I tell him. As he slowly nods, I say, "Don't forget how much I care about you, Miguel. Don't ever forget that."

"I will never forget it," he says. His voice is earnest and strong. "Not for my whole life." I start to take off his gloves, but he insists I keep them, clutching them onto my limp hands. I take them back and start to ride away. "Be careful," he calls as I ascend a steep hill toward my house.

◆

In the weeks following that nightmare day, my emotions run the gamut. Profound sadness comes first, mixed with seething anger. Then the anger ascends while sadness diminishes. Relief makes a showing, and all of my feelings are laced with an effusive thankfulness to God that I am okay.

Once anger has run its course, I am left with sadness alone. This lasts a couple of weeks. It is followed by embarrassment. I feel like one of those women who hears a man's swooning prattle and separates like cling wrap from her own brain. I feel detrimental to my mental health. This sentiment, a sort of baffled shock at my actions, lasts a few weeks. It is followed by more sadness. This time the sadness remains.

As distance and clarity broaden, I come to see a sort of inevitability in my choices. I realize how much I learned from the experience, and I realize that Miguel, without realizing it, had given me something important—the experience of physical reciprocity I had always hoped for.

When I was in high school, a mentor of mine struggled with closet alcoholism and landed in treatment. When he told me how he'd struggled during the years we were close, during the time he'd been a supportive friend to me, I told him, "I'm sorry I wasn't there for you. I was so self-absorbed, I hadn't helped you at all." In response he said, "Tricia, there was nothing you could have done. It was something I needed to do, something I had to live through. There is really nothing anyone could have done to stop it."

In the weeks following my last real conversation with Miguel, I remember this interaction. Like my mentor, I don't think there is any way I, being who I was at the time, could have lived the experience differently.

Before splitting with Darryl, I had not known the deepest depths of loneliness, or had not known them for years. As disconnected as he was from me, Darryl's presence allayed my loneliness to some extent. When I made the decision to end our marriage, and when Darryl, for the sake of his heart, asked that I have no contact with him for a few months, I became desperately lonely.

My loneliness during this time stems, in part, from fear, a sudden fear about making it financially, the fear of being abandoned by everyone I know. I feel like I've jumped from a burning building and suddenly no one stands below me with a net. Most of my support group have rolled their eyes and walked away. My heart twists and convulses. In this state, I let affection for and from Miguel distract me. For a handful of weeks he filled the huge, gaping void in my belly, a void that, on occasion, crept into my throat and made me choke.

Some may wonder how, after such a profound experience of God's presence and love in Oceanside, I could have descended into a mind-bending state of loneliness and fear for the future. All I can say is: I am in good company. Any spiritual person who has not experienced the depths of despair and stumbling, and who thinks she is exempt, better brace herself. It is coming.

But though connectedness to God does not exempt us from struggle, from losing our heads on occasion and breaking our own hearts with our bumbling, it does bathe the experience in love. And throughout the entire debacle with Miguel, I continued to feel that divine love. The love of God.

"Jesus loves women," Martin always said, and that means the clumsy and broken ones too. I came to know this, as the old Quakers said, "experimentally." The sense of beloved-ness that had eluded me so much of my life, as I strove to be good, to earn love, to be a nice girl, continued to fill me at that time of flailing. Not for a minute did I doubt that the compassionate, gracious love of God was there for me. That I was absolutely, absurdly loved, even when I was being absolutely absurd. And maybe, I think, that is the point.

♦

In the weeks following my goodbye to Miguel, as I work through my emotional pot pourri, I am sometimes gripped by an intense compulsion to pray for him. Not a short prayer, but for hours. A mantra runs behind my thoughts as I venture through the day: *Please show Miguel the way to love.* By "the way to love" I do not mean "how to," but "the direction to." I don't mean the way to a certain person or situation, but to whatever and whomever will demonstrate to Miguel true love. My prayer is that God will direct Miguel to love somewhere in this world, so that he can experience it, and dwell in it, and find joy and freedom. I pray this dozens of times a day, in and out like breathing. I have to—something compels me. The compulsion is healing.

A few weeks after I'd talked to Miguel in town, I see him at a distance. This happens on two separate occasions. He spots me as well, and we stare at each other across a wide chasm. Both times, my spirit sags under the brokenness.

Three days before I leave to spend Christmas with friends and family around Newberg, I decide to call Miguel and tell him "*Feliz Navidad.*" I call him from work so he won't know my number. "I will hold you in the light over the holiday," I tell him, "*en la luz.*"

"Oh, thank you," he replies earnestly. "Thank you very much for calling me," he adds.

An hour later, he calls back, asking if I will give him my home number, which I tell him I cannot do.

The next day, as I am running errands for work, I run into Miguel three times within the course of fifteen minutes. The timing is uncanny. We say hello and smile. Next time we wave. He asks if he can drop by my house sometime to visit (I say "*sure,*" knowing he never will). The final time we pass, he seems almost giddy, leaning out of his truck with a huge smile on his face, waving his whole arm like a child. That day he honks his horn as he drives past my house. He has never honked his horn. He seems elated.

I spend three days around Christmas at the abbey, where the compulsion to pray for Miguel grows intense. The mantra-prayer loops in my head for days: *Please show Miguel the way to love. Please show Miguel the way to love. Please show Miguel the way to love.* There had been times in the prior weeks that I had longed intensely to touch him, even knowing how he'd treated me, even knowing his duplicity, and I had to fight the longing. I missed his voice on the phone, the way he said, "Thank you, Baby"; I missed the patchouli smell of his skin and his hair; I missed reading the Sandra Cisneros book with him on my bed and drinking coffee together. I missed the feel of his arms, his earlobes. My body missed his. Miguel had become an addiction.

Over Christmas, a switch inside of me gets flipped. I no longer feel an intense desire to be with him. I still want to hold him in God's love and to pray for him. But I feel a new kind of warmth for him, something separate from need or longing. I know God loves Miguel immensely. It is as if my heart has started feeling some of that love.

During the early part of December I'd experienced a time of pronounced stress. Besides the events of my own life, which, as I've told, were harried, and apart from concerns about facing the holidays twice-divorced, a friend of mine, James Loney, along with three other members/delegates of CPT, was being held hostage in Iraq. They'd been taken captive in late November. Jim was the CPT Canada Co-Director, and I had worked with him on different projects related to Grassy Narrows. I felt a special affinity with him, as we are both writers.

A deadline for the threatened execution of Jim and the others came and went with no news. Nothing was known of their whereabouts. During those weeks I thought of my friend Jim many times each day. Around the deadline, I was fraught with worry, an unhealthy worry for him and the others. As sometimes happens in times of stress, I became sick. Mid-December through early January, I was ill by varying degrees.

As the deadline for the execution of the CPTers passed without incident, my acute fear gradually faded to an omnipresent concern. When I thought of them, I whispered a mantra: *Jesus, have mercy,* over and over. CPTers across the globe were banding together in advocacy and prayer for the hostages. Groups were meeting for prayer and vigils in many parts of the world, calling for the release of these hostages and for the release of thousands of illegally detained Iraqis. But in the far western states at the time there were few CPTers, and I had not connected with groups on the coast who gathered for this sort of prayer and advocacy. I carried my heavy burden for Jim and the others alone. My prayers for them, for peace in Iraq, came out of solitude.[9]

In early January I carry these concerns with me to a meditation group I am attending at the time. Being an introvert, I have barely met the others who attend, but I enjoy the set times of meditation in their company.

With the gong of the bell, I close my eyes and enter into the deepest meditation I have experienced in my life. For me, spiritual connectedness in meditation feels like being entered, like something comes and fills me so full I am swollen with love, with the eternal. It feels like the *me* part of me moves aside to make room for a divine presence so beautiful I want it to stay as long as possible, to keep myself open and undistracted for as long as I can before the me elbows her way back in and closes the door.

In reality, of course, *I* do not exit at all. Instead my *ego* gets out of the way so that my true being can merge with the Being and love underlying everything. I cannot bring on the connectedness. But I can be receptive or unreceptive to it. This experience in meditation is, for me, sensory—an actual physical feeling, not just a state of heart or consciousness I associate with spiritual awareness, which can exist anywhere. The entered-ness I am describing happens only when I sit and get my ego out of the way.

I have experienced this entered-ness on many occasions, but always very briefly, never more than one or two minutes at a time. On this day, it comes for the entire twenty minutes of silence (it is a shorter meditation session than usual). I feel full of God, full to the gills, full to the brim of every quark of every cell of my body. It is a feeling like weight, but not heavy. That morning I am sitting under an elephant, and it feels incredibly good.

My mind remains still throughout most of the session, yet to some extent I am thinking and observing my thoughts. First I feel deeply connected to my friend Jim in Iraq, and then to Tom Fox, who is with him, whom I have never even met. I can sense their presence like they are right beside me, or even inside of me, like the God-force in both my heart and their hearts has pulled us together like strong magnets, across time and space, and in the case of Tom, despite unfamiliarity with one another.

Then I feel Miguel present to me, in a way different than Jim or Tom, but even more present. Perhaps it is actually my spirit being present to him. In any case, I feel as if he is held in the presence of God within me, and I keep holding him there. This lasts a long time—several minutes. It is not quite like thinking, because I am not having thoughts of Miguel so much as feeling a bond with him as I hold him in that light. Later I remember what I'd told Miguel before Christmas: "I will hold you *en la luz*." My brain automatically plays the mantra I'd repeated hundreds of times around Christmas: *Please show Miguel the way to love.* It is as if the prayer is being prayed through me.

During this session, I feel I weigh thousands of pounds. I feel like a twenty-ton boulder, my body a piece of the ancient earth. My hands feel as if they could crush my legs with their weight.

After the bell gongs again, I remain aware of God's presence but no longer entered or "filled." The physical sensations of deep union pass. Still, my eyes remain closed as a member of the group shares a reading.

As I sit reflecting, I think how strange it is, the recurrent, pressing compulsion to pray for Miguel. It is almost like I have a new small task—one that isn't so small: to hold Miguel in God's light, and to love him. To love him at a distance and anonymously, with an almost sisterly kind of love, but to love him the way God loves him. As I think of this driving home, it fills me with a mixture of joy and sadness.

By the time I get home, joy has made its way to the foreground, and I am energized enough to take a beachwalk with my dog, Fiona. After weeks of sickness from colds, fungus-allergies (which I have, that winter, discovered), and the flu, which I'd picked up at Christmas, I have neglected her. I haven't walked Fiona on the beach for over a week. I head toward the sand via one of my two usual routes.

Both routes take me past a hotel where Miguel and his coworkers have been working, a hotel just north of my house, but directly on the beach. It is undergoing a process of remodeling, so many of the rooms are not currently rented to guests, and Miguel and others have done various remodeling jobs there for several weeks. On the route I take to the beach that day, I walk down stairs just fifteen yards north of the hotel. I've been taking this route for months. Though I've taken it several times during the weeks Miguel has worked at the hotel, I have never seen him.

As I reach the sand at the bottom of the stairs, I glance up at the windows on the far end of the hotel's north side. Written on the inside of one of the windows in large masking-tape letters is the message, "Hi Fiona." Miguel had enjoyed my dog Fiona. Instantly I know Miguel has written the message. Still, I give it a double-take, then a triple-take, making sure my eyes have not deceived me. But there it is in masking tape, the greeting Miguel left for my dog, knowing we walk that stretch of beach.

I smile the entire way home.

I had not talked to Miguel in almost six weeks except for my brief Christmas call, and the time I'd run into him on the street right after that. But he has been present to my heart. I know from his message that I am, in some way, present to his. Though I will rarely interact with Miguel again outside of an occasional hello on the street, I know from meditation that morning that I need to hold him in God's light. I take the discovery of Miguel's note to Fiona as a surprising affirmation.

Shortly after this I come upon a Rumi excerpt I had transcribed months earlier: "Dance when you are broken open. Dance when you are perfectly free." With Miguel, I had danced until my heart broke open. Then I had kept dancing. Finally, I had danced until my heart was perfectly free—not free from pain, but free, at last, to truly love.

◆

On a Saturday a few weeks later, in early 2006, I see Miguel. He stops by my work (something he had never done) and talks with me for five or ten minutes, though he doesn't have much to say. He smells strongly of alcohol and has the drooping, yellowed stare of an addict. I thank him for the note to Fiona and he seems to not remember who she is. His eyes are as vacant as a schoolyard in summertime. I tell Miguel I pray for him every day, that I care deeply for him, and he sits looking at me a long while before saying, "You look very beautiful."

But I shift distractedly in my seat. I glance nervously around like a squirrel, wondering if anyone has entered the museum. I feel endangered even talking with Miguel, wondering where his girlfriend thinks he is. In a flush of discomfort, I tell him I need to get back to my job. He asks if he had left something at my house, something he'd been searching for, and suddenly I understand why he's come. "No, I don't have it," I tell him, my voice suddenly cool. As he says goodbye, my heart aches. "Take care," we both say, squeezing one another's hands.

For a full hour after Miguel has left, I half-tremble with fear. Then I sit still for two minutes and pray. Anxiety flutters off like a bird, and in its absence I am left with remorse. I had been so distracted, I had missed an opportunity to give love.

The next week, I see Martin and describe the encounter to him. He sits across the table from me, his eyes sparkling like the surface of a well of love. "When I first got sober," Martin begins, "I couldn't believe how much more stamina I had. I remember, on the first beach retreat I didn't drink, cleaning the entire house on Sunday. I felt so strong. Before, I had been so tired by Sunday, too much drinking."

"After I got sober," he continues, fidgeting with the placemat under his hands, "I would go visit our neighbor up the road, and he would be drunk." His mouth tightens as he speaks emphatically, with passion, eyes wide. "It was like a mirror was held up for me. I wasn't seeing Sandy, then. It was like I saw myself as I had been.

"Now I go see Sandy and he looks great! Full of life!" Martin smiles and pats his hands on the mat. "And I see men in our meetings (AA) who turn their lives around, Tricia. Miracles can happen," he says. "Sometimes we just have to trust."

When Martin hugs me goodbye, I say, "Pray for Miguel."

A few days later, Martin writes me a letter. I receive it on February fifteenth, the day after Valentine's:

> Feb 14, 2006 ~ Happy Valentine's Day
> *Muy querida* Tricia
> Happy Valentine's Day to you & Madison.
> You always leave me with some special love insight after your visits. As I gave you your farewell hug and you asked me to pray for Miguel, I had a real strong feeling that you live and love with a lot of passion. You left me with a touch of your love for Miguel and your prayers for his well-being in the future. You had some intimate times with Miguel so you probably saw and felt his struggle, trying to free himself from a life with addictions and a not-too-healthy relationship with the woman he lives with.
> You are certainly a loving, beautiful woman. But you are also a woman of God. You reflect it in your eyes, in your words, in your whole person. I can see your own pain in seeing someone unable to free himself to seek a life and love with God present in it in an intimate way. I know God is with us no matter what kind of life we live, but we can't suppress the Spirit within us and be at peace.
> Maybe that is why Jesus had a special love for women. They had a longing for the everlasting spirit life, and often didn't find it in their home lives. I was happy seeing you look so good—full of passion and love in dealing with life, ready for the next adventure God will lead you into.
> The other thing I have been pondering, which I've done in the past, is Jesus' commandment "to love one another as He has loved us." He is really telling us how to deal with "loneliness," which is everybody's portion. Even with just a little effort, when we love someone, they can become present to us. Thus my own personal experience, especially this past week, trying to be patient nursing my left leg. It is healing, but slow. Thinking of you and Madison at your home in Cannon Beach has been consoling.
> I know you love like God—you look at the heart. So if I don't make a lot of sense in what I write, know I want to share

my *corazon* with you. I will keep Miguel, your family, Madison, and all your intentions in my heart and prayers.

Love, Martin

The day Martin composed this letter—St. Valentine's Day, February 14—I run into Miguel in the vicinity of the hotel where he is working. As I stride past on the street, I see Miguel standing by his work truck with co-workers but am too timid to shout hello. I keep walking, hoping he'll see me . . . and then I hear my name.

As he reaches me, Miguel puts one hand in mine, and with the other gently pulls my cheek against his. He has just finished work for the day and is sober, though his eyes still look sickly and jaundiced. He wears a cigarette behind his ear and his face is smudged, but soft. He smells good, like fabric softener.

We say our standard hello-and-how-are-you's, and I ask how his English is coming along. It isn't. "I have no one to teach me," he shrugs.

Unlike our last encounter, I feel, this time, present. I feel free. "Miguel," I tell him, "you know that I am your friend and I love you. . . . And God loves you very much." He smiles and pulls me into a bear-hug. He hugs me warmly as I squeeze his arms. "It is good to see you," I offer as we release. "It is good to see *you*," he replies emphatically.

I continue, "You know, God looks at you and thinks . . . "

"He thinks: *That Miguel is a bad guy!*" Miguel interrupts. But I say no. I tell him God sees his heart.

"Thank you," Miguel replies. He nods his head just slightly. "Thank you."

"Don't forget that I pray for you every day," I remind him. "Take care of yourself," I say, "what is that, '*cuidate*'?"

"*Si, ciudate.*"

"Take care of Miguel for me," I tell him. "I want you to take care of Miguel." For a long moment, we look at each other.

"I will remember that forever," he replies.

His friends wait to leave, and he apologizes for having to run. He gives me another hug and I tell him goodbye. As he walks away, he squeezes my hand.

♦

Attachment grips my heart like a fist for the next twenty-four hours. Once again, my body longs for Miguel; I feel physically parched and erotically charged. But unlike past attachments, I hold this one in the light of awareness and compassion, as I am reading about in Sharon Salzberg's book, *A Heart as Wide as the World*. The attachment gradually loses its grip, and I let go as best I can.

At times I rest into a calm pool of trust that God is healing Miguel, even at that very moment, drawing him millimeter by millisecond toward wholeness. I picture Miguel in the future, as an old man with some kind old woman at his side. I see him sober and full of love and appreciation for his children and grandkids. I want him to find his way to that love, I want it to envelop him and infuse him with life.

Other times, I wrestle with my own desires. I want to touch and be touched, *now*. When I become a tight tangle of longing, I sometimes meditate, kneeling on the prayer bench Martin made over thirty years ago and recently gave to me. I focus on breathing or whisper a mantra, sometimes audibly, sometimes inaudibly: *Jesus show me the way*, or *Jesus have mercy*. On one occasion I focus on a dazzling sun-stenciled cloud outside my window. As I watch it drift, my breathing calms, my heart loosens, the fever in my body begins to cool.

One evening I take a walk to the beach at sunset. The sky is alight with ambrosial gradations of golden rose, cornflower-blue, and white—a Maxfield Parish evening. The sun hovers on the horizon, a gigantic disc of fire. Light gilds the water between broken expanses of navy, and bleaches the breakers an unearthly white. I sit on a large driftwood log and talk aloud to God. Suddenly I find myself weeping.

It dawns on me that I cannot escape loneliness. There is simply no going around it. It must be walked through. And there is no escaping the experience I shared with Miguel, because of what it did in me, because I carry God's love for him in my soul. I cannot put it out of mind, or tuck it away in a drawer like an ugly painting

I don't want anyone to see. Something was born inside of me during my time with Miguel—a chick hatching out of an egg. It was an essential, enormous part of who I am that I had kept hidden and inaccessible most of my life—in my youth out of shame, and in my married life out of necessity and a commitment to monogamy. It was the passionate, sexual, physically alive part of me, and it had wanted desperately to be born. It had always been a significant part of who I am, yet I had forced it into dormancy. Once it was born, it was born.

But birth is hard. It is also, inevitably, messy.

Sitting on that log, night draping slowly around my shoulders, I decide to forgive myself the mess.

The Wind Blew So Hard
this New Years Day,
foam tumbled in billows on the beach,
sand clung in small peaks to grass—
sad, last-ditch efforts, barbed
sacraments of intransigence.
Walking home, I thought
of Saint Teresa, flirtatious young
nun, old reformer of orders,
keeper of a woman's mystic
secret. When time came to quit
la vida vieja,
preening chatter of parlors,
swaying vanity of youth, did
it come as a stroke or a gale?
A whisper or a shout, fierce
and adamant? Did the raven-haired
beauty wake to stillness, or to a man's firm
hip on her dream-tossed mind,
equatorial pull unyielding? This new
year comes like a winnowing.
Corruption slowly unbraids
from glory before my eyes.
Dead leaves stagger while sea birds play.
Hillsides crash, and still,
the gulls rise.

CHAPTER NINE

Grace Notes

On an August afternoon in 2006, my friend Connie and I head to the public pool, hitting it in a stroke of good luck on a rare day when swim lessons are cancelled, getting the pool all to ourselves. We swim laps and float, we hang on the side of the pool like young girls, knees bent in front of us, while Connie, a writer and designer of educational materials, tells stories from her college days in the '60s. We hang that way till the soles of our feet turn gray.

On the way home we stop at the market for lettuce. "I would much rather have cheesecake," I offer as we pass a decadent display of desserts. I am nursing a badly bruised heart from someone I dated for several weeks in late spring, a gentleman named Gilberto I didn't want to part with—a good man, someone far more delightful than cheesecake. We had met at the museum when he assisted with a translation project as a volunteer. In the absence of the man, the bakery-case confection makes a tempting stand-in. Steeling myself, I walk on by. I am too broke to buy cheesecake, and I've just swam alongside the fifty-six-year-old Connie who hasn't an inch of cellulite. *Be strong.*

My car is parked at Connie's, less than a block from the beach, and I decide to take a beach-walk before driving home. Connie heads inside to help her friend John on the computer, and I turn toward the sea.

On the foggy beach I watch a man play catch with his son, a couple with braided arms staring toward the murky sunset, a family clustered around an elaborate sand village, the children caked in sand from head to toe. Feeling ridiculously lonely, humorously lonely, I turn back toward Connie's. I laugh at the way a beach town can make one feel so surprisingly bereft—like everyone in the world is having a good time except you.

Then stepping up to the driver's-side of my car, I notice a small Coleman ice chest perched on the front seat. Stuck to the top is a yellow post-it that reads: "Homemade Blueberry Cheesecake for Tricia." By coincidence, Connie had made it the day before. It is even low-fat.

When I enter the house to thank Connie, her friend John stretches out his arms and whisks me off the entryway landing like I am Ginger Rogers and he is Fred Astaire.

I give Connie a hug, then smile the whole way home.

♦

Two weeks later, I show up on Connie's porch looking like a war widow. My eyes are puffy and bloodshot as I sit waiting for her to return from a walk. I hang my head in a wad of tissues.

"Well, hello there," Connie says on approach.

"I'm grieving," I state melodramatically. Over two months earlier I had made an offer on a lot, a lovely slice of woods in a river valley about thirty minutes south, and was working on a plan to build a cabin or modest house on it. Many variables had to mesh for the dream to become reality, and I'd been waiting on final numbers from my builder-friend. I had just met with him and the numbers were not good. About $18,000 over-budget not good. And with my budget, $18,000 is a deal breaker.

"What is it?" Connie says as she opens the door. We take off our shoes as she turns on a light and shuts the door gently behind me.

"My little house dream is gone," I dramatically retort.

We ascend stairs to the top story of Connie's abode where she resides, the first story being guest quarters. I drag my self-pity into the front room and heave it onto her couch. I tell my story.

"Well, $18,000 doesn't seem insurmountable," says Connie optimistically. I'm not sure whether to roll my eyes or take my hope out of the box where I've stashed it, somewhere in the vicinity of my liver.

"Are there things that can be put off till later," she continues, "costs that can be cut? Do you know what Peter has bid for different jobs?" Connie has restored and resold several houses in her time. The woman knows construction costs. I drag myself down to my car for the bid, then return.

"Okay." Connie studies the sheet of paper like a radiologist with an X-ray in her hands. "Is the house one-story?" she asks. "I see $6,000 right here," she says as I nod yes. I sit staring at the floor, my head in my hands. "You can do the interior and exterior painting yourself."

I pull out my little hope box and set it on the table.

"And here's another $1,500. You don't need landscaping."

I lift my head and take the lid off the box. Dishwasher goes. Brand-new fridge and range go. New cabinetry and countertop go. Professional floor installation goes. "You can find used things and install the floors yourself," Connie assures. In the end, she's trimmed over $10,000 from the bid!

But that still leaves us several thousand dry.

"How much do you pay for rent?" Connie asks.

"Eight-hundred and fifty a month."

"So if you and Madison move in downstairs while the house is being built. . . . "

I start multiplying 850 by nine to ten months. Connie stands up and takes me on the downstairs tour.

Less than two months later, Madison and I move in.

◆

My friend Shonna recently said, "Sometimes we don't get the thing we want; we get the thing we need instead."

It appears I got a house.

It all began when I saw an ad in the paper for a "free house," a house that needed to be moved. I didn't actually get the free house (lots are so expensive around Cannon Beach I couldn't afford the land to put it on), but the ad set a process in motion.

In talking to a builder friend about real estate and the logistics of moving a house, I learned I could buy land a ways south of Cannon Beach, close enough to commute my three days a week to work, and build a tiny house. My monthly mortgage payment would be within range of what I paid to rent a mediocre two-bedroom apartment whose knotty-pine ceilings turned green with mold if I didn't keep after it. With my mold allergy, the place was a death trap.

My parents and I hatched a plan: they would co-apply for the mortgage, since with their financial status, no down payment would be required, and I would pay the house payments and oversee the building process. Down the road, we would refinance and shift the loan to my name.

A house! I say.

◆

Driving to see the lot we eventually purchased, I passed six bodies of water: one bay, three rivers, and one creek right across the street from the property. The ocean is fifteen minutes away. The blue hills rising on either side of the winding, river-valley road were as layered and mythic as the Appalachians, with trees and wildflowers velvety in their crevices, and horses, cows, and sheep cropping up in the flatlands between. River and creek wound through the valley, sparkling. En route I passed a quaint shingle factory and a family farm with a sign out front for "Flowers, Garden, Fresh Eggs." The landscape itself felt like an embrace.

The lot was gorgeous. A steep, three-acre plot of woods shaped like a piece of pie. The house site, which sat just off the road, was on the narrow end of the slice, making the lot unsuitable for anything but a very small house—as in *small* small. Though the neighborhood had been zoned in 1970, the year I was born, the lot had never seen a house. Most people don't want to buy three acres and build something *small* small.

I am not most people.

♦

I've come to think of Connie as one of the "grace notes" in my life. Not only are the grace notes "notes of grace," but they play a role like grace notes in music. In music theory, grace notes are "notes of short duration before the sounding of longer-lasting notes which immediately follow them." In my life, these notes are people, sometimes present only for a spell, whose actions or friendship set off and somehow set the stage for a long-lasting change. In music, grace notes are often glanced over. Unless we're paying attention, we can miss the grace notes, not noticing how they create the character and beauty of a piece. Grace notes are subtle.

Throughout most of my life, I did not hear the grace notes until they'd long since faded. In telling my story I did not mention them because during the events I was narrating, I was not aware of their role. At the time of those events I could not see how the grace notes set off and set the stage for the dominant strains of my life. I could not see how God had given them to me like a good composer gracing a piece with purpose and direction and beauty.

My second-grade teacher, Ms. Laurie Miller, was a grace note. She was a big-boned, vivacious woman with a red Afro and freckles by the millions. Wearing loose-fitting calico dresses and large-framed glasses, she had a smile that looked like God herself shining down. Ms. Miller played guitar. I remember James Taylor's "Shower the People" and her booming, fearless voice. She was so alive, so different. Ms. Miller was the only teacher I had in school that I truly loved.

After my second grade year she left the school to move to San Francisco and teach. *San Francisco.* At the time it sounded so exotic to me, even at the age of seven. Though I regretted losing Ms. Miller, I was entranced. I wanted to live in a place like San Francisco someday, to have such life in me that it burst out all over everyone like sunshine. I couldn't stop thinking about Ms. Miller and the places she would go, the mysteries of her fearless, joyful life. I wanted to follow in her footsteps. It is the first I remember of having a hero and a dream.

♦

Jane was a grace note. She taught me voice lessons at sixteen. Jane had studied opera in Italy, as well as psychology. Besides teaching people to breathe from their diaphragms and sing by opening up the throat, Jane did counseling from an out-building her husband had constructed across from their house, an airy, tidy, custom dwelling he had also built. To compensate for the cost of my lessons, I cleaned Jane's office and house. I remember the place strewn with worn Asian rugs and framed artwork, pottery and stained-glass lampshades. Jane was tall and stately in appearance and wore not a hint of makeup. She had short, close-cut gray hair and wire-framed glasses, and she donned linen pants and jackets of loosely woven fibers. She was one of the few women I knew who'd attended graduate school.

Jane sometimes sang at my home church and was obviously a person of faith, though our relationship didn't include discussions of faith. Judging from the expanses of bookshelves I dusted in her house and office, she was also an intellectual and embraced beauty, whatever and whomever the source—in art and music and literature. As my eyes scanned the shelves of books, I saw Jüng and Thoreau, novels by Virginia Woolf and D. H. Lawrence, and countless names I had never heard of. I saw thin volumes of poetry. Her vast record collection was dominated by classical composers I had likewise not heard of, and whenever I arrived to clean, some spellbinding tune awaited my ears.

Jane was not afraid of what fundamentalists would have called "the world" yet embraced God. Because I grew up in a fundamentalist environment that was fairly anti-intellectual and anti-art, Jane was one of the first people I knew who fully embraced faith *and* the finest offerings of the secular world. As a young person, I admired the way she seemed keen and open in mind and heart and senses, so fully alive. When she and her husband were away from home, I'd clean their house pretending it was my own and I was a keeper of timeless ideas, a lover of the boundlessly creative human spirit.

♦

The next grace note was Margaret. When I met Margaret she was almost eighty years old and, though a brilliant woman, a few years past her intellectual prime. Still, the expansive generosity of her heart had grown to a formidable force. During the last year of my marriage to Alex, I was referred to Margaret for counseling. A retired youth counselor and a Quaker, Margaret offered her services free of charge to as many people as she could fit into her tight schedule.

For several weeks, Alex and I went to Margaret for counseling. We sat at her lace-covered kitchen table in the retirement condo Margaret shared with her husband. Alex and I acted polite, both out of fear and dissemblance, and Margaret, I'm sure, saw right through us. But she would pray with us before we left, holding our hands and speaking in her slow, measured tones, asking God to protect us in God's "care and keeping," and the place where my hand met hers felt holy. The power that passed from her to me was, I think, the purest emanation of divine love I had experienced in a long time. The charge lasted only five or ten minutes. But for those few minutes I felt that everything would be okay, because nothing could compromise God's all-embracing, all-forgiving love for me. As I left Margaret's house, this sense of beloved-ness clung to me like perfume, but the scent gradually faded, minute-by-minute, as it met the elements of my life.

After Alex and I stopped seeing Margaret as a couple, I went to her on my own for a few years with varying consistency. Margaret rarely said anything earth-shattering to me. Yet age and spending a lifetime steeped in grace, a lifetime that included the sudden loss of her college-aged daughter to an unexplainable disease, had made her a healer. Her slow movements, her careful words and touch, her tender look of acceptance—they all healed.

Of the things Margaret said to me, I remember mainly one. Eight months after I had left Alex, around the time I admitted I would never return and that I was getting a divorce, I told Margaret how good I felt. I told her that, despite the views of other people, I felt no guilt. Margaret looked at me like I had made a discovery. Her eyes brightened. She said in her most matter-of-fact voice, "Tricia, it sounds like God is setting you free."

◆

While living in Scotland I saw a tiny classified ad in *Sojourners Magazine* from a female prisoner requesting correspondence. An inner nudge told me I should write to her, but I ignored the impulse. The magazine had been out for several weeks. *Sojourners* had sent it to Darryl as a complimentary copy since he had drawn an illustration for the issue, and the magazine had taken weeks to reach Scotland. I figured the poor lady was overwhelmed with mail by that point. I continued to hold off the nudge.

Pretty soon the nudge started to feel like a jab in the tender place between my ribs. I ignored it three whole weeks before I submitted. I wrote a letter to Bonnie, who, it turns out, had not received a single letter before mine. Thank heavens for the jab. Thank heavens both for Bonnie and me.

Bonnie was from Louisiana. I never saw her in person or by photo, and I never asked about her crime. But from hints in her letters, and by the tenor of her voice on the phone (we talked by phone after her release), I surmised she was African American and had been incarcerated for a minor drug offense. Bonnie was in her late forties and had a twenty-something son she didn't see. By the time I wrote to her, she'd been in prison almost four years and was over two years from release.

For over two years Bonnie and I wrote steadily, describing our goings-on and struggles. We offered whatever encouragement we could to one another, mostly lending the compassion of an openminded friend. Bonnie said she prayed for me, and it seemed she prayed for me a lot.

I lost touch with Bonnie in 2001. It was after her release, when she was living in Texas, struggling to find a steady footing in the outside world. She was working full-time and battling endless allergies and fatigue.

In 2006, Darryl had a message on his phone. It was Bonnie calling to tell me hello, to say "how important you were to my life." She did not leave a number, and she was no longer at the number I used in 2001. But her voice sounded buoyant and strong. Bonnie sounded, finally, free.

Bonnie was a grace note not only for her love and embrace of my person, but because gaining her friendship taught me to follow the nudge, or the "inner light," as Quakers call it. My friendship with Bonnie showed me that I was being led, and that the source of the leading was guiding me to love.

◆

Listening back on my life, I hear the grace notes, and many of these from my parents. They are notes of memory redolent with joy and generosity, times when love was so abundant that the notes leap out at me now. They shimmer amid the more somber tones I've recalled of childhood.

I recall coming home from grade school one day to discover Mom had hidden dozens of hand-me-down Barbie clothes throughout the house for me to find. I remember Mom washing my hair in the kitchen sink and letting me take an Oreo from the jar when she had finished. I remember the handmade furnishings in the handmade dollhouse Mom crafted, the wooden-spool tables, the tiny upholstered chairs and curtains. I remember Mom praying next to me when I'd fallen from a bicycle and gotten a concussion. I remember countless times when she kneeled to "rub my head" or to soothe the ache of growing pains with nimble fingers. I remember Mom pulling me out of school one day in 1985 after discovering a poem I'd written about suicide. I remember her taking me to meet with the counselor who was a healer and a friend. I remember when I traveled to Mexico as a teenager and was achingly homesick because I hadn't received mail the first week, and I remember a letter arriving the next week and then every single day of the summer thereafter—almost every letter from Mom. I remember arriving home from my trip to find she had bought me an entire wardrobe of quirky thrift-store clothing that I loved. I remember Mom praying in the corner of the hospital room as I struggled to give birth to Madison. I remember laughing convulsively with Mom after she disguised her voice to a telephone salesman.

I remember my dad laughing convulsively while watching the TV show "Laverne and Shirley" after I'd been tucked into bed as a small child, and I remember feeling amid his laughter that all was right with the world. I remember singing beautiful three-part harmony with my dad and sister in church. I recall relief at Dad's ability to explain "story problems" in mathematics. I remember the good-natured way Dad let me and my siblings laugh at his expense. I remember Dad carrying the food and camping gear on a youth-group backpacking trip in order to lighten my load, and being the only kid on the trip to eat grilled steak. I remember Dad taking me to dinner in the months after he'd moved to Oregon, and on a motorcycle day-trip to view covered bridges. I remember him taking Madison on cherished "Grandpa adventures" to Bi-Mart. I remember the many times Dad expressed pride and confidence in me, in Madison.

My young life was riddled with grace notes, like a good Scottish reel. Late do I hear them ring.

♦

Martin is a grace note.

I go to visit Martin about a week after he's undergone eye surgery. He wears a pair of dark glasses as he enters the guesthouse kitchen where I'm fixing toast with peanut butter, making myself at home. "You've heard of Stevie Wonder?" he says. "This is Stevie Gonzales."

We walk to our usual spot by the pond and take a seat. The weather is mild for late August, overcast and humid, and Martin talks to me about recuperating, and about silence. In the days following his surgery, while staying at a friend's cabin next to the abbey, he'd turned off his hearing aids. "Sometimes you need silence," he says, and I know just what he means.

After a few minutes of talking about his surgery and recovery, about the frailty of the body, he says, "I want no limitations." He leans forward in his chair. "Yesterday, I was talking with a guest about the risen life—how I really believe it, you know? There has to be something beyond this life." I can see my reflection in his sunglasses, and the shape of his eyes through the lenses. "We have a connection that goes on, even when we're apart, and we always will. It's like that when I listen to Tricia's silent music. It's like my spirit just flies over mountains, over to Cannon Beach, and I am right there with you. That's what I mean by the risen life, being present to each other in the spirit.

"You know, love is important, and being with people. Like right now, I love being with you in person—seeing you smile, looking at your eyes." I keep my eyes focused on his, my elbows resting on my knees as I lean forward. "But I don't care what anyone says, love is about the spirit, the deepest connection is spiritual. And you're going to experience that with a lot of people in your life. People will come and go, but with some people that spiritual connection will always be there."

He asks how I'm doing with my heartache, referring to the recent break-up with Gilberto, and I tell him it has been a hard time. "Well, you look great," he says. "Loving people is just going to hurt some of the time." His brow furrows with compassion.

I smile and shake my head, looking to the ground. I don't want to hear about it.

"But I'm serious," Martin continues. "You wouldn't be able to write the way you do without suffering. It is suffering that gives you *unction*." He laughs, knowing how much I resent this particular speech. "Love is just something we have to endure. It will bring suffering same as it will bring joy. But we have to just endure it, and suffer with it, and then spread the good part around."

He tells of a young priest who recently died of cancer, and another longtime friend who suffered a recent, debilitating stroke. So many people who love them are hurting because of their love. Loving, suffering, losing. That seems to be the course of things.

Martin and I talk five minutes more. "I have a loaf of bread for you," he says as we get up to leave. "You can wait in the chapel while I get it."

In the church, I take a seat. I watch Martin walk through the chapel, hobbling slightly to the far exit, bowing at the altar before walking on. I think of how close he is to the end of his life and what a blow it will be to lose his friendship.

But then my thinking shifts. I imagine Martin as a spiritual presence. I imagine feeling a connection with him, talking with him, after his spirit had merged with light. Suddenly I'm confident

Martin will still be with me in some form even after he dies—the spiritual connection unending.

When Martin comes back to the chapel, I stand up. "I have a question for you," I say.

"What is it?"

"If you get sick, or if something happens to you, do the people here know to call me right away?"

"Yes," he says, smiling and nodding. He takes hold of my arm. "Don't you worry about that."

At the back of the chapel, beside the exterior entrance, Martin hands me the brown bag that holds my bread. "You are wonderful!" he says. He gives me a quick peck like my grandma used to do, and we hug. "We are never far apart," he says, handing me a silver rosary with a pendant of Our Lady of Guadalupe. "When you suffer, I suffer, okay? I am always right with you. Right here."

I walk to my car slowly that evening and hang the rosary on my rearview mirror, grateful for the westward hills rimmed in gold, the maternal moon, broad and white as a magnolia flower. As I drive toward home, I can see her behind me, guiding me. I drive away from the abbey as I have dozens of times, cognizant of the emptiness of leaving, the fullness of having been. And yet this time, a knowing part of me remains.

A couple of weeks later Martin sends this letter:

> Sept 12, 2006
>
> . . . I know I said this before but I love to tell you that you are like the Risen Jesus in the forty days before the Ascension. He always came appearing at different times & places. So you become so present to me very strongly in different ways and places. So it was this morning as I was attending and celebrating the Eucharist. I could feel your spirit just pouring in and out in a mysterious, loving way. . . . See, you and Madison are not alone. Thanks for letting me share your life.
>
> Love, Martin
>
> P.S. I'm keeping alert so I won't miss you if you make one of your risen life appearances.

◆

Madison started high school at the public school last fall. She's pulled A's, become a dedicated member of the Speech Team, and adopted a more colorful vocabulary. Until we move to the new place, I drive her to the school bus. When the bus pulls up, she steps out of the car, tells me "I love you," climbs aboard the bus, and takes a seat. Almost every day as the bus pulls out of the lot, Madison waves to me and blows me a kiss.

I've become friends with her dad, who's offered to help me and Madison move to the new house, and who's lent a corner of his shop to store our bargain, vintage claw-foot tub, a fortuitous Craigslist find. Madison has inherited Alex's eye and ear for comedy, and the two speak a humor language all their own. He's also teaching her to drive. As she prepares to back up a Subaru on the farm he owns, he patiently instructs her to put the car in reverse, to look behind, to softly give it some gas. She smiles at me through the car's rear window.

◆

Of late, my mantra or prayer chant has been: *Where there is hatred, let me sow love, let me sow love, let me sow love, let me sow love.* I often chant it while I'm walking, or when crocheting, weaving the words over and under and into the knots of yarn. Recently I crocheted a blanket for Madison this way. When I gave it to her for Christmas, I told her I had sewn love and prayers into it. "*O-kay . . .*" she said, in the drawn out way of teenagers. "Whatever, Mom." She was obviously moved.

This piece of St. Francis' prayer expresses the longing of my soul these days, since resentment makes an appearance in my heart too often. But it is hard to nourish resentment when praying the old words: *Where there is hatred, let me sow love, let me sow love, let me sow love. . . .* While praying this prayer, it is hard to recite the venomous, unfair scripts that sometimes play in our heads about the people who have hurt us.

Where there is hatred, let me sow love, let me sow love, let me sow love . . . .

♦

Every four or five months I see Miguel, usually driving past in a car as I am walking. Every time, we wave. Every time I remember, again, to pray for him, and that God receives my prayers and loves Miguel. Sometimes I'm reminded of the relationship I shared with him and am struck anew by the insanity of it. I shake my head. *What, for the love of God, were you thinking?!*

But then I step back a few feet. I recall glimpses of God I saw in Miguel and Miguel's very flawed but honest efforts to love. I recall how his best efforts felt. I think how the experience broke something free inside of me, something that had been hidden and bound my entire life—the sensual, sexual, fully feeling part of me. I think how the all-embracing love of God I felt at the time that relationship unraveled convinced me that journeying to God and to love is not about getting it right. It is about openness and presence and being with God right here, right now, wherever we are.

Really, the whole thing makes a lot of sense.

♦

Thomas Merton wrote, "Life's one imperative is to become who we are." Ron Rolheiser, in an article Brother Martin sent me, said, "To be truly ourselves, truly recollected and centered is to touch and feel the memory of God in us. That inchoate memory is what both fires our energy and provides us with a prism through which to see and understand."[10]

I love the word *recollected* in this excerpt. It conjures in my mind a reverse, time-lapse film reel: a shattered statue, crumbled to a heap of stone, being gathered back up into a flawless work of art like the Venus de Milo.

For many entangled reasons, reasons for which no one is to blame, the earliest years of my life were a crumbling away. I think that is true for many of us. We are not shattered all at once as if a wrecking ball has hit us, but we undergo a slow erosion, leaving fragments of ourselves scattered here and there along the road. Passersby have to dodge the wreckage so as not to tear up the bottoms of their cars.

I do not recall someone explicitly encouraging me to be alive as the sensual person I am, deeply aware of sights and smells and tastes and sounds, of the passions and of *eros*. The explicit messages I heard commended either silence or shame about the body and its constellations of feeling. The people sending me alternative messages were subtle, like Jane, and sometimes I could not hear their voices for the din of accumulated shame that drowned them out. Now I see their significance.

Somehow I am managing to "become who I am," as Merton put it, thanks to God, the grace notes, and many other things including my parents' acceptance of me, which seemed late in coming but has now bloomed. Their support of me has never been more generous or more impacting—my house a case in point. Would I have been able to become who I am without their dawning, if incomplete, acceptance? At this point in my life, I think I would have. But I would have carried with me a grief that could not be comforted, as do all children who don't have the acceptance of their parents. As it is, my grief has dissipated.

"Who I am" is deeply physical and sensual and alive in my body. I know now that God loves this about me, despite voices saying that sensuality, being fully awake physically and emotionally, is bad or at best weak. I have heard this most often from male voices, though women chime in too. I have heard it frequently from the church, in a tone either of condescension or accusation. A quote from Dorothy Sayers tells how unlike Jesus' voice it is:

> Perhaps it is no wonder that the women were first at the Cradle and last at the cross. They had never known a man like [Jesus]—there had never been such another. A prophet and teacher who never nagged at them, who never flattered or coaxed or patronized; who never made arch jokes about them, never treated them either as "The women, God help us!" or "The ladies, God bless them!"
>
> . . . There is no act, no sermon, no parable in the whole Gospel that borrows its pungency from female perversity; nobody could possibly guess from the words of Jesus that there was anything 'funny' about woman's nature.[11]

Darryl sent me this quote. He said "here's a quote on 'how Jesus loves women.'" It was one of his many gestures of friendship and forgiveness. We are good friends, Darryl and I. Thanks to God.

◆

"Why does Jesus love women?" spiritual director Vivian asks.

At the time, I've been seeing Vivian for spiritual direction for about a year and a half. She is a flaming red-head with pale skin, a small nose, and a lyrical voice. I could picture her as a fairy one-twentieth her size, though she is a strong, confident woman. She has a spritely smile that makes her eyes twinkle.

I've just described to her the break-up with Gilberto, a delightful and passionate man, someone gifted and big-hearted whom I hated to let go.

"I don't want to care for someone if it's going to feel this way," I tell her. "It is too great a risk to my heart. I can't open my heart to someone again—not for a very, very long time." I pull another tissue from the box and dry the tears under my eyes. She sits quietly across from me, spinning a hammock of spaciousness where I can reflect and let go.

"Sometimes it hurts a lot, doesn't it?" Vivian says.

Then, after several moments, she asks: "But why does Jesus love women?"

The question surprises me, though it is one I should be prepared for. I look down at the tissue wadded in my hand as I think. Finally I look up at Vivian's eyes. "Because they keep loving," I say. "They keep loving, and loving, and loving . . . even when it hurts. They don't close down their hearts."

◆

Loneliness does seem to be "everyone's portion," as Martin wrote. This is the lesson I have most resisted my entire life, pressing hands to my ears and trolling "la, la, la," like a two-year-old ignoring the babysitter. I have resisted loneliness the way an alcoholic resists sober, painful, awareness. Take the drink, the drug, and feel the pain slip away. That is the path of the addict.

My main addiction? Unwise relationships, I'm afraid, relationships that fend off loneliness for a spell, helping me to banish the pain I most fear, if only for a year, a day, or one bed-time hour. Coming to this realization about myself has taken thirty-some years. But the realization, the awakening to what is real, is the gateway to liberation, right? It seems I've opened the gate.

Loneliness is always near. I walk alongside it, asking Jesus to walk alongside me and to bring comfort. If Jesus experienced ardent love, Jesus also experienced rejection, and most surely the lingering ache of loneliness. How does Jesus love women? By knowing the ache of love unfulfilled and by nodding compassionately at our broken efforts to find fulfillment. By understanding the capacity of a heart kept open—a capacity for love, but also for pain. By embracing all the sensations of human life and revealing their goodness. By loving, loving, loving, without addiction, without believing lies, and without buying the idea that love requires self-abasement, as I have often done. Jesus loves women by saying, "I love you. Love others. *Be love.*"

I am resisting the urge to banish loneliness by trailing down paths of fantasy about how much better life would be with this or that or another relationship. But the thing helping me side-step that fantasy path isn't will power. In a moment of grace-inspired clarity, I'll catch myself knee-deep in illusion, and I will pray for more grace. *God, fill me with your grace and help me. I need grace, I need grace, I need grace.* And grace comes.

Martin says that the twinge of loneliness many people feel in this life is evidence of the awakened soul. It comes from an awareness of one's infinitude. We are creatures of eternity who can never fully be satisfied within the confines of this life, he explains. Or as his favorite author Gerald May put it, "We have had God's breath in us since the beginning, and God knows that the fulfillment we long for will come from nothing other than God's very self. Nothing less than God will satisfy the yearning that God has planted within us."[12] Because our yearning after God is always, to some degree, unquenched in this lifetime, loneliness is our common portion. In Martin's sense, loneliness is akin to spiritual longing or restlessness.

I never could buy this characterization of my loneliness. How could my loneliness be so lofty when it really came down to wanting a loving partner to sleep with at night? *Spiritual longing?*—I think not. Yet I've come to see the connection between this kind of loneliness and what Martin speaks of.

One kind of loneliness is a manifestation of spiritual yearning. Another kind of loneliness is a withdrawal effect of addiction.

This second kind of loneliness results when we lose or are deprived of a relationship to which we have become attached—a friendship, a parent/child relationship, a romantic relationship, or a relationship with some other addictive element like one's job, an image of oneself, or even a drug. In relationships characterized by attachment, we *use* the thing or person to which we are addicted to fulfill our desire. Frankly, my loneliness has most often been of this kind.

But the reason I become addicted to things in the first place, the reason anyone becomes addicted, is because we displace our intense yearnings for spirit onto other things. This desire is the purest expression of our God-like nature, of God *in* us. And this desire can only be met in our spirits. Yet God, eternal Spirit, is illusive and mysterious and cannot be controlled or used. We cannot rally God to meet our longing *right now.* So in our impatience, we strive to meet our inborn, spiritual desires with anything we *can* marshal, anything we *can* use—from food, to children, to "good deeds," to entertainment, to work, to sex. These stand-ins take us captive as addictions. We all have them.

I frequently feel the withdrawal effect of loneliness because of lost relationships. This withdrawal effect is no more holy than the tremors one gets when breaking with caffeine. I *want* the drug of touch, of long gazes and whispers on the phone, of sexual embrace, of feeling mutually, intimately appreciated by a fellow human being. I want it the way an alcoholic wants booze.

Yet I have had the grace-moment of clarity. I can see that the press and sting of my misplaced longing will oppress me until I seek the real fulfillment of my desire, which is spiritual.

I will always have natural desires: the desire to eat, the desire for sexual satisfaction, the desire for community and companionship. The point is to meet these desires without becoming an addict—*which sounds so much easier than it is*. The point, for this very reason, is grace.

◆

So while sexual intimacy has been my drug of choice, it is, like many things we abuse, profoundly *good*. At the place where my feet stand, I'm more convinced of this than ever.

And what, at the end of this narrated journey, do I consider my sexual ethics?

My sexual ethics surely begin with this: *Sex-Is-Good*. From there I head in a somewhat traditional direction, then take an important detour. You could call my position "nuevo-traditional."

I affirm that the wild, exposing relationship of sex is powerful. It can impact us in ways—negatively and positively—that we don't recognize for years. It is also risky, in this STD age, and can lead to pregnancy. Therefore, sexual intimacy is meant to be paired with deep emotional intimacy and long-term commitment. Sex apart from emotional intimacy and commitment is usually unhealthy, in my observation, and has precipitated more than a little pain and embarrassment. The differences between being loved by someone and being used for sexual gratification can blur in the heat of an erotically charged moment, but down the road, we most certainly feel the difference, if we are honest with ourselves. And knowing we have been used, or that we have used another person, generally *hurts*.

On the other hand, the expression of sexuality in the context of trust, non-domination, and true, committed love is glorious. It is absolutely holy. In this context, the wildness of sex, the complete unveiling of our souls and our selves, brings about an unparalleled sharing between two people and a sacred kind of freedom.

Our sexuality is linked with our spirituality. We cannot expose ourselves the way we do in sex without our spirits and emotions wanting to become involved. For this reason, many people close themselves off from their spirits and emotions as a means of protection during less-than-healthy sex, and this closing-off spills over into other arenas of their lives. It is a full-service defense, and it is astoundingly common, especially among women. This sort of shutting-off of our deepest selves is not good, to state the obvious. It erodes our souls.

My detour, then, comes here (and I realize this may put me in creative tension with many Christians, including my publisher).

Some forms of sexual expression paired with deep emotional intimacy and true, committed love, do not run parallel with the hard lines of a marriage certificate; and commitment and marriage are not necessarily coexistent.

I have been witness to the use of sex to dominate and subjugate—within marriage. I have also experienced marriage detached from commitment. I'm afraid my experiences are woefully common. On the other hand, a relationship of deep emotional intimacy, commitment, wholeness, and love can exist apart from a marriage certificate, and sometimes does for practical reasons. As a result, I see overstressing marriage as *the* way to legitimize or de-legitimize sexuality as problematic.

Sex is beautiful. It is wild in the best sense, in the sense that it is like nature, and so close to God. It is also potent and can be harmful to our souls. As with most ethical paths, I believe the path to healthy sexuality is not ultimately about rules and hard lines. It is about seeing clearly and honestly, and letting spirit guide you. But since we're sometimes unable to see clearly, especially when in the throes of romance or sexual attraction, it may sometimes be healthy to lay down clear lines, following "the letter of the law" until the fog rises. Then, once we have internalized healthy boundaries, we can see clearly enough to live by the spirit that guides us. The ultimate goal, however, is to see clearly, to see far, to part with illusions. The goal is to find what is healthy, what promotes our wholeness and the wholeness of others, and to move in that direction.

◆

When I take Martin to see the site where my house will be built, he leans over, puts his hands on his knees and *laughs*. "Wow" is all he says. He looks around at the forest, the tiny patch of level ground, a home-site. He shakes his head and laughs again. Finally he remarks, "Me and the monks will have to come here for retreats!" Then he gets very quiet. "Listen," he says, holding his hands out in front of him as if to stave off all human sound, "all you can hear are the birds, the wind, and the creek. It is like being kissed by the earth!" We stand listening to the variant bird songs drifting through the trees. "With all these birds, you will have lots of company!"

On the way back to the beach cabin where the seventy-and-older monks are staying for a night of retreat, I keep an eye out for swimming holes. I watch the light play all around, glistening on the river, burnishing a hillside where it rises above lingering morning mist, cutting the landscape into a patchwork of shadow and brilliance.

Out of nowhere Martin says, "Sometimes I am hypnotized by the word *love*." He chuckles softly and gestures with the sunglasses clutched in his hand. "I just say the word over and over again—LOVE, LOVE, LOVE."

Epilogue

On this night in September, in the year 2007, the full moon hovers protectively above my house, a house Madison and I have named—in the Scottish manner of naming houses—Casa Luna, or "moon house." It is a small blue home with a covered porch looking, in one direction, toward the mountains and creek, in the other, toward a vast expanse of woods. On this porch sits a rocker, providing an ideal perch for drinking morning coffee, reading a book, or meditating on the birds, the myriad shapes and textures of leaves. The hills across the valley from Casa Luna make a dramatic backdrop for cloud formations, which sidle past them almost every morning, assuming gauzy, transient configurations.

I have learned that the Native people of this area, the Tillamooks, who lived along the coast for centuries before European settlement, used these hills as vision-quest territory. Their villages dotted the shoreline, clustering at the mouths of rivers and streams where the ocean offered its bounty. But the young people, when the time came "to fast and receive their power," would venture into these mountains to encounter the Great Spirit and receive blessings.

I can see why.

Since moving to this place in June 2007, my spirit has been opening, connecting, quieting, filling with joy like never before. This is transforming ground. In this community I have found people with whom to share poetry and practice meditation and dance, and I experience God in the trees, the birds, the waters I encounter on daily walks, in the people I meet in my far-flung neighborhood. I can now see how love imbues everything, how as Richard Rohr says, "everything belongs." I've begun to see how nothing stands outside of God's presence, how no separation exists between the "secular" and the "sacred." There is *no profane thing*. Jesus loves women, because women and other outsiders often grasp this reality better than those invested in maintaining the lines.

Frequently when I sit on my porch and stare up at the hills or investigate the slow, seasonal evolution of the woods, I remember hours spent at the abbey doing the same. I remember my dream to find a place in this world as nourishing to me as that place. About Casa Luna, what can I say? I suppose most fitting would be: *Thank You.*

Many generous friends made Casa Luna what it is. Friends labored all day to put down flooring or paint the walls, friends gave me cabinets and fixtures they no longer needed, and friends located necessary building supplies and used appliances with uncanny timing. My brother helped install them. My stove was actually sitting on the side of the road in the rain as I drove past it one Thanksgiving Day, on my way to dinner with friends Bill and Brenda—the stove a perfectly promising cast-off by all appearances. When the owners assured me that it worked ("Just needs a new element!"), three of my friends whisked it into a van and stored it for me until the day it was installed in my kitchen.

Casa Luna has a candelabra light-fixture whimsically refurbished by an artist friend, a delightful cranberry-red claw-foot tub Alex helped me secure, a huge porcelain sink given me by Connie, a new dishwasher provided by my parents, and bamboo floors pieced together from remnants found on Craigslist that I painstakingly installed with Bill and Brenda. The walls' bright colors come from others—from Mom and Donna and Gilberto, who painted with me. Casa Luna is sunny, cozy, and *beautiful*. It is bathed in spirit. It is a sacrament of *philos* running deep and wide.

On this night I sit at the back of my house before a swelling campfire, listening to the crackle of sparks, the creek across the street and the still symphony of the woods. My body feels caressed by the fire and the ambient night. Through windows at the back of the house I see Madison—tall and dark, so grown-up—seated in the glow of my bedroom talking with a friend on the phone. Soon we will make and eat s'mores.

Gilberto, the break-up guy mentioned earlier, the guy more delightful than cheesecake, has become my best friend. He will come to visit and roast marshmallows. As I wait, chipmunks in our ancient cedar tree chirp a few times more then retire to their bedroom in the enormous trunk. Stars gradually blink to life overhead.

How could this world not be enchanted? How could the endless voice of the universe not know my name, and love me?

Notes

1. Evelyn Underhill, *The Spiritual Life* (Harrisburg, Pa.: Morehouse Publishing, 1955).

2. Frederick Buechner, *Now and Then* (San Francisco: HarperSanFrancisco, 1983).

3. Frederick Buechner, *The Sacred Journey* (San Francisco: HarperSanFrancisco, 1982).

4. Thomas Kelly, *A Testament of Devotion* (San Francisco: HarperSanFrancisco, 1992), pp. 14-15; gender-exclusive pronouns for God have been changed.

5. My doctoral dissertation was a study of the spirit-language in John and 1 John using social-scientific methodology and the anthropological model of patron-client relationships. It was published in 2002 as *Spirit in the Writings of John: Johannine Pneumatology in Social-Scientific Perspective* (London: T & T Clark, International).

6. "Hesychasm" refers to a method of contemplation traced back to early Eastern Christianity. Hesychastic prayer is characterized by short, repetitive prayers synchronized to one's breathing, the classic hesychastic prayer being "Lord Jesus Christ, have mercy on me a sinner."

7. Frederick Buechner, *Telling Secrets* (San Francisco: HarperSanFrancisco, 1991), p. 95.

8. Richard Rohr, *Everything Belongs: The Gift of Contemplative Prayer*, rev. ed. (Crossroad Publishing, 2003).

9. Three of the four CPT hostages, Norman Kember, Harmeet Sooden, and my friend James Loney were freed on March 23 after 118 days of captivity. Quaker Tom Fox, the only American among the hostages, was killed on March 9, 2006. For an in-depth story of the CPT hostage crisis, see Tricia Gates Brown, ed., *118 Days: Christian Peacemaker Teams Held Hostage in Iraq* (Telford, Pa.: Cascadia Publishing House, 2009).

10. *The Catholic Northwest Progress*, Nov 30, 2006, p. 8.

11. Dorothy L Sayers, *Are Women Human?* (Grand Rapids, Mich.: Eerdmans, 1971), p. 47.

12. Gerald May, *Addiction and Grace* (San Francisco: HarperSanFrancisco, 1988), p. 112.

The Author

Tricia Gates Brown received a PhD in New Testament Studies from University of St. Andrews in 2000 and started to teach in her field before halting her academic course to pursue writing. She has been actively writing and publishing since. Tricia has published two non-fiction books as well as essays and poetry in several periodicals. She is a columnist for two publications and is currently at work on a novel.

In late 2009, Tricia married her best friend, Gilberto Arciga. They reside in a woodland cottage called Casa Luna in the Nehalem River valley and co-own a landscaping and garden-design business.

CPSIA information can be obtained at www.ICGtesting.com
Printed in the USA
LVOW070306131211

259151LV00004B/11/P